SOUTHERN BIOGRAPHY SERIES
William J. Cooper, Jr., Editor

Mary Boykin Chesnut

# Mary Boykin Chesnut

## A BIOGRAPHY

*Elisabeth Muhlenfeld*

Louisiana State University Press

BATON ROUGE

Copyright © 1981 by Louisiana State University Press
All rights reserved
Manufactured in the United States of America

Designer: Joanna Hill
Typeface: VIP Bembo
Typesetter: G&S Typesetters, Inc.

LIBRARY OF CONGRESS CATALOGING IN PUBLICATION DATA

Muhlenfeld, Elisabeth, 1944–
  Mary Boykin Chesnut.

  (Southern biography series)
  Bibliography: p.
  Includes index.
  1.  Chesnut, Mary Boykin Miller, 1823–1886.  2.  South
Carolina—Biography.  I.  Series.
CT275.C548M84   975.7′03′0924 [B]   80-26610
ISBN 0-8071-0852-9 (cloth)
ISBN 0-8071-1804-4 (paper)

Louisiana Paperback Edition, 1992
07  06  05  04  03  02  01  00  99  98    10  9  8  7  6

The paper in this book meets the guidelines for permanence
and durability of the Committee on Production Guidelines for
Book Longevity of the Council on Library Resources. ∞

For Mary Brosey Showalter
and in memory of
Nellie Smith Herring—
my grandmothers

# Contents

# Foreword

MARY CHESNUT IS remembered only for one incomparable book she wrote on her experience of the Civil War. "But one cannot read more than a page or two," as her biographer says, "without wishing to know more about the author herself." That alone would be enough to justify a biography. Mary Chesnut's reading public has grown greatly since the first fragmentary and scrambled editions of her work appeared earlier in the present century, as has the curiosity and puzzlement of her readers about the author of this nineteenth-century classic.

Food for curiosity and puzzlement exists in abundance. Mary Chesnut was a complex and paradoxical personality, and her book often does more to multiply than to answer the questions that it raises about the author. Among them are the puzzles of how such strong antislavery sentiment was bred in the very heart of a slave society and how such vehement feminism burst out of a thoroughly patriarchal order. Here was an essentially secular-minded intellect in the midst of a deeply religious community, an independent-minded intellectual planted in the elite of a traditionalist social system. She loved city life and lived a rural life. Her interests were cosmopolitan and her existence parochial. She could at times be as arrogant and ambitious as the males she scorned, yet she always had an eye for appealing men and the capacity to charm when she chose. These are but a few of the traits that challenge all the talents a biographer can muster.

Mary Chesnut has been singularly fortunate in her biographer. Elisabeth Muhlenfeld knows more about her subject than anybody ever has and uses her knowledge with the subtlety, grace, and intelligence that characterize her essays on William Faulkner.

Her mastery of the sources is grounded on close study of all the surviving Chesnut manuscripts, correspondence, and related materials. Her command of the evidence has been enhanced by her work on the transcription and collation of the surviving parts of the original Chesnut diaries and the version of the 1880s. In addition Professor Muhlenfeld has prepared a superior edition of Chesnut's unpublished novels and other works, available in microfilm.

In the preparation of a scholarly and full edition of the Chesnut book, under the title *Mary Chesnut's Civil War*, the present writer found the work of Elisabeth Muhlenfeld indispensable. Of prime importance were the values, the skills, and the example of literary scholarship that contributed to and often challenged the historical values and principles that the editor brought to the work. These values were not always completely reconcilable. But the literary scholar forced the historian to acknowledge that he was dealing with a literary as well as a historical document. In this service and in her admirable biography of Mary Chesnut, Elisabeth Muhlenfeld has placed American literature as well as American history in her debt.

C. VANN WOODWARD
Yale University, 1980

# Acknowledgments

IN 1975 WHEN I ARRIVED in Columbia, South Carolina, my friend Noel Polk placed a book in my hand before I had even set foot on the university campus. "Read this," he said. "Mrs. Chesnut is a remarkable lady." The book was the Ben Ames Williams edition of *A Diary From Dixie*. Within a week, James B. Meriwether, director of the Southern Studies Program at the University of South Carolina, had enthusiastically described the possibilities for research on the Chesnut manuscripts in the South Caroliniana Library, and had introduced me to C. Vann Woodward, who was spending a semester as a visiting professor at the Southern Studies Program to begin work on his new edition of Chesnut's book, *Mary Chesnut's Civil War*. Thus, from the first, my interest in Mary Boykin Chesnut has been nurtured and supported by scholars who have long counted themselves among Chesnut's admirers. In the course of work on the biography, I have come to realize that those admirers are legion, and each of them to whom I have gone for help has been unfailingly generous.

Foremost among those who have given assistance and encouragement are the descendants of Mary Boykin Chesnut's nieces and nephews. Ellen Butts, McCoy Hill, Sally Bland Wilson, Sally Bland Johnson, Barbara Glover Carpenter, and Katharine Glover Herbert, owners of the literary rights to Chesnut's manuscripts, graciously granted permission to quote from the manuscripts and from related materials in numerous manuscript collections. Mrs. Butts, Mrs. Hill, Mrs. Wilson, their mother Sally Bland Metts, and Kate Williams Tabor have discussed the project with me at many stages, and have shared with me their knowledge of Camden and their memories of family members and traditions. Mary

Ames Bolton Alfriend kindly permitted me access to the Mary Williams Harrison Ames papers. Mrs. Herbert gave me copies of two Chesnut manuscript volumes in her possession—a letterbook and daybook. The estate of David Rogerson Williams IV has allowed me to use material in the S. Miller Williams papers. Martha Williams Daniels has helped in so many ways, from providing genealogical information and anecdotes to pointing out errors and passing along information, that by now it is impossible to adequately thank her. These people made the project possible; for the opportunity to know them and to work with them, I am deeply grateful.

The staffs of numerous libraries and institutions have answered inquiries and provided me with information and access to materials in their collections: the Library of Congress; the Thomas Cooper Library, University of South Carolina; the William R. Perkins Library, Duke University; the Louis Round Wilson Library, University of North Carolina at Chapel Hill; the Robert W. Woodruff Library, Emory University; the National Portrait Gallery, Smithsonian Institution; the Museum of the Confederacy; the Virginia Historical Society; the Mount Vernon Ladies Association; the Maryland Historical Society; the State Historical Society of Wisconsin; the Atlanta Historical Society; the Historic Columbia Foundation; the Kershaw County Court House; the Kershaw County Historical Society; the South Carolina State Department of Archives and History; and the South Carolina Historical Society. I am especially indebted to the staff of the South Caroliniana Library and wish particularly to thank its director, E. L. Inabinett, and Allen H. Stokes, manuscript librarian, as well as Marlene Sipes, Eleanor M. Richardson, and Carolyn Bodenheimer. The South Caroliniana Library houses the bulk of the Chesnut manuscripts; moreover, its collection of material related to South Carolina is unsurpassed and has been indispensable to this work.

For the information and assistance they have given, I want to thank Mrs. A. H. Ehrenclou, Eileen Gregory, John Alexander Moore, Edwin Arnold, Ellen Arnold, Dianne Cox, Leland Cox, Ann Hampton, Gene Waddell, and Edward D. C. Campbell, Jr.

To each of the people who carefully read early drafts of all or part of the biography, I owe a great debt; each offered criticism that strengthens it. James B. Meriwether's contribution has been immeasurable; he encouraged the project from the start, discussed it with me by the hour, led me to sources, and helped me smooth prose and clarify thinking on many points. Thomas Dasher, Stephen Meats, and Clyde Wilson brought to the manuscript a broad knowledge of Chesnut and her milieu. Matthew Bruccoli, Raymond O'Cain, and Joseph McElrath generously shared their expertise in related fields. William J. Cooper, Jr., editor of the Southern Biography Series, Louisiana State University Press, made invaluable comments and suggestions. Beverly Jarrett, assistant director and executive editor, and Martha L. Hall, managing editor, who copy edited the text, have done an excellent job and have made the whole process of seeing a book through to publication an enjoyable one. I have indeed been fortunate that people of such calibre have been willing to contribute so much. As Mary Boykin Chesnut would say, my lines have fallen in pleasant places.

To C. Vann Woodward, I offer very special thanks. The foreword he has written is only the most recent of many, many gifts of his time, his incisive command of the subject, and his encouragement. Two young people, Allison and David Muhlenfeld, also deserve very special thanks. They cheerfully allowed me to work whenever I needed to, and hugged me when I needed to stop.

Mary Boykin Chesnut

ONE  # Perspective and Retrospective

LATE IN THE EVENING of May 18, 1861, Mary Boykin Chesnut was in a hotel room in Montgomery, Alabama. The day had been a warm one, particularly for a woman dressed in the heavy hooped and frilled fashions of the period, so she was glad to sit by lamplight and enjoy the cool air brought by darkness. As had been her habit for three months, now, since the day in mid-February when Jefferson Davis was inaugurated president of the newly formed Confederate States of America, Mrs. Chesnut took out an elegant red leather-bound, gilt-edged diary with a little brass lock, and jotted down the events of her day. As the wife of the first United States senator to resign following Abraham Lincoln's election—a man who was now an influential member of the Confederate Provisional Congress—Mary Boykin Chesnut had already watched and recorded the firing on Fort Sumter. For the next four years she would continue her journal in any notebook she could get her hands on; finally, after W. T. Sherman's incendiary march through the Carolinas and Robert E. Lee's surrender, she would describe the bleak aftermath of war in the back of an old recipe book.

On this particular day—a typical one during this chaotic period—Mrs. Chesnut had just returned from a quick trip south to Conecuh County to visit relatives. Traveling on an uncomfortable boat, plagued by mosquitoes, then riding overland through the close Alabama night by buggy had made her ill, so once back in Montgomery, she determined to curtail her social activities somewhat. Still, it was necessary to return eight or nine of the calls that had been paid her during her absence and to put in an appearance at dinner. "I could only manage to eat cold asparagus—& black berries" she wrote, perhaps unconscious that her very menu—asparagus, that most aristocratic and cultivated of vegetables, and blackberries, so common that they grew wild—well reflected her catholic tastes.[1] After dinner, always served at two or three in the afternoon, she went for a drive with her friend Varina Davis, whose new role as First Lady of the Confederacy had already begun to chafe a bit: "drove out with Mrs Jeff Davis—*She* is very queer—She *preferred* Washington & her friends to being Mrs President—I dont wonder!"

Returning about eight o'clock to her lodgings at the overcrowded Montgomery Hall hotel, she looked forward to a quiet evening. But Mary Boykin Chesnut rarely had a quiet evening. Although she was neither young nor beautiful, at thirty-eight her charm, her intelligence, the irreverent delight she took in all the foibles of mankind had always drawn people to her, and she enjoyed a reputation wherever she went as a brilliant conversationalist, a woman of "literary" leanings, a lady whose drawing room was likely to hold attractive and important people. So tonight, as happened almost every evening, several friends dropped in. When they had finally gone, she seized a moment of peace to make notes in her diary about her visitors:

> came home at 8—Mr Browne [William Montague Browne, former editor of the *Constitution*, aide to Jefferson Davis, Confederate assistant secretary of state] & Mallory [Stephen R. Mallory, Confederate secretary of the navy] insisted on my going to the reception at Mrs Toombs [wife of Robert Toombs, first Confederate secretary of state]—but I did not—Mr Hunter called [R. M. T. Hunter, former U.S. senator and speaker of the House, Confederate secretary of state after Toombs] sat some time—The Judge [Thomas J. Withers, South Carolina delegate to the Provisional Congress and Mrs. Chesnut's uncle] joined us .... then Miles [William Porcher Miles, former U.S. congressman, South Carolina delegate to the Provisional Congress] & then Judge Frost [another South Carolina delegate] & then Jemison [Robert W. Jemison of the Georgia senate]—I had a pleasanter set than I should have had at the levee—Tho Mrs Browne said every body asked for me .... Mrs Fitspatrick [wife of Benjamin Fitspatrick, former U.S. senator from Alabama] & Miss Howell [Mattie Howell, Varina Davis' sister]—

Mrs Taylor [daughter-in-law of President Zachary Taylor] Jessie James—Mrs Clayton [wife of Henry D. Clayton, Alabama delegate to the Provisional Congress] who told Washington news.

After recounting snatches of the evening's conversation, she added: "I with a horrid pain in the chest sit here so lonely."[2]

Within the next three or four days, all the politicians, lawyers, doctors, military men, and their families who had crowded into Montgomery would leave, to reconvene in Richmond, Virginia, the new capital of the Confederate States of America. Directing her servants to pack up her Paris dresses, Mary Boykin Chesnut would return to the comparative isolation of Camden, South Carolina. Within a month, she too would go to Richmond. Calling herself a "close observer . . . of men and manners," she would watch history unfold around her.[3] By turns strong, gay, ill, lonely, she would record it.

The woman we know today as the author of the most famous firsthand account of the Confederacy died in 1886 in Camden, South Carolina. She died quietly, and because she had no immediate family, little notice was taken of her passing. Ten or fifteen years thereafter, few people remembered her. A handful of elderly ladies and gentlemen scattered across the country had been her friends during the Civil War years and recalled her as a colorful and sometimes controversial figure in Montgomery, Charleston, Columbia, and Richmond. In those cities she had been at the center of countless conversations, a lady whose drawing room had functioned during the Confederacy as a sort of informal salon toward which generals and politicians and their ladies gravitated to talk and gossip, to mourn, to debate, to enjoy her company. Mrs. Chesnut's four nieces and nephews, the children of her sister Kate, remembered her as their beloved "Aunty," a family character about whom they fondly told stories. To a few citizens of Camden, the name Mary Chesnut called up pictures of General Chesnut's widow, an eccentric old lady with a caustic tongue, given to wearing her husband's worn-out trousers when she worked in the yard.

One of those who remembered her well was Miss Isabella Martin, a venerable spinster schoolteacher in Columbia who had in her possession the journals Mrs. Chesnut had kept during the Civil War, and a group of nearly fifty notebooks that contained a revision of those journals. Miss Martin kept them in a box under an armoire in her bedroom.[4]

When, in the last year of her life, Mrs. Chesnut had settled upon Isabella Martin as the right person to whom she could entrust the journals, the choice seemed an ideal one. Isabella was considerably younger than Mary but old enough to remember many of the people and events about which she had written. As a girl in her early twenties during the war, Isabella had admired the brilliant Mrs. Chesnut unabashedly and had impressed Mary in turn with her own intelligence. Over the years, the friendship grew. In the twenty years after the war, Isabella had established a school in Columbia that achieved a reputation for distinction. Thus, in Mary's eyes, she had proved her capabilities as an efficient and hard-working woman—one who would oversee the publication of the journals with care and dispatch.

In fact, Mary Chesnut became so fond of Isabella after the Civil War that as she revised her journals in the 1880s, she expanded Isabella's role in them. By converting what in 1864 or 1865 had been her own thoughts into dialogues between herself and Isabella, and by having Isabella comment wryly at times in the revision, Mary used the younger woman as a device to deemphasize her own pre-eminent role in the journal. Thus, the Isabella Martin to whom Mary entrusted her manuscripts was in part a character in Mary's imagination—the "irrepressible Isabella" of the journal.

When the journals became the responsibility of Miss Martin, she was nearly forty. The daughter of a devout minister, she had, with the passage of time, grown less irrepressible and more proper. In her role as pillar of the Washington Street Methodist Church and as a locally renowned educator, she became somewhat hidebound by propriety. She was also extremely busy. Several years, perhaps eight or nine, elapsed after Mary's death before Miss Martin actually took possession of the journals.[5] After reading them through, she contacted publishers, but when she received no enthusiastic response, she simply stored them away. The publication of the journals must have seemed less and less desirable as she grew older; they were filled with irreverent remarks and unflattering descriptions of people whose families still lived in Columbia and Camden. Even if she were to publish them, Isabella Martin felt she would have to edit the journals extensively, smooth them, quietly eliminate the curt passages that might hurt someone's feelings. In fact, she wrote to Francis Warrington Dawson of the Charleston *News and Courier*, assuring him that she would, of course, rewrite them completely. It may have crossed her mind that the best possible way to honor Mary Boykin Chesnut's name might be to destroy the journals.[6]

But she did not destroy them. As a teacher and a scholar, she sensed their historical value. In 1900 she quoted briefly from them in a short memoir of one of Mrs. Chesnut's Columbia friends, and in 1903, she lent a few passages dealing with hospital work to the editor of a book entitled *South Carolina Women in the Confederacy*. Very likely, Isabella Martin would have been content to continue to regard Mary Boykin Chesnut's journal as a private and somewhat awkward treasure, best displayed in this piecemeal way. But quite by accident in 1904 she met a New York writer and journalist whom she found congenial. Like Isabella, Myrta Lockett Avary was southern born and devoted to charitable works, an independent woman who had of necessity managed successfully to support herself.[7] Mrs. Avary had written a memoir, *A Virginia Girl in the Civil War*, so in the course of polite conversation, Isabella Martin told her of the Chesnut journals. Myrta Lockett Avary was looking for literary projects that might be profitable, but more than that, she was extremely interested in the history of her native region. Thus she asked Miss Martin to show her the journals and after reading them insisted that they should be published immediately.

The New York firm of D. Appleton agreed at once to publish the journals, and in very short order the work was prepared for the printer. Mrs. Avary handled most of the business details, and Miss Martin wrote an introduction and corrected a typescript that had been hastily prepared in New York. Partly because of limitations imposed by the publishers, but also because Miss Martin regarded as private many sections of the journal, less than half of the work was included; most of the passages dealing with Camden and Columbia were cut, and the remainder was edited with a free and heavy hand. A working title for the book was *With the Heroes of Dixie*, but Appleton arranged for serialization in the *Saturday Evening Post*, and when the first of five long excerpts appeared on January 28, 1905, it did so under the title *A Diary From Dixie*. Capitalizing on the publicity provided by the serialization, Appleton abandoned the less-than-satisfactory working title and adopted that of the *Post*. *A Diary From Dixie* was first published in March, 1905.[8]

Despite the fact that the market was saturated with southern memoirs in 1905, and despite the severe cutting and editing, *A Diary From Dixie* received favorable reviews. Most reviewers acknowledged that Mary Boykin Chesnut's book was by far the best of its kind and mentioned the personal charm of the author. One reader wrote directly to Miss Martin:

> The "Diary" is quaint, picturesque and beautiful beyond description, and if I should ever visit South Carolina again I would never leave the State until I had visited her grave. It has never been my happiness to meet so remarkable a woman, and her life is a heritage of glory for woman, dainty, piquant and beautiful. The world owes you a debt for bringing the Diary to light. It is more interesting than any love story, and excites in my mind an interest and admiration for Mrs. Chesnut that is little less than idolatry. No wonder every one sought her presence.[9]

Other readers were equally charmed with the author of *A Diary From Dixie*. Ben Ames Williams who read *A Diary* as background research for *House Divided*, his novel about the Civil War, was so drawn to Mary Boykin Chesnut that he based his heroine, Cinda Dewain, on her. When Williams discovered that the published version of the journal was heavily cut and that the manuscripts still existed, he obtained permission from the heirs to the journal to prepare a new, more complete edition. Williams' edition, published in 1949, did indeed include more than half again as much of the journal as Martin and Avary's had.[10] But just as the first edition, overseen by an old lady anxious to "protect" the writer's memory from her own indiscretions, had distorted Mrs. Chesnut's work, so did the Williams edition, prepared by a novelist eager to apply cosmetics to the journal. Williams cut over 100,000 words from the manuscript, revised wording, imposed twentieth-century punctuation and grammar, and silently added words, even sentences, of his own. Like the first editors, Williams did not include the information that the "diary" he was editing was in reality a much expanded, changed, and thoroughly restructured version of the original journal.

After its first publication in 1905, *A Diary From Dixie* became increasingly known, admired, and quoted by historians. And with the advent of the longer Williams edition, Mary Boykin Chesnut's book enjoyed an even wider reputation. Unaware of the extent to which *A Diary* had been rewritten twenty years after the war, historians used it to cite conversations "recorded" by Mrs. Chesnut as verbatim quotations from various dignitaries of the Confederate elite, and to applaud her remarkable objectivity and her ability to select just the right incidents and anecdotes. One reviewer of the 1949 edition praised her selectivity: "What the diarist saw, and saw so clearly, she put down without malice and generally, consciously or unconsciously, because the happening contributed to her picture of her time." The author was so successful, the reviewer added, that "One gets the feel of the time as if one were living in it."[11]

What these historians and reviewers were responding to in *A Diary From Dixie* was, in fact, Mary Chesnut's carefully planned work of literature, not an accident. Edmund Wilson sensed as much. In *Patriotic Gore*, he acknowledged the literary aspects of the book, if not the conscious artistry with which she wrote it: "The diarist's own instinct is uncanny. Starting out with situations or relationships of which she cannot know the outcome, she takes advantage of the actual turn of events to develop them and round them out as if she were molding a novel." Wilson acclaimed the book "an extraordinary document—in its informal department, a masterpiece." And although he believed that it had been written day by day in the midst of war, he assessed *A Diary* as a structured literary work.[12]

With the recent publication of C. Vann Woodward's edition of the revised journal, *Mary Chesnut's Civil War*, we can at long last appreciate Mrs. Chesnut's book in its entirety, as she wrote it.[13] Woodward makes clear the relationship of the book of the 1880s with the journals written during the Civil War. Thus, after nearly a hundred years, readers can see the intricate ways in which Mrs. Chesnut arranged and pointed up her material, creating the "extraordinary document" Wilson praised so highly.

The atmosphere and emotional tone of the revised Civil War journal are, of course, uniquely those of its author. Mary Boykin Chesnut was a remarkable person in her own day and would be considered so in any era. As an educated woman of an old and respected family, she was representative of her class and her time; but intellectually she was distinctly unrepresentative. Because she could perceive her place in the broader social and historical perspective, she often found herself set apart from most of her contemporaries. Thus, necessarily, she was in many respects a lonely woman, and she developed the habit of writing as a means to integrate the passionate, social side of her nature with the intellectually objective side.

From the beginning of secession, she recognized the depth of the political and social upheaval in which her region was engaged, and she felt herself qualified by education, social position, and native intelligence to report what she observed. Following the war and the loss of the Chesnut fortunes, she was able to assess the war and the society it had devastated. During the next twenty years, she taught herself to write by completing three novels; then she undertook the seemingly endless task of rewriting her war diaries.

Although she never finished polishing her revised Civil War journal to her own satisfaction (the manuscript she entrusted to Isabella Martin was not yet ready for a printer), it represents achievement of a high order. Lyman Butterfield, historian and editor of the Adams Papers, has called the Chesnut journal "the best written by a woman in the whole range of our history . . . in the same top bracket with that of Sewall, Byrd, Cotton Mather, John and John Quincy Adams . . . . Even in their company her book remains unique as a revelation of a woman's mind and heart; in short, a great book by a great lady." [14]

As she revised her journals, Mary Chesnut wrote to Varina Davis that she was trying to impose objectivity on them, to leave herself out, and to focus instead on the world around her. [15] But one cannot read more than a page or two without wishing to know more about the author herself. How was she educated? What social forces or private meditations worked upon her so that she grew into the witty and paradoxical woman who could write such a book?

Information on which to base answers to these questions is scant. [16] Mrs. Chesnut kept no diaries before or after the war. Most of the personal letters she received were periodically consigned to the fireplace. Although she was widely known—and loved—in her own time, she was certainly not famous. Thus, when her correspondents were conscientious or prudent enough to save Chesnut letters, they were usually the prim and formal communications of her husband—the statesman, the Confederate general—not the long, gossipy letters of his perceptive wife. The details and even the broad outlines of her life must be pieced together from few sources. Nevertheless, when the patchwork has been carefully sewn together, a woman emerges who is "a great lady" indeed. And just as her journal illuminates her world for the twentieth-century reader, so her life—compelling and indomitable—informs and illuminates her work.

STATESBURG, SOUTH CAROLINA, in 1823, the year Mary Boykin Miller was born, was a small community already proud of its role in the history of a nation little more than forty years old. The town was situated in the middle of the state, and its earliest settlers were in the area well before the Revolution. They had first established trading posts with the Indians and then had begun to carve out large and profitable plantations in the back-country wilderness. The settlement was remote from Charleston, the state's cultural, intellectual, and economic center. Caught up in the events of the Revolution, the citizens of Statesburg faced the hardships and irritations of British military rule with courage born of isolation and independence. With practical dispatch honed from their familiarity with the area, they resisted the British both covertly and openly. The rolls of the partisan bands of Francis Marion and Thomas Sumter included many names from Statesburg, and by the early 1820s, the heroic adventures of these men and their families had grown into a rich fabric of legend, passed from the participants themselves to their children and grandchildren. Thus the established families of Statesburg, their friends, relatives, and business associates in Camden, several miles to the north, all possessed a feeling of intimacy with history and a sense of prosperity and respectability fairly earned and hard won.

Mary Boykin Miller was born into this community on March 31, 1823, at Mount Pleasant, the plantation home of her mother's parents.[1] Her mother, Mary Boykin Miller, had been nineteen for less than a month when this her eldest child was born; her father, Stephen Decatur Miller, thirty-four, had already buried a much loved first wife and two sons. A lawyer by training, he had served a term in the United States Congress and was, in 1823, a senator in the South Carolina legislature. Both parents were to have a strong and positive influence on their daughter. Each brought to the child a heritage that stressed the importance of family, honor, and a deep respect for the values of honesty and duty. Equally important to Mary's development, both parents enjoyed life thoroughly and took pleasure in observing human nature with an objective but good-humored eye.

Stephen Decatur Miller was not by birth a member of the up-country elite. Born on May 8, 1788, in the Waxhaw Settlement, a small community near the North Carolina line in Lancaster District, he was the son of Margaret White, of Scotch-Irish descent, and Charles Miller, English. Both of Stephen's parents were Presbyterians whose ancestors had emigrated to this country prior to the Revolution. Because his people were not prominent and because they kept few records, little is known about them. They seem to have been yeoman farmers, later described by Miller as "respectable & unambitious." However, despite meager funds, Stephen and at least two of his brothers received good educations.[2] Stephen attended a neighborhood school, where he was taught classical literature and the scriptures. In 1808 he graduated from the newly founded South Carolina College in Columbia. From 1808 to 1811, he read law with John S. Richardson, who kept offices in Statesburg and nearby Sumter. Richardson was elected attorney general of South Carolina in 1810, and the following year Miller was admitted to the bar and took over Richardson's practice. Tall, slim, dark, with a rather harsh voice and an expressive face, Stephen Decatur Miller had achieved a reputation as a man of promise in his early twenties.

In 1814 he married Elizabeth Dick of Sumter, and in 1815 his first child, Elias Dick Miller, was born.[3] Two more sons, John Richardson and William Smith, followed in the next three years, but both died in infancy or very early childhood. At the age of twenty-nine, Miller was elected to Congress in 1817 and went to Washington, leaving his wife and children at home; but in January, 1818, he learned that his wife was very ill, and immediately returned to South Carolina. When she recovered enough to travel,

Miller took her back to Washington. Elizabeth Dick Miller died the following year, and at the end of his congressional term Miller returned to Statesburg and resumed his law practice.[4] On May 9, 1821, he married seventeen-year-old Mary Boykin. Although she was hardly more than a child herself, the second Mrs. Miller took over the mothering of her husband's six-year-old son, Dick.

Stephen Decatur Miller's new bride was of an old and respected South Carolina family. The first Boykin had emigrated to Virginia in 1685; Mary's own father, Burwell Boykin, had been brought at the age of four to South Carolina in 1755. As a resident of the Camden area, Burwell Boykin shared the hardships suffered by Whigs during the British occupation from 1780 to 1781 under Lord Rawdon. Along with two of his brothers, Boykin served as an officer in the American forces, riding with Generals Francis Marion and Thomas Sumter. Boykin was a successful planter and amassed a fortune large enough to enable him to leave considerable property to each of his children at his death in 1817. Mary, one of thirteen children, was born in 1804.[5] The family was a close one, and when Stephen Decatur Miller married Mary, he was accepted into the fold—the newlyweds probably lived at the Boykin plantation, Mount Pleasant, until Stephen bought Plane Hill, one mile away, in 1824.

Thus Mary Miller spent her early childhood surrounded by her mother's family, including many children: her mother's younger brothers Burwell, William, and Alexander Hamilton were twelve, ten, and eight when she was born; her Aunt Charlotte was six, and her own half-brother Dick was eight. But perhaps of all these relatives, the one who meant the most to Mary was her grandmother, Mary Whitaker Boykin, for whom she had been named, and who took the child under her wing at an early age and instructed her by example in the arts and duties of running a large plantation.[6] Almost fifty years later Mary wrote informally to her own nieces and nephews, describing her life on the Boykin plantation with her grandmother. As was always the case when her memories were vivid, her thoughts spilled onto the paper so quickly that she punctuated them almost entirely with dashes:

The old slave days of which Mrs Stowe has given the horrible account are gone. Grandma was a queer product of any thing of such
bad repute—She was a christian—She did unto others &c—I was
with her all days—her Shadow—the oldest grand daughter &
named for her—her pet—We began early. She read her chapter—&
we had our breakfast. . . . There were eight chambers in that
old house—& they were generally filled. So the breakfast was a Serious affair to the lady at the head of the table—afterwards—We fed
our chickens—we inspected our dairy—We ordered dinner.

Many of Mary's memories centered on the slave community
and the constant round of activities going on in the "Yard":

One day in the week was given over to cake & pastry making—
then we descended to the store room—next to that was the loom
room—where the weaving never stopped—Once in the store
room—I was happy—negroes came from the plantation—for
Medicine for shoes—for clothes—for hours she [Mary's grand-
mother] was ministering to their wants—We measured a shirt or a
pair of pantaloons by holding them up & guessing if they would fit.
They gave us a stick the size of the foot—& we stuck [it] into a pair
of shoes. We concocted all manner of physic—& gave out sugar—
vinegar to bathe heads in with brown paper—& heard all their
stories—then—began cuting out clothes—Grandma stood by a
table—& sung hymns & cut out Negro clothes all day—& I ran up
& down & carried them up to the sempstress room—where half a
dozen stiched away from Morn til dewy eve—then I sat on a table
& read novels to them—they knew the old books pretty well—&
asked for the tales they liked best—They sung old baluds. then I
learnt cruel Barbera Allen—& Lord Lovel—the head sempstress
used to sing—& talk—& sometimes crack any sleepy headed
youngster with her thimble—the wool seemed so thick we used to
hope it did not hurt—very much.

Mary's childhood was filled with plenty, and she was carefully
taught that abundance carried with it the responsibility to share
one's prosperity with friends and with less fortunate neighbors.

There were five or six milk maids—& there were pails upon pails
of strawberries & raspberries—& cotton baskets of peaches & ap-

ples in the Store room—& cherries & plums—it seems now—that
stoning—& peeling—& preserving & eating never ceased—in
those days of rude plenty—We drove to Camden seven miles in a
huge carriage—lined with red Morocco & it was not a pleasant
odour on a hot day—& it swung about too on its springs—& it was
packed to its utmost limits—it took cakes & tarts & sausages—&
hams to every body who needed them—besides taking us—Aunt
Betsey in a beautiful new white muslin sat on a cherry tart—which
was too much for the carriage box—& ought to have been handed
back to the footman—she was not in love with Grandma's charity
that day We often turned back—loaded down in this way if we met
a negro coming for physic or sugar or shirts or molasses—or a tale
That he wanted to tell Missis by herself. & then we proceeded in a
very bad humour to church—because 'Ma was so preposterous
about those negroes—"let them wait or come sooner" my aunts
said. If Grandma has not gone to Heaven—it is an empty place—
No mortal is there . . . . She died when I was eight.[7]

Before she had any formal schooling, then, Mary had learned a
great deal about the role of the plantation mistress, and had come
to know the slave artisans and house servants on the Boykin plantation well. In the same memoir, she says of the head "sempstress," "I know now that Leah was a slave—but I could not have
found it out then for myself." At her parents' house, Plane Hill,
she also spent many hours with servants; there she taught her
mother's butler to read while "sitting on his knife board."[8]

Mary herself had been taught to read long before she was old
enough to attend school regularly—most probably by her mother—
and in addition to the practical education provided by her grandmother, she was told and read countless stories by her young
aunts and uncles, her parents and grandmother. As an adult, she
recalled particularly her own fascination with her older brother
Dick, who told her stories that she later realized were literary classics, dramatized for a child's delight. Dick also gave his little sister
simplified explanations of the political realities of the day:

See this line—which he drew with with the toe of his boot across
the passage at Plane Hill—"The constitution draws this line & says
to old Hickory so far shalt thou go & no farther"—"See"—& he

stepped his new boots over—"Old Hickory steps over—& takes the bags of money from the Bank—& says—by the eternal—that for your line—stop me if you can"—Then he would read—& declaim to Stephen & myself following him round like puppies do a big dog. . . . Day after day he used to declaim . . . to Tebe & me—often standing on the gate post. When he was exhausted—he went off into the woods & under a tree would play the flute for hours. In the afternoon he would say—"little Sissy dress—& let us go & call on Aunt Charlotte"—she being his lady love. We went up the hill hand in hand—he telling me wonderful stories out of the Arabian nights.[9]

Mary, eldest granddaughter of the Boykins, first child of her parents' marriage, and Stephen Decatur Miller's first daughter, seems to have been the pride of the family. Her father, in letters to his friend and political mentor, Governor David Rogerson Williams, had even "betrothed" his infant daughter to the ex-governor's grandson, David. But Senator Miller was unable to spend much time with Mary, who remembered him as "never" being at home. Miller's political fortune was rising, and as head of the state senate judiciary committee in 1824, he introduced into the state senate a resolution that became the foundation of the States' Rights party in South Carolina.[10] Largely due to his championship of states' rights, Miller was elected governor in 1828.

In the years of her father's governorship, political associates from throughout the state visited frequently at Plane Hill. Although Governor Miller was inaugurated in a full suit of homespun and prided himself on his image as a man of the people, he began to redecorate his house with elegant furniture and fabrics, ordering tables of "the Very finest Egyption—Marble" and beautiful curtains and mirrors shipped from New York. And Mary's life, which had centered on the routines of her parents' handsome home and her grandmother's plantation, began to expand outward from the familiar worlds of Statesburg and Camden. During Miller's term of office, his family joined him in Columbia, the state capital, for extended visits. Mary's formal schooling probably began in Columbia, for in later years she would mention friends first met at schools there run by Mrs. Henrietta De Leon and Mrs.

Sarah Faust.[11] But it is likely that Mary at ages five and six attended Columbia schools only briefly, perhaps as a visitor, and that the primary responsibility for her education rested still with her mother. Nevertheless, she was learning a great deal that would be invaluable to her as an adult. Politics was in the air she breathed. Snatches of conversations overheard by the child suggested to her that political issues were an important and natural facet of adult life. Glimpses of distinguished ladies and gentlemen, to whom she was no doubt proudly exhibited, introduced her to many of South Carolina's most influential people. Even the preparations for teas, dinners, and parties she watched behind the scenes familiarized her with the social role she would later fill so easily and well.

Prohibited by state law from serving more than one term as governor, Miller successfully sought a seat in the United States Senate in 1830. His politics were radical, but very much in accord with the public opinion of the day in South Carolina. The federal tariff act of 1828, the "tariff of abominations," infuriated South Carolinians. Following the beliefs of Miller and his political allies, they regarded the tariff as unjust and unconstitutional. At Statesburg in September, 1830, Miller, a powerful speaker, coined a phrase that became the rallying cry of the Nullifiers: "There are three and only three ways to reform our Congressional legislation, familiarly called, the ballot box, the jury box and the cartridge box." Elected to the refrain "the ballot box, the jury box, or the cartridge box," Miller went to Washington once again, this time leaving a family that now included Stephen Decatur, Jr., born in 1825, and Catherine, born in 1827. (Sarah Amelia was to be born in late 1831.)[12]

While her father was gone, Mary began school in Camden, seven miles from home. During the week, she stayed with her aunt and uncle, Elizabeth Boykin Withers and Thomas Jefferson Withers; each Friday, a carriage from Plane Hill called for her and took her home for the weekend. No evidence exists to indicate which school Mary first attended, though she was certainly going into Camden to school in 1832. However, in 1833 a young Vermont woman named Stella Phelps opened a school for young ladies on Lyttleton Street that Mary attended for two years. Stella Phelps had been well educated at Emma Willard's Troy Female

Seminary[13] and quickly made a reputation in Camden and throughout the state as an excellent teacher. Mary later described her thus:

> Our Principal—Miss Stella, was tall and thin, with blue eyes,
> and a clear, straight forward look in them; dark hair, what there
> was of it; beautiful hard white teeth—a fair complexion—a fine
> face withal, from its honest, pure, expression. [She was] flat
> chested, awkward and ungainly with a certain unmistakable dig-
> nity of bearing, which commanded our respect.
>
> A rigid Presbyterian, not a shadow of injustice or unfairness ever
> came near her.
>
> . . . . . . . . . . . . . . . . . . . . . . . . . . . . . . . . . . . . . . . . . . . . . . . . . .
>
> We had huge fire places at each end of our school rooms. And I
> dare say our poor school mistress accustomed to better behavior,
> was driven wild by our undisciplined conduct. We were in the first
> place hopelessly restless. And to go up and warm, or to go out and
> drink water presented two very convenient means of stretching our
> young legs.
>
> Having drunk the bucket of water dry, or slopped it all over the
> floor, the next move was to ask permission to fill it at the well. Her
> patience was inexhaustible. Certainly my two years with this excel-
> lent woman were invaluable to me.[14]

One Friday when the carriage from Plane Hill arrived to pick up
the child family servants called "Little Missie," her teacher accompanied her to spend the weekend. At home, Mary overheard a
conversation between Miss Stella and Senator Miller which impressed her deeply:

> My father whose manner to women was always courteous, nay,
> flattering, was saying the most complimentary [things] to Miss
> Stella. She was cold, calm, unbending. She said "the governing
> principle of her life was Duty."
>
> . . . "When I marry—I doubt if I ever shall know any thing of
> love as a passion; it will be from a sense of duty."
>
> "God forbid any woman should marry me from a sense of duty,"
> piously and fervently cried the padre. "I married from a sense of
> beauty. And you see. It was the wisest thing I ever did in my life."[15]

The woman's role as demure, dutiful, subordinate to man that was
carefully and formally taught to all young girls of her place and
time would never sit comfortably on Mary's shoulders. Instead,

she embraced the passion and fervor with which her father approached all things domestic, and she adopted his "sense of beauty," his love of the attractive, the appealing, as her own.

Even when Stephen Decatur Miller was away from home, the relationship between father and daughter remained strong. When he was in Washington, Mary wrote to him every Saturday on her weekend vacation. One such letter survives, written shortly before her ninth birthday. It suggests that other traits later to characterize her adult life were already being formed in the girl: a frankness which, in later years, was sometimes to spill over into indiscretion, an interest in politics, and even, perhaps, an eagerness to read the newspapers.

> Plane Hill    March 3    1832
>
> MY DEAR FATHER
>
> It gives me great pleasure to write to you every saturday when I come home Mother says she received a letter from you this morning and says you have been speaking on the tariff I will read my Fathers speech when it is published. . . . Kitty says if she dont dare to ask you for things who can she ask are you not her Father she says and she will ask you as much as she pleases. You must think of me some times
>
> Your affectionate Daughter
>
> MARY B. MILLER [16]

Thus Mary kept in close contact with her absent father, and he, whom historians portray as a fire-breathing nullifier, seems to have remained emotionally tied to his family in South Carolina. His letters home bespeak a man intimately concerned with the day-to-day lives of his children, and longing to be with them, perhaps because he remembered his earlier sojourn in Washington which had ended with the death of his first wife. [17] Suddenly, in 1832, his two surviving sons, Dick and Stephen, were stricken with a serious illness and, with no warning, the older boy died at the age of seventeen. Stephen was made deaf by fever and would never completely regain robust health. Dick's death was a severe blow to his father—the boy, a sophomore at the South Carolina College at the time he died, had been bright and popular. Mary later wrote of him: "Still I constantly meet old friends & acquaintances of his who speak of him with such affection & regret. He was a boy of brilliant promise—handsome, clever, ambitious—untameable spirits. . . . One curious trait borne witness to by all—he fought to win—or to whip—& he fought about any or every thing as it happened—but he rarely lost his temper—he began the row laughingly & so ended."[18]

In November, 1833, Stephen Decatur Miller resigned his seat in the Senate, pleading ill health. Although he never resumed political activity, he remained an active man from 1833 until his death, probably from yellow fever, in 1838. It seems likely, therefore, that some of his ill health was of the spirit—the rewards of national politics in the 1830s were simply insufficient to make up for the family separations, and this man who cared so much for his family was unwilling any longer to live apart from them.

From the time of her father's return in 1833 until the spring of 1835, Mary Miller's life was much like that of any schoolgirl of her era. Kitty joined her at Miss Stella's school, and the two sisters must have explored the Camden area on afternoon outings—perhaps wandering over the crumbling Revolutionary redoubts still visible on Hobkirk Hill, the site of a bloody battle between the British commander Lord Rawdon and General Nathanael Greene in 1781, perhaps pausing to watch schoolboys play cricket on the commons that dotted the town.

Camden, a small community during the Revolution, had become a city of more than one thousand in the 1830s. Visitors arrived by stagecoach or booked passage up the Wateree River on one of the boats owned and operated by the large cotton plantations that surrounded the town—boats that carried cotton and other products to market in Charleston and returned bearing goods and materials ordered by the planters. A commercial center, Camden's most impressive building was the market which boasted a steeple that housed the town clock. At the steeple's peak was a striking weathervane representing King Haiglar, a Catawba Indian chief, who had frequently visited the area, called Pine Tree Hill, in the 1750s. Overseen by King Haiglar with his bow eternally drawn against the wind, the streets of the town were busy by day, filled with farm wagons, ladies' carriages, shoppers on foot, servants carrying messages or doing errands for their masters, lawyers going in and out of the courthouse opposite the market, and the cows and hogs that grazed and rooted along the streets and in the public squares. Occasionally a small group of Catawba Indians came to town, remnants of the Indian nation who had lived here before white settlers came. Every evening at nine, Mary could hear the bell on the town clock—which at other times served as market bell and fire alarm—ringing a curfew to signal that slaves must be off the streets.

In the summers, Mary and her sister probably went to hear her father speak at Fourth of July ceremonies in front of the Cornwallis House, a large, traditional frame house which had been the town's first mansion. Built in 1780 by Joseph Kershaw, grandfather of the famous Civil War general, it was still unfinished when General Cornwallis took it over in June, 1780, to serve as British Headquarters during the occupation of Camden. After the Revolution, the commons in front of the mansion became the site of civil and military gatherings. In the winter, the Miller girls, chaperoned by one of their numerous Camden relatives, could go to the annual Camden Races that attracted planters and their families from all the neighboring counties. And during the Christmas season, they could shoot off firecrackers in a traditional celebration of the holidays. Once or twice during her childhood, the winter weather was severe enough to freeze small ponds, and Mary could watch local gentlemen who had been to northern colleges demonstrate the strange sport of ice skating. In the winter of 1835 the Wateree River itself was frozen over at Camden, a circumstance that, as far as anyone could remember, had happened only once before.

Each year on the first of May, Mary and her friends danced around the Maypole at a festival inaugurated by her teacher, Miss Stella, which quickly became a favorite social event among the young people of Camden. One spring afternoon, perhaps during this period, Mary was sitting with her aunt when she saw a "very handsome old man" who was introduced to her as Colonel Chesnut of Mulberry. "I was in my earliest youth in the days of the first primer," remembered Mary in 1876. The colonel impressed her with his "stout bay horses—his friends mounted out rider—& his bull dogs—lazily trotting along." [19] Mary's parents were both well acquainted with the Chesnuts—the Boykins had been their neighbors, friends and hunting companions since Revolutionary days—and Mary had probably already met the youngest Chesnut child, James, who was a friend of her uncle Alexander Hamilton Boykin. In the spring of 1835, James was a senior at Princeton; five years hence, he would become her husband.

It was during 1835 that Stephen Decatur Miller sold Plane Hill to his young brother-in-law Alexander Hamilton Boykin and determined to move his family to Mississippi, where he owned cotton plantations. The decision to move west was one which many planters of the Camden area—and indeed of the state as a whole—made during the 1820s and 30s. Much South Carolina soil had become depleted, and as the Indian tribes of Alabama and Mississippi were forced farther west, the rich lands of the deep south states presented new opportunities for fortunes to be made.

For the last several years, Camden residents had watched as countless families migrated to the West and Southwest. As early as 1828 the town newspaper had reported the streets of Camden "literally choked with wagons, carts" and other vehicles, many en route to new settlements. By 1835 such movement had become commonplace; one editor saw some eight hundred westward bound people pass through the town in a single week. [20]

Nevertheless, the proposed move seems an odd step for Miller to have taken. He was, after all, principally a lawyer rather than a planter, and he was leaving a state where he had enjoyed singular honors. Furthermore, he who had resigned from the Senate for reasons of health, was leaving a relatively healthy environment for a climate which fostered illness, particularly malaria and yellow fever.

Miller's reasons for choosing to move were undoubtedly complicated. His political life in the state had been bound up in the states' rights and nullification controversy, which, by 1833 with the Clay compromise tariff, had become a less emotionally charged issue. Certainly by the time John C. Calhoun openly espoused the doctrine of nullification in 1831, Miller had been forced out of the limelight by the stronger politician. Prior to 1833 Miller had owned land in Mississippi that was being planted by overseers,[21] and he must have been attracted to the challenge of undertaking a new enterprise much as he had so willingly battled the nationalist economic principles of the federal government ten years earlier. His uncertain health may have prompted him to improve his financial position as quickly as possible. By ability laced with a generous sprinkling of luck and energy, he had risen from modest beginnings to prominence in the state, and had married into the planter aristocracy; perhaps he cherished the idea of cementing his position as a member of that aristocracy himself. Two of his wife's brothers, Francis and William Whitaker Boykin, had established themselves in Alabama, and Miller had no doubt watched their progress carefully. Whatever his motives, once the decision was made, he was faced with the difficult task of relocating a family. Living conditions on his Mississippi plantation were not lavish—indeed they were primitive—transportation was difficult, and the climate was unhealthy during the summer months.

The Millers determined that regardless of the whereabouts of the family, Mary had reached an age when she was ready for more rigorous schooling than Miss Stella could provide; her father had long wished for her to learn French. Accordingly, in the spring of 1835, he accompanied her to Charleston and enrolled her in a fine French boarding school run by Madame Ann Marsan Talvande, an indomitable character and an excellent teacher. Mary, now twelve, probably came back to Camden for the summer (for her mother and the younger children remained there through 1835) and then returned to Madame Talvande's for the fall term. At Christmas that year, perhaps as a going away party, Mrs. Miller gave a ball for her sister Charlotte, which the two youngest Chesnut sisters, Emma and Sarah, attended.[22] It was probably shortly after the New Year in 1836 that Stephen Decatur Miller first took his family to Mississippi, leaving Mary at school in Charleston.

THREE 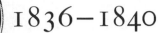 1836–1840

MADAME TALVANDE'S FRENCH School for Young Ladies was one of the most respected schools for girls in the Southeast. Located in a fashionable section of Old Charleston, the school occupied two large townhouses connected by a walkway and gardens. Both have been carefully preserved, and look today much as they did when Mary was a student at Madame Talvande's in the 1830s. One of the houses opened on Tradd Street by a porte cochère, and as Mary later described it, "must have been a grand establishment in its day; so thick were the walls and so fine the wood carving, not to speak of the sculptured white marble mantle pieces." The main floor of the Tradd Street house served as "State drawing room . . . finely furnished in French style with mirrors, to the superfluous point. The walls were papered with the story of Paul and Virginia [a sentimental French novel popular at the time] depicted in every color of the rainbow on a back ground of gorgeous tropical scenery." The other house, which fronted Legare Street, was frame, an excellent example of the traditional Charleston house "with its three tiers of Piazzas open to the breezes from the East, South and West." On the main floor of the Legare Street house was the schoolroom; boarding students lived on the floors above. Mary found much about the school to her liking. She delighted in the flower gardens and the orchard of flowering trees planted between the houses. But the high brick walls "surmounted by rows of broken glass bottles" that surrounded the grounds seemed to make the place "a Convent in its seclusion." And although today the Legare Street house is known for its famous Sword Gates of iron grillwork, in the 1830s there was only a narrow green door in the wall which, in Mary's eyes, "suggested a Nunnery."[1]

If from the street Madame Talvande's had something of the look of a convent, the atmosphere inside (which Mary would later preserve in her unpublished, largely autobiographical novel, "Two Years—or The Way We Lived Then") was usually lively—even deafening:

> Of Pianos more or less ill-used there were one or two in every room in the house. From "morn till dewy eve" the sound of their drumming and strumming abated not. Singing, taking lessons, practicing.
>
> As you entered the Hall door—every imaginable sound of *Musique manquée* burst forth or was shut off, by the opening or shutting of doors; dominated generally by the deep, gruff, growling voice of the old man, who gave singing and guitar lessons in the small parlor; round the corner of the brick house passage, came portentous sounds, for there a younger and more energetic Frenchman strenuously battered to his heart's content, a loud Piano—if one may be allowed such a contradiction in terms. We were perfectly accustomed to this Babel—and cared as little for it as a Miller does for the racket of his Mill.[2]

In the company of eleven other "young barbarians," Mary lived in a large room on the third story. Windows on three sides provided a view of the Battery and beyond it, the bay. One side of the room was lined with dressing tables and washstands; another housed the ubiquitous piano, on which someone "of a conscientious turn of mind, was always practicing; oftenest with wide stretched mouth singing her solfeggios."[3] When privacy was desired, the girls improvised screens and bed curtains of their petticoats; when they had just returned from an afternoon at the theater, the same petticoats became stage curtains for an amateur production.

Madame Talvande's school was expensive; basic tuition was $500.00 a term, and there were additional charges for special subjects and outings—dancing lessons, $34.00 per quarter; drawing, $68.67, including supplies; and music lessons, $33.75. Therefore, its more than a hundred students were, for the most part, from wealthy families. When Mary Miller first arrived there, she was only twelve. From the outset, however, she seems to have been a natural leader and a particular favorite of the headmistress, Ann

Talvande, whose standards of social and scholastic conduct were extremely (indeed, to her students, terrifyingly) high. Mary's regular seat in the dining room, for example, was at Madame's right hand; when the famous Bishop England dined, as he did every Wednesday, she was not relegated to a lesser table, but rather moved one seat to enable the bishop to sit next to Madame. Thus, once a week the up-country girl participated in conversation between her teacher and one of the foremost Catholic divines of her time. Mary must have been, even at thirteen and fourteen, reliably proper and a notably charming, witty conversationalist.[4]

Aside from what Mary herself wrote about it in the 1870s, little is known about Madame Talvande's school. The curriculum seems to have been somewhat broader than that of most girls' schools of the day. Mary studied literature, music, history, rhetoric, and natural science (including chemistry, botany, and astronomy) as well as singing and dancing. Above all, she learned to speak French so fluently that she was occasionally taken for a native of France, and to read as readily in French as in English. German, too, was taught, and Mary emerged from Madame Talvande's able to read German and to write beautiful German script.[5]

In a society where the role of women was carefully delineated and women were, by both law and custom, dominated by men, Madame Talvande's school was a community of women, ruled and operated by women. It was an environment in which Mary excelled, and in which her talents for leadership could be exercised. As significant to Mary as the scholastic opportunities was the social environment in which she found herself. Here under one roof were the daughters of sea island planters, Huguenots and Carolinians of English descent. Separated from family for the first time, Mary also formed close ties with two servants who mothered her: Maum Jute, the self appointed "Maumer" to her favorite students, and Dédé, an elderly woman the color of "handled ivory" who had come to Charleston when her master fled the slave uprisings in Santo Domingo at the turn of the century. For Dédé, particularly, the attachment was very strong, and Mary vowed to her that she would buy her as soon as she was able.[6]

Many of the girls with whom she went to school remained lifelong friends, among them Sue Petigru, who was later to become the novelist Sue King, and James Chesnut's niece Mary Serena Chesnut Williams, who became Mary Miller's closest girlhood friend.[7] The two Marys had undoubtedly known one another in Camden, for Mary Williams, whose mother had died when she was a baby, had spent much of her life at Mulberry and Sandy Hill with her grandparents, James and Mary Cox Chesnut. Now in Charleston, Mary Williams was occasionally called on by her young uncle, James Chesnut, Jr., who had recently graduated from Princeton. In the summer or fall of 1836, he became interested in his niece's vivacious friend Mary Miller—then thirteen. Mary may at first have regarded James as the beau of her young aunt, Charlotte Boykin, for Camden gossip had linked the two together the preceding year; Mary Williams had been convinced that James was likely to marry Charlotte. Nevertheless, Mary Miller and James Chesnut were soon seen walking together on the Battery, and eventually news of this reached Mary's father, who determined that his daughter had best be removed from temptation—or at least from the prying eyes of scandalmongers—and placed once again under the supervision of her mother.[8]

Accordingly, in the fall of 1836, Mary was taken with her whole family (who had returned to Camden for the summer months) to Mississippi, a journey that took four or five weeks, and which was accomplished in a landau drawn by four horses, accompanied by two saddle horses, a baggage wagon, and a number of servants. Mary was to use the trip to Mississippi as a structuring device in her novel "Two Years—or The Way We Lived Then" written in the 1870s, but she also described the trip in her 1876 memoir of her sister Kate, "We called her Kitty":

> We drove out in a Landau—which could be closed if necessary—& four spanking bays—father & Mother rode on horseback a great deal—& when they were tired of that Stephen & one of us girls were too thankful to get out for a gallop. We were four children in there—& as a rule our parents seemed to prefer their own company to ours—for we did not often get their horses—We stopped at the roughest places—Some times had all to sleep in one room—Sally's principal pleasure as we passed a village was to sing at the top of her

voice—a song called "The choctow nation pretty little wife & a big plantation" & as we were rather an unusual turn out even with[out] Sally's vocal efforts I think every living thing would come out to watch us pass.[9]

Mary, who regarded the trip as a punishment, began her journey in a pout, but natural good spirits soon got the better of her, and she found the trip a revelation; in a very real sense, her sensibilities were being awakened. Not only did she learn a great deal about the hardships of frontier life, but she also grew "intimately acquainted" with her own family.[10] She began to see and know her father and mother in a new light—as human beings in their own right—and appreciated for the first time the ties that bound her parents together:

> As usual the heads of the family had been on horse back all the afternoon the day the[y] arrived at home—a sudden change had taken place in the weather—cold north wind &c—When the horses stopped at the door—with out waiting to be helped Mother jumped as was her custom—but her knees were stiff from the cold & long ride & she fell like a log—in one second we were all there—but father pushed us aside—he carried her in the house  That was my first lesson as to what a man's love means—I can never forget the tones of his voice—as he tried to rouse her—& we tried all remedies—he told her she was his life—That he could not face life a moment with out her. Angel was the worst word in his mouth—& as she revived he continued to whisper these things in such excitement & intense anxiety—I was dumbfounded. I knew nothing of death—I did not understand her danger—I was thinking how awfully he is in love with her—She was nearly thirty—he twenty years older.[11]

In Mississippi, too, she learned firsthand of the plight of the Indians of the Old Southwest, for the Millers' nearest neighbor was the famous Choctaw chief, Greenwood LeFlore. Son of a Frenchman, Louis LeFleur, and an Indian woman, Rebecca Cravat, LeFlore was educated in Nashville and moved to Mississippi about 1820. Elected a chief of the Choctaws two years later, he had been in the forefront of the Indians' unsuccessful struggles to retain their land. Although by the early 1830s most Choctaws had migrated west,

LeFlore remained in Mississippi and established himself as a plant-er. By the time the Millers moved to Mississippi, he had succeeded notably on the white man's terms, and had become one of the area's largest land- and slaveholders. Thirteen-year-old Mary Miller was not impressed by his status as a planter. For her, that was a commonplace. But his tales of his Choctaw brothers and their hopeless battles with "Christian" politicians sparked all her romantic sympathies.[12]

Too, for the first time, she began to understand some of the anomalies of the slave system on which her life was based. "I received there my first idea that negroes were not a divine institu-tion—for our benefit—or we for theirs—At any rate Kitty said some girls shamed her for owning so many negroes—& we proud-ly told each other that the more we had the better it was—We liked them all—& they seemed devoted to us."

Mississippi, compared to Camden and Charleston, was primi-tive: "We had then three plantations—& several hundred slaves—but it was hard to make ourselves . . . comfortable—it took ten oxen to haul up any thing from the river." The plantation was lo-cated in north central Mississippi in what is now Carroll County, seven miles from Carrollton on the Yalobusha River, a tributary of the Yazoo. The family lived in a log house of two rooms con-nected by an open passage way. Fine linens, silver, and china had been brought from South Carolina, but the furniture consisted of pine beds, tables, and six chairs. Mary's room was a clapboard leanto, and when she sought to build a retreat down on the banks of the bayou, where she could go to read and escape the family for a time, she was advised to beware of rattlesnakes, bears, and pan-thers. One night, wolves collected under the house, "barking and howling, and roaring like a pack of hounds, knocking against ev-erything and sniffing as if resolved to get in somewhere."[13]

Despite such hardships, Mary adjusted quickly and contrived as best she could to devise diversions and outings and to meet new friends. However, she was to remain on the plantation only about six months before she was taken back to Charleston and enrolled again in Madame Talvande's school. Apparently the same charm that had attracted James Chesnut worked equally well in Mississippi. "Stephen & Kates school people gave a ball we went to it—& all danced . . . & then there were mysterious whisperings—& I was packed up—& taken back to Charleston. Some of the men I met at the ball—& I do not in the least remember any of them—wrote to me—& were fool enough to give the letters to Willis [her father's body servant]—who did not think they were fit for Missy to wipe her shoes on. So the letters were answered—& I did not hear of it until several years after." Mary's mother pointed out to her husband that his daughter could be trusted, that men could be found everywhere, and that Mary was likely to find a better sort in Charleston than on the Mississippi plantation. Bowing to his wife's logic, Miller escorted Mary back to Charleston in the spring of 1837.[14]

The trip began with a carriage ride to one of the boat landings on the Yazoo River. There passage was engaged on a small boat that carried father and daughter down the narrow, muddy waterway to Vicksburg. At Vicksburg, they transferred to a Mississippi steamer bound for New Orleans, and in New Orleans took yet another boat to Mobile. From Mobile they journeyed to Pensacola and then, by various stage lines, to Macon, Augusta, and eventually Aiken, South Carolina. The final lap of the trip was by train over a route opened only two years before, which must have seemed luxuriously fast after so many days of travel. In Charleston, Miller left his daughter once more under the protection of Madame Talvande and returned to Mississippi.[15]

For the next six months or so, Mary was very much isolated from her loved ones, for this year the family remained on the cotton plantation in the two-room "double log house" all summer. One by one, each member of the family except her father fell ill with what was probably yellow fever; her mother was considered "desperately ill." Alarmed, Miller brought his family to Charleston in the fall of 1837, and established them in the Planters' Hotel for the winter, leaving his wife with a carriage and two servants. Kitty was placed at Madame Talvande's with her sister, and Sally, the youngest, attended as a day student. Mary was to remember this winter as the best of her life. She and Kitty went home every Friday night and remained with their mother until Monday after breakfast. "Mother invented every manner of excuse to come & see us—& to take us out walking with her."[16]

Charleston in the 1830s had been the economic, social, and cultural center of the Southeast for a hundred years. It was a city famed for its beauty, and for Mary Miller it was—in contrast to rural Mississippi—an enchanting environment. On weekends and half-holidays, when she could escape from Madame Talvande's for an afternoon, the city offered her virtually limitless entertainment. In addition to the routine pleasures of streets lined with shops, there was always the possibility of something unexpected. Traveling menageries frequently came to town, and once, to her horror, she saw the captured Seminole chiefs Osceola and Micanopy being exhibited to the public in the courtyard of the Planters' Hotel. "There they were—like a monkey show—with a crowd of boys and negroes looking on—The Indian Warriors. Micanopy who was of Falstaffian proportions, bodily and mentally, sat eating and drinking and laughing. Not so Osceola. His was the saddest face I ever saw. Under that red skin it seems there was a heart to be broken. . . . For the poor savage—there is no friend. It seemed to me that my country had not dealt magnanimously with these aborigines of the soil. And I found the dignified Osceola a sad spectacle."[17] Such incidents were important to young Mary Miller's development, for she was beginning to conceive a deep-seated hatred for slavery in any form or disguise—a hatred that would often, in future years, set her apart from her peers. But such sobering incidents were few; this was, for the most part, a season for merriment and adventure, and there was little time for quiet contemplation.

Naturally gregarious, Mary was pleased by the opportunities that Charleston afforded her—to enter society, to stroll with friends along the Battery, to join in the annual Race Week festivities, and once a week, to dance with proper young men in an elegant "longroom":

> I remember how we looked. Our dresses did not go much below the calf of the leg, so there was no hiding an ugly foot or ankle;

these dresses were also scant and narrow; we wore with short waists large buckles and broad belts; and the eider down cushions in our huge sleeves made us looked winged.

Our hair was plastered down on each cheek, leaving the ears standing out like handles to a jug or "walrus ears"; and then it was done up in what was called a "French twist" and on the top of the head it was arranged in one high puff. This does not sound very enticing. But if we were not lovely, the men did not find us out, and we were perfectly satisfied with ourselves.[18]

It was Madame Talvande's policy to accompany her students to concerts and plays on Friday and Saturday nights, to see (as Mary later put it) "whatever was worth seeing—& a good deal besides." Plays were a particularly welcome diversion because the fun could be duplicated night after night: "We continued to perform a travesty of the last play, every night in our rooms, (in all the freedom of night gowns and counterpane robes of state trailing behind, with most ingenious devices to simulate male attire)."[19]

For Mary, trips to the theater offered more than fuel for the imagination. They offered the excitement of romantic encounters: "As soon as we were all seated in solid phalanx flanked by Miss Anne Johnson—& her deputies on every side would come some nice young man who had considerately gone for Mother & persuaded her to come too—& Mad T would be requested through him or them (for some times there were two of them)—to allow myself & my sister to sit with our Mother—if there was a box at the Theatre—it would be very nice. Madame thought our Mother very indiscreet—but she dared not refuse."[20]

The most persistent "nice young man" to accompany Mrs. Miller and her daughters was James Chesnut, Jr., who was by now reading law in the office of the prominent Charleston lawyer James L. Petrigru. This winter James and fourteen-year-old Mary fell in love. For James, the emotion was no doubt a real one; he was twenty-three and had been an eligible bachelor for several years, moving in society in Charleston and Camden as well as Philadelphia and Trenton, New Jersey (where his mother's relatives[21] had frequently entertained him while he was at Princeton). For Mary, however, James represented her first serious entry into the glamorous world of belles and beaux, and her feeling was one of excitement rather than love. She "looked on him as a sort of half holiday—could any man want to be any thing more delightful to a school girl?" There were other young men in her life, for she later wrote of receiving several proposals, but at fourteen and fifteen she relegated marriage to the cloudy future.[22]

The excitement, frolic, and romance of this period were cut off abruptly on March 8, 1838, by the death of her father. Miller, who had spent the winter in Mississippi, had become ill, and was preparing to depart for South Carolina when he died at the home of his nephew Charles M. Hart in Raymond, Mississippi; his last wish had been to see his wife and children.[23]

Mary, her sister Kitty, and her mother were stunned. The thirty-four-year-old widow turned to her many brothers and sisters for comfort and help, and returned to Camden to recover from the shock and decide what course to take. Mary, too, in the sober atmosphere of mourning began to think seriously about the future. James Chesnut loomed large in her thoughts. He had declared his love for her, and she, in turn, confided her own love for James to her closest friend, Mary Williams. In September of 1838, she began to keep a daybook and, on the flyleaf, wrote the initials MC and MMC in the time-honored fashion of girls in love, to see how her new initials would look should she marry.[24]

Miller's estate proved to be encumbered by debts; Mrs. Miller faced the necessity of selling the plantations immediately, and determined to proceed west without delay. Prior to leaving for Mississippi, however, she and her daughter made a brief trip to Charleston where, on October 8, a poem signed C and entitled "To Miss M on leaving for Mississippi" was carefully copied into the daybook—James Chesnut's parting gift to Mary:

> Sweet is the incensed breath of morn,
> That lately wooed some vernal flower—
> More grateful yet the sign that's borne,
> In sorrow at the parting hour,
>     for those thou leavest behind.
>
> Bright are gay hopes glittering beams,
> Gilding o'er our youthful sky;

Yet brighter still the tear that gleams
With chastened beauty from thine eye
    for those thou grievest to leave.

Dear are those scenes, we loved so well,
Of earlier joys, of younger years;
But dearer far the kind farewell
Thy flowing feeling fondly bears
    To those thou lovest well.

And happy they whose friends ne'er fall,
Whose cares are few, whose hopes still live—
Happier still are those, than all,
Who feel, for them, that thou wilt give
    A tear or sorrowing sigh.

On the next page of the daybook, though probably several weeks later, Mary copied these lines, very likely her own:

'Since then I have wept bitter tears
    And roam'd through far & foreign climes,
And changeful scenes, through dreary years,
    Have taught me to forget old times—

I have forgotten many a face,
    And many a haunt of early youth,
But one dear memory keeps it's place—
    Thy love's first glow & earnest truth—

In the midst of all this sentimental verse, Mary wrote a comment suggestive of her later incisive diary entries of the Civil War years: "How untrue to say youth is the happiest season of our life: It is filled with vexations, for almost all our ideas are false ones; they must be set right—and often how harshly!" Mary Miller, whose clear intelligence and straightforward approach to life had been evident from her earliest letters, was no longer a schoolgirl, and there was nothing in her relationship with James Chesnut, Jr., to induce her into flights of moonlight and roses. Instead, he was a constant in her life: established, mature, intelligent, admiring, and above all, stable.

A few days before leaving on her second trip to Mississippi, Mary received from James a "most elaborate composition—offering himself." [25] She was not allowed to read the letter, but was in-structed by her elders to write a note of refusal. She did so, only to receive a second letter protesting that no answer was needed. Mary later remembered:

> They made me answer & say *No* I could not accept any body at fifteen . . . they seemed satisfied—Next day we went to Columbia on our way to Mississippi—We remained there a week—& I re-ceived a letter from Mr C of the most decided kind—quite grateful *at not* being refused—here was a row—they accused me of not being candid . . . . This time Aunt Charlotte wrote the formal refusal—& I copied it—she put "hopes that can never be realized"—& after they read it—I ran my pen thro "never" & substituted *not*—Never being a long word—So I had plenty to think of out West—& I gave my mind to it. [26]

Mary and her mother went first to Alabama, where they dis-cussed the settlement of the estate with Mrs. Miller's brother, Francis Boykin. [27] On November 15th, they reached New Orleans, where Mary wrote a poem in her daybook which suggests that she had begun to care deeply about James, and was surprised at—or perhaps afraid of—the depth of her feeling. The poem ends thus:

> Some difference of this dangerous kind,—
> By which, though light, the links that bind
> The fondest heart may soon be riven;
> Some shadow in love's summer heaven,
> Which, though a fleecy speech at first,
> May yet in awful thunder burst.

Reaching the Mississippi property about the first of December, mother and daughter found the situation worse than they had sup-posed, and in mid-December, Frank Boykin wrote to his brother, Alexander Hamilton Boykin, in an appeal for help—"to stand up to Sister as we should and ought to do." Mrs. Miller felt that Hamilton's presence would undoubtedly enable her to save five or six thousand dollars, and Frank wrote, "If you don't the chances are gloomy." A forced sale was scheduled for March 1, 1839. [28]

While they waited for Hamilton to arrive, Mary and her mother had nothing to do: "In Mississippi—in a double log house—We were surrounded by accomplished house servants—cooks—chamber maids sempstresses—butlers—footmen." Mary made only one visit, to a neighbor ten miles away, but returned to find that a favorite elderly servant had died unexpectedly in her mother's arms, and Mrs. Miller had taken to her bed in a fit of nerves. Still, that one visit had provided Mary with the means to survive her exile; she brought back an odd assortment of books and read everything from chemistry to Jewish history to wile away the days.[29]

Once Mary's uncles Hamilton and Burwell Boykin arrived, they and their brothers acted in concert to assist Mrs. Miller; in March, a power of attorney was given to two Mississippi gentlemen signed by five of the Boykin brothers, and a family anecdote holds that at one point in the negotiations for sale, it was necessary for Hamilton to draw a pistol and lay it on the table before the other party was willing to sign the requisite papers. The Mississippi lands were finally sold in June, for $97,050.00, and from that sum, the claims against the estate were settled.[30] Prior to the actual sale, Mary and her mother returned to South Carolina.

Mary, now sixteen, once again saw James Chesnut, and the two agreed—probably secretly—to marry. But James was about to leave for Europe. His older brother John had contracted measles in the course of a brief military campaign in Florida against the Seminoles in 1836, and complications of the disease had led to a serious pulmonary condition.[31] Doctors had prescribed a trip to Europe so John could consult specialists in France, and James was to accompany his brother. Hours before he was scheduled to sail from Charleston, he wrote Mary a love letter. That he was about to leave Mary filled James with emotions unfamiliar to him. Normally reserved, practical, he found himself invaded by thoughts of the small, slim, dark-eyed girl who had promised to marry him. His words to her suggest that he was not yet sure of her love for him, that he did not quite understand her.

> I have been living for the last few days, very much at variance with my usual life, in a world completely ideal. The forms that filled my fancy & eye were phantoms, yet bearing likeness most strong and true to something that *is* in nature, something too of flesh & blood and which is the idol of my soul . . . . Ah! dear girl you know not how much I love you. If I could breathe my whole soul into a single word, I would tell you. But of this you care not to hear. I have

taken the liberty of sending you a diamond ring, which I ask you to accept and to wear. I promise to ask you to accept nothing more for six long months, therefore do receive it & wear it for me.

For several more sentences, James continued, revealing a command of language that would win him acclaim as an orator in future years, but revealing also a formality that Mary would sometimes find stilting. His final words suggest that his fiancée had insisted on secrecy and drama in this courtship: "My sister Sally will deliver you a package containing this letter & the ring, without knowing what it contains or speaking aught about it, as you so desire that my communications shall be sent. I go, and bear with me the treasure of your image. Adieu, may the choicest blessings of heaven be showered upon you, & its care be with you & all that are dear to you."[32]

Mary must have answered the letter quickly, for on June 28 James wrote her a long letter from Paris that began by thanking her for a letter just received, written more than a month before. Mary had apparently alluded to Camden gossip which seemed to suggest that James had been indiscreet enough to mention his love for her to his best friend, Tom Ancrum, and James's second letter is filled with concern lest this unfortunate turn of events temper Mary's affection for him.[33]

While James was gone, Mary was busy with visits and short trips, but these six months were, for her, essentially a period of waiting. Clues as to how she filled the days may be found in the weekly letters that James's relatives wrote to keep him abreast of local gossip, and to remind him of the family's love and concern. Mary Williams' long, sentimental letter of the first of July mentioned seeing Mary Miller. "Mary showed me a beautiful ring, which she seemed to prize very much, altho' she would not wear it constantly. I told her that was nonsense, for every one was pretty well convinced if you didn't give it to her, you had a right to her." In Camden, then, Mary was shy about wearing James's ring, but in July and August she went on a tour of resorts in the area, the springs to which well-heeled southerners flocked each summer to escape the intense heat and its accompanying malaria and yellow fever. Before she left, she confided to her friend that she would wear the ring all the time once she got away from Camden.[34]

The illness of John left the entire Chesnut family in a state of suspense and dread. Each family member privately feared that John's lung infection would soon prove fatal. At first, Mary Miller seems to have visited the Chesnuts regularly, but the gloomy atmosphere may eventually have palled on her. She was young and healthy—and John Chesnut was, for her, no more than an abstraction. By fall, she had apparently begun to avoid the Chesnuts, at least occasionally. One letter from Mary Williams asked archly after her health. Despite her recent reluctance to visit the Chesnuts at Mulberry Plantation, she had been reported dancing every dance at a party a night or two later. In November, Mary Williams wrote to James that "Mary was with me yesterday, as gay as a lark . . . . Grandpa had sent for her to come & see him—he seems to be quite attached to Mary—but she is as shy as a squirrel of him."[35]

Meanwhile in Europe, John stayed in France waiting vainly for his doctors to effect a cure; James went to England, Scotland, and Ireland. Both brothers wrote home frequently to assure their parents that John's health was indeed better, but the letters sound as if James and John were trying to convince themselves. Discouraged, they booked passage home in September and consulted doctors in New York and Philadelphia, who gave hopeful prognoses. In October, for example, John wrote from Philadelphia that "Dr. Jackson has relieved me *altogether* of my apprehensions—He says 'there is nothing to keep me from getting *perfectly well!*'" Nevertheless, John died on December 27, a few weeks after his return.[36]

His death was a tremendous loss for the family; John had been a social, political, and military leader of the Camden area, and he left a wife and six small children.[37] For James, the death of his brother had important consequences. John had been the elder son of Colonel James Chesnut of Mulberry, the son who, it had been assumed, would inherit Mulberry and who had for fifteen years been assisting his father in the running of his large plantations and the management of his several hundred slaves. James, fifteen years John's junior, had been trained in the law and had not thought in terms of managing the Chesnut lands and fortune. Now twenty-four, his responsibilities had been multiplied many times by John's death.

Mary's fiancé, suddenly the Chesnut's only son, had been born on January 18, 1815, the thirteenth and youngest surviving child of James and Mary Cox Chesnut. His mother, forty when he was born, had herself been born in Trenton just prior to the Revolution to Esther Bowes Cox and Colonel John Cox, a Revolutionary hero; she had been a girlhood friend of Nellie Custis and thus an intimate of George Washington's household. James Chesnut, Sr., was one of the wealthiest planters of the South Carolina up country; his father John Chesnut was brought to the Camden area as a boy about 1756, and prospered first as a merchant and then in planting.[38] He, too, had served honorably in the Revolution, and had borne to his death the marks of shackles he had been forced to wear while a prisoner of the British. There had been few years after 1783 in which a Chesnut did not hold public office in the state. Thus James Chesnut, Jr., was raised with the understanding that he would, as a matter of course, do his duty by seeking opportunities to serve South Carolina in a political or judicial role.

Educated first in Camden in a school run by the Reverend Jonathan Whitaker, James was then sent to the Richland School at Rice Creek Springs to prepare for Princeton. Letters from home constantly stated and restated the creed by which he was to live: "It becomes you my dear Son, to make the most of your situation . . . your position in life *demands* of you, to be able to meet your contemporaries, on the great Theatre of Life, well prepared to sustain yourself, & the reputation of your Father & grandfather committed to your charge—it is the most sacred trust." And again: "Let me impress on your mind that your position here will be very favourable as you grow up, unless, by your own follies, you do something to forfeit the stand you will enjoy by inheritance & other circumstances."[39]

Duly instructed, James entered the Princeton sophomore class in 1832. He arrived well prepared for the formal college education of the day. In a letter of recommendation from the headmaster of Richland School, his accomplishments at age seventeen were carefully outlined: "He has read the usual portions of Virgil, & Cicero's

Orations, & all of Horace, & some parts of Livy in Latin. Graeca Minora & the extracts for the Memorabilia in Majora in Greek; & finished Algebra, or the greater part of it, & proceeded to some extent in Geometry in his mathematics. As a scholar he possesses highly respectable talents, & attentive habits—As a young gentleman his conduct has gained him general esteem—in his moral habits he is, as far as we know, unexceptionable."[40]

Nevertheless, in his first year at Princeton, James failed to satisfy his family's expectations. His mother expressed concern over his grade report in August, 1833: "This does not *quite* satisfy me I have set my heart upon your distinguishing yourself, so has your father & you must not disappoint us—I flatter myself that your behaviour being marked 2 instead of 1 as formerly may have arisen from the little disturbances on the 4th of July which I suppose the faculty are obliged to take notice of: but do my dear James study hard. & do credit to yourself and friends." By the following year, James *had* distinguished himself, and was chosen by his debating society to deliver the Fourth of July oration—a decided honor. In 1835 he delivered an oration at his class's graduation. His entire family journeyed north to be present at his commencement.[41]

James probably remained in Camden for much of 1836, perhaps assisting his father while his brother John was involved with military duties in Florida. After John became ill and returned, both brothers went on a tour of the Virginia springs in August, hoping that the mountain air and mineral waters would cure the older brother. By December of that year, James had agreed to accept an appointment as aide to Governor Pierce Mason Butler, but was forbidden to do so by his father. Instead, he went to Charleston to read law with Petigru (and, not incidentally, to strike up a friendship with Mary Miller). His delivery of the Fourth of July oration of 1837[42] marked his first public appearance in Camden, where he began to practice law the following year. He was, then, in 1840, a superbly educated young man who had already shown great promise and who, by virtue of his birth, had every prospect of great wealth; he was, in short, an eminently desirable match for any young woman. To Mary Miller, whom James loved very deeply, marriage meant all these things; but it also represented the

stuff of which the novels she so loved to read were made—a satis-
factorily "happy ending" to a girlhood romance.

Mary turned seventeen on March 31, 1840. Three weeks later,
at eight o'clock on the evening of April 23, she and James were
married at Mount Pleasant, the old Boykin home where she was
born. The day before their wedding, he wrote to her, trying in his
formal way to reassure her.

> It seems that I cannot see you, though my heart longs for it. Will
> you read a note from me? I see a world of preparation going on
> around me, as if in contemplation of some great event—and I pre-
> sume you, living in the very focus of all the turmoil, see visible
> signs of an approaching *era*. Tomorrow ends the career of my bach-
> elorship—and do you suppose I feel no solicitude at the prospect?
> Little on my own account, believe me, but much on yours. The
> happiness, so far as depends on human forethought, of one dearest
> to me will be entrusted to my keeping. It is the assumption of no
> trivial charge. You will sacrifice much, & I assure I feel it. I must
> believe you love me, and so believing, do you think that one of *any*
> sensibility could do less than resolve, and feel some confidence in
> the resolution, to make the first object of his life, effort for your
> happiness?[43]

Because the Chesnuts were still in mourning for John and the
Millers had so recently lost their father, the wedding was, as Mary
later described it, a private one—only fifty or so guests stayed in
Statesburg overnight.[44] There was no wedding trip; after festivi-
ties lasting about a week, James took Mary to live at Mulberry, the
Chesnuts' beautiful country home three miles south of Camden.

FOUR 1840–1860

THE HOME TO WHICH James took Mary was in many respects a self-contained community headed by two strong figures: Mary Cox Chesnut who was sixty-five in 1840, and James Chesnut, Sr., sixty-seven. Two of James's unmarried sisters, Emma, twenty-eight, and Sarah or Sally, twenty-seven, also lived at Mulberry, so seventeen-year-old Mary moved into a family in which there were already three women older than herself—three women who found it easier to regard her as a child than as a young married woman. She could assist her mother-in-law in the management of the home and "yard," as she had helped her grandmother and mother, but she was not really a necessary part of the household. It was perhaps inevitable that as soon as the first surge of excitement wore off she, the outsider, began to chafe at the position in which she found herself. She could make herself be as *busy* as she pleased; there were always friends and family members to be entertained, and a continual procession of Chesnut grandchildren coming to make extended visits. But she could not consider herself genuinely useful, nor could she, by any stretch of the imagination, see herself as the center of attention—a position to which she had been accustomed since birth.

Thus, during the next twenty years, Mary's feelings about Mulberry and her husband's family were often mixed. In the revised version of her Civil War journal, her descriptions of life at Mulberry indicate both intense appreciation for the virtues of country living and irritation at its restrictions:

> From my window high—(I sit here in the library alone a great deal) I see carriages approach. Col Chesnut drives a pair of thor-

ough breds—beauties—mahogany bays—with shining coats and arching necks . . . .

Mrs Chesnut has her carriage horses and a huge family coach, for herself, which she never uses. The young ladies have a barouche and their own riding horses. We have a pair, for my carriage; and my husband has several saddle horses. There are always families of the children or grandchildren of the house visiting here—with carriage and horses—nurses—children—&c &c. The house is crammed from garret to cellar without intermission.

Now—as I sit here writing I see half a dozen carriages under the shade of the trees—coachmen on their boxes, talking, laughing &c—some hookling, they call it. They have a bone hook some thing like a crochet needle—and they hook them selves woollen gloves—Some are reading Hymn books, or pretending. The small footmen are playing marbles under the trees.

A pleasant, empty, easy going life. If ones heart is at ease. But people are not like pigs; they cannot be put up and fattened. So here I pine and fret.[1]

The patents to the land on which Mulberry stood had been granted in the eighteenth century by King George II, and the property had been in the Chesnut family since well before the Revolution. This was choice land, beautiful and fertile. Four hundred years before Mary Boykin Chesnut lived there, the area had been an Indian ceremonial center, and was the earliest proposed location for the settlement that would come to be called Camden.[2]

The mansion itself stood about a mile above the Wateree River, at the end of an avenue of live oaks. Of a simple and classic design, the house had been built to last for centuries; its roof was slate, its walls were two feet thick, constructed of bricks made from kilns on the plantation, and the broad steps leading to its piazza were marble. Begun in 1818, the three-story house was completed in 1820 and by 1840 had served as the winter residence of Colonel and Mrs. Chesnut for twenty years. Because of the massive trees that framed the house, it did not appear particularly large from a distance. But visitors who entered Mulberry were struck by the spaciousness of its rooms. The finest feature of the house was its grand center hall, from the rear of which a magnificent cantilevered staircase rose in an elongated spiral to the upper stories.

To the right of the entrance hall were the drawing room and the dining room; to the left, the library, Mary Cox Chesnut's bedroom and its adjoining nursery. The second and third stories each had six large bedrooms. An unusual innovation in a house finished in 1820 was a water system designed so that a "hydraulic ram forced fresh water through hollow tupelo logs to tanks in the attic, from which gravity feed supplied several bathrooms and basins."[3] The new Mrs. Chesnut was ensconced in a beautiful front room on the third story which quickly became a retreat and sanctuary for her, and a vantage point from which she could watch the changing seasons modulate the lovely grounds that surrounded the house. When she felt she had been slighted or insulted, or when she had simply become tired of the company of the older women in the house, Mary spent countless hours in one of the deep window seats in her room, observing the world around her.

A Scottish gardener had been hired to design and supervise the laying out of the grounds when Mulberry was built. Under his eye, the massive old oaks native to the area had become a natural backdrop for carefully planned walks and drives lined with flowers and boxwood hedges, now overseen by Cuffer, the head gardener, and his assistant Yaller Abram. Mary's favorite view across the east and south lawns was of a portion of the yard which had once been a deer park and which looked to her like a "primeval forest."[4] But she also loved the jessamine and Cherokee roses, which obscured the fences, and the cultivated gardens, preferring always those flowers which gave off heady perfumes: violets, roses, gardenias.

As Mary came to take her place at Mulberry, she found that she was living in a world that was, quite simply, perfectly appointed. The ground floor of the house contained storerooms, pantries and a renowned wine cellar. Behind the main house stood the kitchen and laundry in a long two-story brick building which also held sleeping quarters for many of the house servants. Mulberry's head cook, Romeo, was Charleston-trained; he and Big Judy, the pastry cook, were regarded by the family as treasures. Because of their skill, the Chesnuts maintained a reputation for cuisine second to none in the Carolina up-country. Beyond the kitchen stood the brick cottages of more house servants. There too were the ice-house and the smokehouse overseen by Daddy Abram, who Mary would later assert was a kinder and better man than Harriet Beecher Stowe's Uncle Tom. Mammy Rhody's dairy, near the smokehouse, was supplied by a herd of English cattle which Colonel Chesnut had imported. The stables and barns, northwest of the house, were the charge of old Quash and Scipio; both the old Colonel and his son set great store by horses, and Mary herself loved to ride and so came to know Scipio well. She would later describe him in his old age as "six feet two—a black Hercules—and as gentle as a dove."[5]

Under the capable and unquestioned generalship of Mary Cox Chesnut, the entire household ran like a well-oiled clock which Mrs. Chesnut wound every morning by the apparently simple device of giving detailed daily orders to her head cook, pastry cook, maids, and seamstresses, who in turn oversaw the work of twenty-five house servants. In actuality, old Mrs. Chesnut had for forty years taken a personal interest in the upbringing and training of each servant, and had established in the house a routine which was as unvarying as it was gracious.

In the 1840s, the wife of a plantation owner had a complex, demanding, and more than full-time job. Mary Boykin Chesnut had been well trained for this role, but at Mulberry, she found herself essentially superfluous. By the time she awakened, the house had already been swept and dusted, the brass already gleamed; three o'clock dinner had already been planned and begun. Not even the arrival of a half dozen unexpected visitors required anyone in the family to lift a finger. There was always food sufficient for guests, and each guest room was kept in constant readiness by a maid appointed for that purpose. Should Mary wish to take on any duty or task, she could only do so at the expense of usurping someone else's province.

Once she became a member of the family, Mary found herself pampered as she had never been before. James's old nurse, Betsy, stepped quite naturally into the role of lady's maid, treating Mary with gruff affection as one more of her charges:

> My dear old maid, is as good as gold, and pretty much of that color. She has a sour and discontented air—but it is only a way she

has—She chooses to wait on us because "she nussed Mars Jeems—and she likes me . . . . She is as noiseless in her ministrations as the White Cat—she brings water and builds up a fire—she lets that burn down to warm the room. She then makes a positive bonfire—and says—sternly—"Aint you gwine to git up—and fust bell for breakwus done ring."

Which mandate, if I disregard—She lets me sleep as long as I please—And brings me—Oh! such a nice breakfast to my bedside.

While I loiter over my breakfast she gets my room in what she calls "apple pie" order—When I am in my dressing room and bath she sweeps and dusts. It all seems cleaning and getting to rights by magic no trouble or disorder—Mrs Chesnut [has] the art of training servants.[6]

Servants did everything for her. Of the butler at Mulberry she would later write, "Eben . . . would be miserable and feel himself a ridiculous failure—were I ever forced to ask him for any thing."[7] Always appreciative of luxury, Mary adored being waited on. Had these servants been hers, had she been able thus to feel responsible for them, she could perhaps have enjoyed her position thoroughly. Instead, she found herself unable to shed the feeling of being a perpetual and somewhat unwilling guest, and she regretted what she grew to call her "useless existence."

The senior Chesnuts presiding over Mulberry were a noteworthy pair. James Chesnut, Sr., Mary described as "kind—and amiable when not crossed. Given to hospitality on a grand scale—jovial, genial, friendly, courtly in his politeness. As absolute a Tyrant as the Czar of Russia the Khan of Tartary—or the Sultan of Turkey." Already approaching seventy, the old Colonel had firmly set opinions. He forbade any woman in the family to wear a red dress, refused to allow his horses to be driven faster than a slow trot, and would not tolerate the appearance of an onion—however well disguised—on his table. He treated everyone with an elaborate courtesy which made disagreement impossible. He had been called "the Young Prince" in his youth; at his father's death in 1818, he had assumed the throne and enjoyed his reign thoroughly. His daughter-in-law, who thought him an anachronism, was frequently annoyed at his royal pronouncements but nevertheless developed a deep affection for him—an affection which he seems to have reciprocated.[8]

Mary Cox Chesnut was, in her own way, as strong a character as her husband. In Mary Boykin Chesnut's eyes, she was something of a paradox, a woman who had undergone tremendous suffering, sustained by a seemingly iron will, and yet who professed to view the world through rose-colored glasses. "In the soft luxurious life she leads, she denies herself nothing that she wants. In her well regulated character she could not want anything that she ought not to have." She acceded with grace to her husband's demands, but held her own: at her marriage she had agreed never to place an onion on the table if he, in return, would refrain from smoking in the house. The bargain was kept scrupulously.[9]

Old Mrs. Chesnut had been a semi-invalid for many years. Nevertheless, she operated on the principle of duty, spending hours every day cutting out baby clothes for the infants born to Mulberry slaves, and then apportioning the unmade garments into the work baskets of her daughers and daughter-in-law. "She is always ready with an ample wardrobe for every new comer. Then the mothers bring their children for her to prescribe and look after when ever they are ailing. She is not at all nervous. She takes a baby and lances its gums quite cooley and scientifically. She dresses all hurts—bandages all wounds."[10]

By 1840 Mary Cox Chesnut had borne fourteen children and buried ten of them; she had raised several grandchildren as well. She had been a beautiful young woman, with auburn curls and delicate, aristocratic features. Her childhood had been spent on her father's estate, Bloomsbury Court, on the Delaware River near Trenton, New Jersey. During the Revolution, Bloomsbury Court had served at different times as headquarters for Lafayette, Greene and Washington, and her father, John Cox, had maintained close ties with Washington and other Revolutionary heroes after the war. Prior to her marriage, the crowning moment of Mary Cox Chesnut's life had been her role as one of the six young ladies who welcomed Washington to Trenton before his inauguration. Now old Mrs. Chesnut prided herself on her impeccable manners. Always serene, unruffled, she rarely criticized anyone outright, but when witness to a transgression of good breeding would say, "Ah—you were not brought up at Bloomsbury." [11]

Mrs. Chesnut superintended Mulberry and, in the summer, the simpler establishment at Sandy Hill several miles to the northeast with apparent effortlessness. Winter and summer she read incessantly, a fact that her daughter-in-law, also a lover of books, noted with wry humor: "Mrs C has a greediness of books such as I never saw in any one else . . . . Economy is one of her cherished virtues. And strange to say she never buys a book—or has been known to take a magazine or Periodical. But she has them all—they gravitate toward her—they flow into her room. Every body is proud to send, or lend any book they have compassed by any means fair or foul. Other members of the family who care nothing whatever for them buy the books, and she reads them." [12]

Had Mary come to know Mary Cox Chesnut in any other role than as mother-in-law, the two women, though widely separated in age, would probably have been good friends. But Mary and her mother-in-law threatened one another, and so at times lived together in what amounted to a cold war. Old Mrs. Chesnut fought the war in a way which Mary considered particularly insidious: she was *too* good, too solicitous, too polite, too virtuous. Thus she contrived to make her daughter-in-law feel petty, foolish, or inadequate in such a manner that Mary was never quite sure whether a battle had been fought or not. Mary, as strong willed as the older woman but far more impetuous, fought the war erratically, by turns trying to be equally good and polite, then losing her patience and becoming outspoken, sarcastic or even, upon occasion, openly rude.

For the most part, Mary Boykin Chesnut spent the early years of her marriage aimlessly. She was growing into full adulthood in a quiet, self-satisfied world that was fundamentally at odds with her gregarious nature and inquiring, somewhat iconoclastic mind. For diversion, she frequently ordered Quash or Scipio to bring around her carriage and drive her into Camden to visit or shop. But Camden was by no means an exciting or enlightened environment. One resident described the town in the early 1840s as quaint, with "dingy frame buildings and sandy streets."

The sidewalks, innocent of brick or flagstone and fringed with grass which was a receptacle for cigar stumps and trash, were interlaced with projecting gnarled roots, no lamps to light the path, and, when the trees were in leaf and the stores closed at night, it was Egyptian darkness. Hogs, horses and cows roamed at will through the streets.

There was no apparent effort to make the stores attractive. They had low ceilings and small windows, and large dry goods boxes were placed in front to accommodate idlers and loungers, who passed their time whittling and gossiping. Inside these same stores, however, the shelves were filled with the products of the looms of Britain, France and Germany. The merchants were shrewd, substantial business men whose credit in the northern markets was second to none. The citizens were well-to-do and looked it, enjoying life in a rational way.[13]

Once in Camden, Mary could visit her mother, who remained in South Carolina for several years. Her sister Kate attended school in Camden for a year or two after Mary's marriage, and when her youngest sister, Sally, was sent to school in Charleston, Kate left school and spent a great deal of time with Mary. Kate was an important outlet. The two sisters had always been close, and Kate, who admired her older sister inordinately, was becoming a beautiful young woman. Though Mary was the more outspoken, Kate shared her views of men and manners, so it was to Kate that Mary could vent her frustrations, confide her hurts, and express her sometimes irreverent opinions. Furthermore, Kate was one person who needed Mary, and to whom Mary could be of real use. The young Chesnuts took Kate under their care—James enjoyed directing her reading, and when opportunity presented itself, Mary delighted in chaperoning her to dances and parties in Columbia and Charleston.[14]

Trips to Columbia and Charleston, though, were infrequent. Most of Mary's time was devoted to endless afternoons spent in what old Mrs. Chesnut called her "sewing society," making clothes for the slave children and engaging in desultory and boring small talk. Even gossip was tame, for her mother-in-law refused to hear ill of anyone—a trait Mary found infuriating. Her own family loved to trade stories and happily passed judgment on everyone.

Mary roundly declared, "I praise when I love and abuse when I hate." But she dared not do so in the presence of any of the Chesnuts. Away from them, she played the guitar and sang the old ballads she had learned as a child. Sporadically, she would enthusiastically undertake to teach some of the children of the Chesnuts' slaves to read—an enterprise everybody seemed to regard as noble, although the practice was illegal in South Carolina. But she was overzealous, holding her young charges to the task long after their attention had waned.[15]

Whenever she was unable to visit her mother or Kate; whenever James was busy; whenever, in short, she could make time to do so, Mary read, and in her reading found the society she longed for, the intellectual stimulation her surroundings denied her. Her tastes were eclectic. She liked both ancient and modern history and read an impressive amount of it, always anxious to obtain the most recent publications. She read the great essayists of the seventeenth and eighteenth centuries, as well as her contemporaries. Her school years at Madame Talvande's, with their weekly "piece days" when each girl had to declaim a passage, had left her well versed in the histrionic and melodramatic poetry of the eighteenth and early nineteenth centuries, and though she recognized its theatrical elements, she would sometimes find herself moved by such sentimental verse until her death. But she treasured far more the classic works, which she had come to know on her own: Chaucer's *Canterbury Tales*, the plays and poetry of Shakespeare, the works of Spenser, Sidney, Donne, Milton, Dryden, Swift, and Pope. Possessed of an excellent memory, she could recite long passages of her favorite poets, and frequently quoted the poems of Goldsmith, Byron, Keats, Shelley, Coleridge, Wordsworth, Scott, Robert Burns, Campbell, Moore, and Tennyson. She read French as readily as English and knew well Rabelais, Fontaine, Voltaire, and the great French playwrights. Interested in German writers, she kept abreast of the works of Schiller and Goethe, reading them in German and comparing the originals with French and English translations.[16]

These works—many of them available to her in the library at Mulberry, others part of the growing library she and James amassed—were read and reread, committed to memory, pondered, quoted. But Mary also began a program of regular reading in religious works, in an effort to improve her character, to curb her wayward temper and to combat her growing uncharitable feelings toward her new relatives. When she was angry or depressed, she would retreat to her bedroom and read the Bible and the sermons of Joseph Hall, bishop of Norwich, or of Jeremy Taylor. Often she copied out long passages to study and remember. Mary was by nature a thoroughly secular person, far more interested in the people around her than in religious matters. And yet she had been imbued with a simple faith in God both by her Protestant parents and the Catholic teachers and clergymen to whom she was introduced as a schoolgirl. She loved the serenity and panoply of church services and attended church regularly. But she was as eclectic in her religious preferences as in her other tastes, and felt allegiance for no particular church. Sometimes attending Bethesda Presbyterian Church in Camden to which both the Chesnuts and her mother's family, the Boykins, belonged, she also visited other churches to hear ministers she particularly liked. Once a month, a missionary minister came to preach and perform weddings and baptisms at the little Negro church on Mulberry Plantation. Mary often attended these services and sometimes felt they brought her closer to the pure meaning of Christianity than did the more reserved churches of the gentry.

James usually avoided church, a fact which Mary regretted, but she felt that he was a much better Christian than other men who appeared every Sunday. In fact, Mary Boykin Chesnut believed that religion was quite properly an intensely private matter. She took very seriously the biblical injunction that prayer is best conducted in one's closet, and was inwardly critical of anyone who displayed his piety too openly. Thus, Mary rarely discussed or quoted from her readings in the works of famous theologians. (The prayers and religious passages she recorded in her private diary of the war years would almost all be removed as she revised the journal for publication.) But her daybooks and diaries and the breadth of her biblical knowledge all bear witness to the fact that these readings were a sustained and unquestionably earnest effort on Mary's part to develop her religious sensibilities, and to deepen her faith.

However seriously Mary pursued theology, she certainly found far more solace in novels—books considered by many of her friends and relatives to be at best frivolous and at worst decadent. Most of the novels sent to her when she was a student at Madame Talvande's had been confiscated as unsuitable for a schoolgirl, and Mary's mother-in-law placed novels she regarded as immoral under lock and key at Mulberry. But Mary herself perceived novels to be the most interesting works in all literature. As a girl she had read the Waverly novels of Sir Walter Scott and the romances of Bulwer-Lytton and G. P. R. James. She had been a confirmed lover of Dickens since the publication of *The Pickwick Papers*, which she had read at Madame Talvande's as it reached Charleston in numbered installments.[17] Now she read Sterne, Fielding, Jane Austen, Charlotte Brontë in English, Victor Hugo, George Sand, Dumas père, Balzac in French, Goethe's novels in German, and much popular fiction, often devouring a book a day. From them she was learning a great deal about the workings of human nature and society.

Because she approached literature—and particularly fiction—personally, subjectively, she was also comparing herself and the people she lived among with the characters about whom she read, noting how far her life had veered from adventure and romance. Always her own severest critic in private, though outspoken and self-confident in company, she viewed her own assets rather harshly. Mary Boykin Chesnut was by no means beautiful—certainly not by the standards of her day. She was conscious of being short (a full portrait made from a daguerreotype when she was nearly thirty suggests she stood perhaps five feet) and admired height in the men and women she knew. She would later describe herself following a very tall friend, General John Preston, as a "very small steam tug" towed by a "huge seventy-four gun ship." Her features were strong, and she regarded herself as rather plain. But her portraits reveal a handsome woman with dark, deep-set eyes—eyes she called her "only decent feature" and observers described as sparkling. She had a wide, clear brow and high cheekbones. Her nose was too broad for conventional beauty (she felt it was most unattractive and called it "pug").[18] Her mouth was full and well shaped, falling naturally into lines suggesting a ready smile above a soft, rounded chin. Her figure, which would thicken a bit in middle age, was soft and well-proportioned; in all, Mary Boykin Chesnut was a woman eminently attractive, whose expression proclaimed her intelligent, good-humored and warm.

In Mary's eyes, her young husband looked the part of the romantic hero, but he lacked dash and spirit. He was tall and slim, with handsome features—the wide brow, intelligent eyes, and high cheekbones of his father, the long, narrow jaw of his mother. He stood markedly erect, and even in repose often seemed rather formal and stiff. Like his father, his manners were faultless; like his mother, he rarely lost his temper. Reserved by nature, he was almost self-effacing, the quintessence of the private man of reason. Loath to show his emotions, he relaxed completely only occasionally with children, or with the horses he loved. James, like Mary, was an inveterate reader, preferring history, the classics, and the romantic poets; Mary often passed along books to him or read what he had just finished, looking forward to long discussions in which she could match her perceptions and her wits against her husband's.

At the time of their marriage, James Chesnut, Jr., was just beginning a lifelong career of public service. His election in 1840 to represent his district in the state legislature necessitated travel to Columbia, but except for brief visits to friends around the state, James and Mary seem to have stayed at Mulberry for most of the next five years. In her writings of later years, Mary never discussed this period of time. The young couple may have been exceedingly happy. It seems far more likely, though, that these were years of vague dissatisfaction, perhaps mild disillusionment as Mary discovered that by marrying James she had by no means achieved independence and had in large measure given up the excitement of being a marriageable belle. Certainly this period in her life lacked drama, and Mary was a woman with a flair for and a love of the dramatic.

In the summer of 1845 she fell ill, and it was decided that a trip north to the fashionable watering spots of Saratoga and Newport would improve her health. Since James's sister Emma was also ill (she would die less than two years later, probably of tuberculosis), she planned to accompany them, and other Chesnut family members may have gone too. The party sailed from Charleston on Sunday, July 15, and a letter from Emma to her father the following Friday announced that "soon after crossing the bar the ladies, with the single exception of Mary, all got sea sick." The letter continues: "James & Mary are here, with us, but I do not know whether they are going to Sarotoga or not. I have not seen Mary since she came from the boat—in this immense house we might as well be miles apart, for I do not know where to find her. It is impossible to tell you how much Mary has improved, it is really wonderful. She was not at all sea sick, went to every meal, & laughed & talked with any body that was well enough to join her—I cannot say how I am exactly upon the whole."[19] Emma's letter suggests that she felt a real affection for her sister-in-law, but it also suggests Mary's illness had not been serious, for on a voyage that made everyone else seasick, Mary had been conspicuously hearty; the pattern of sickness alleviated by a departure from Camden was one that was to reemerge occasionally until the last years of Mary's life.

Mary and James did go on to Saratoga and Newport and then, a month later, sailed for England, much to everybody's astonishment. When the senior Chesnuts heard the news, each was prompted to write a letter immediately. Colonel Chesnut was practical: "Your determination to sail for London was so unexpected to us & I expect, so sudden that you have not prepared yourself with letters of credit, or introduction, which might become necessary, should sickness or protracted stay or any other cause render them necessary." Mrs. Chesnut was less formal, and most solicitous of Mary. "We were impressed at the intelligence of your going to Europe as quite impossible. Both Mrs. Miller and myself felt our hearts a little troubled at first, at the idea of the ocean being between us, but soon came to the conclusion that if Mary was not as well as you expected after trying the Bathing then it was the best thing you could have done."[20]

How profoundly Mrs. Chesnut misread her daughter-in-law is revealed by her next statement: "I did not expect her to mend much at New Port after hearing of the bustle & crowd of the place for I know excitement would injure Mary . . . . I trust she will return quite well, if you do not let her fatigue herself too much with sight seeing." Like most mothers, Mrs. Chesnut feared that her son did not take enough care of himself: "Indeed my dear Son tho you have kept it to yourself—I suspect you needed the voyage as well as Mary . . . dont let Mary walk too much—you know tis one of the things the Dr objects particularly to." This last admonition suggests the possibility that Mary's illness may have resulted from a miscarriage.[21] In any case, the trip to London seems to have been made on impulse, and the impulse was very likely Mary's. Having gotten away from Mulberry for the first time since her marriage, she must have been delighted at the idea of a side trip to Europe.

In London, Mary found the English accent "so pleasant to the ear"; she had long been an Anglophile, following the latest trends in English literature and politics as closely as she followed the career of young Queen Victoria—who, Mary noted, had like herself married in the spring of 1840. The Chesnuts dined at the American minister's, and shopped for books to bring back to South Carolina.[22] Mary's love of beautiful things endeared Parisian fashions to her, and she returned with a wardrobe of dresses à la mode.

Having once tasted travel to social centers, Mary Boykin Chesnut managed thereafter to make visits north as often as possible. Her husband had numerous relatives in Philadelphia, New Jersey, and New York. His mother's sisters had all married men of great distinction, and Mary was thus introduced to Philadelphia society by Sarah and John Redman Coxe, perhaps that city's leading physician, and by Elizabeth and Horace Binney, a lawyer of national repute. In New York and New Jersey her hosts were the sons of John Stevens, one of the state's most illustrious and wealthy citizens, founder of the Pennsylvania railroad system. James and Mary were regular guests at the Stevens estate, which comprised much of present-day Hoboken. In 1847 they visited Philadelphia and Saratoga and in 1848 were again in the north.[23]

This visit in the summer of 1848 was prompted by another illness of Mary's—this time of a serious nature. A mid-August letter from Thomas Jefferson Withers (her aunt's husband who had, before her marriage, acted as Mary's guardian and who would appear frequently in *A Diary From Dixie* in his irascible old age) to James Chesnut, Sr., provides clues as to her health. Withers had waited to write until he had actually seen Mary and could vouch for her recovery: "Mary seemed better than usual [when she arrived in New York]—But she has suffered intensely since, and we were not free from concern about her for several days—She is now relieved from all pain & nausea, and is stationary longer only from debility. Whether the journey to Saratoga will be prosecuted by them I know not." [24]

If Mary and James went on to Saratoga, they did so only briefly, for by early September they had gone to Philadelphia to consult doctors there about Mary's health. James's father wrote urging that they stay in Philadelphia until October, "by which time, all the effects of [the doctor's] prescription can be well ascertained," and suggested James hire a "good female attendant" for Mary. To his daughter-in-law he wrote pleasant, newsy letters, passing along word of her mother and sisters. In one such letter he wondered why mill ponds should "make places sickly?—the water looks so pretty," and happily announced that "This is the anniversary of our wedding—only fifty two years ago I had the supreme felicity of making Miss Molly Cox, Mrs Chesnut—oh what a change for a blooming girl to! become the bride of a Southern slave driver." [25]

Such letters expressed Colonel Chesnut's affection for Mary. He was anxious to cheer her, for this illness brought with it (or perhaps was exacerbated by) very low spirits. In Mary's daybook—into which she copied uplifting quotations—the entries of 1848 are filled with items such as extracts from the sermons of Bishop Hall and biblical verses that hold out hope for heavenly rewards even though life on earth is filled with misery. [26] On page after page is recorded one or another statement of St. Augustine, Jeremy Taylor, or Francis Bacon, each exhorting man to attend to the duties of the world. Mary seems quite deliberately to have taken herself in hand, occupying herself by searching out such quotations and determinedly copying them, to pull herself out of despondency.

The Chesnuts remained in the North through September, but

this time Mary had been away from Camden so long that, for the first time in her life, she felt homesick: several poems copied in the daybook in September center on the theme "there's no place like home." Back in South Carolina, James and Mary moved into their own home, Frogvale.[27] The modest house on Union Street in Camden, of a simple but very unusual and interesting design, had been completed while they were away. Always feeling herself cut off from the world at Mulberry, Mary must have been pleased to be in town.

For the next several months Mary was as busy as she wanted to be. The details of setting up housekeeping for herself, buying and arranging furniture, and overseeing the laying out of grounds, all served to distract her from her depression. Her favorite sister, Kate, had in 1846 married James's nephew, David Williams, the same David to whom Mary's father had jokingly "betrothed" her as an infant. David was the brother of Mary's childhood friend Mary Williams, and had spent much of his youth at Mulberry with his grandmother and grandfather Chesnut. He and Kate had just produced their first child, Serena. Mary was charmed with the baby and pleased to have her sister nearby. Her youngest sister, Sally, was by now a belle and needed chaperoning to parties and dances. The railroad had finally reached Camden in November of 1848, and it was therefore possible to leave home with relative ease—to shop in Columbia for a few days or even to make a quick trip to Charleston simply to see a play.[28]

By August, 1849, Mary's spirits seemed to have improved. Into her daybook she copied an unidentified poem she felt characterized her well:

> He was a minstrel—in his mood,
>   was wisdom mixed with folly;
> A tame companion to the good,
> But wild & fierce among the rude,
>   And jovial with the jolly!

And in early September, preceding an inspirational quotation from Archbishop Robert Leighton on "repentance," she wrote: "Yesterday—instigated by the devil I said most unchristian & hateful things—May God forgive me—& grant me power to refrain in future from such sinful conduct . . . . I wish I could impress all this upon my mind & heart but I forget in the hour of temptation—September 5th 1849."[29] Apparently, she had allowed herself to become "wild & fierce among the rude" but her response to her own misconduct no longer hinted of depression.

By 1850 James Chesnut's importance as a political figure in South Carolina had grown. He, with Maxcy Gregg, was sent from Kershaw County with representatives from several southern states to the Nashville Convention in June. Their purpose was to consider the Wilmot Proviso (prohibiting slavery in any territory acquired from Mexico) and what southerners considered to be other acts of northern aggression against slavery. Chesnut, in his wife's words, "represented the conservative and moderate wing of the southern rights party."[30] While he was in Nashville, Mary wrote him a letter which suggests that as early as 1850 she was extremely interested in his political activities and accustomed to debating politics with James and to disagreeing with him. She referred directly to the fact that she was "not the *hearty* lover of slavery this latitude requires": "I shall not dilate upon the Nashville convention merely to fill up paper—as I am not *sound* on certain important *topics* now so constantly discussed—indeed so very heterodox am I—that I principally *hate* the abolitionist for their *cant* & abuse of us—& worse than all their using this vexed question as a political engine & so retarding beyond all doubt the gradual freeing of our states which seemed to be working its way down in Maryland & Virginia."

Slavery, she felt, was wrong, and yet she found herself despising the abolitionists for using a moral problem as a political bludgeon. James's position at the Nashville Convention had quickened her interest in politics, and she found herself questioning her own political beliefs: "I was amused last night with the *exactly* opposite stories told by the [Columbia] telegraph & the [New York] Herald as to what was going on in Washington—I think I am in danger of turning a regular somerset in *my* politics & transferring my allegiance from Mr. Calhoun right away to Clay [Calhoun had died two months earlier, in March] . . . Webster I cannot *go*—you must *make* time to write me long letters as I am *intensely* curious as to your movements." [31]

In the same letter she betrayed her role as housekeeper: she had taken advantage of her husband's absence to make "a great change for the better"—characteristically in her favorite room, the library, and had "thoroughly placed every book & every paper in its place." One of James's servants, "old Dick," had been helping her, and she told her husband with great glee about the aging slave's political opinions:

> He assisted this morning in taking up the library carpet & regaled me in the mean while with the glories of his old Masters time—he can only sigh that you cannot be seen & known by your grand-father—you are just the grandson he wanted . . . . Dick *avers* that the old gentleman did so long for a "*Statesman*" in the family—& he says *triumphantly* you evidently are the *man*—again he *did so* love a *true true* gentleman—& you know how much *of a one* Mars James is—he harangued upon the fluctuations of your popularity—its ebbs & flows—Dick has a demagogue's reverence for that "many headed, monster thing" the opinion of the mob.

James's political popularity clearly pleased Mary, and she would continue throughout the years to collect and cherish praise lavished upon her husband, and to bristle at criticism of him. Her own sense of worth became increasingly identified with his success. By the early 1850s, her family had scattered: Kate and David Williams remained in South Carolina, but lived in Society Hill, a small town on the Pee Dee River; both Mary's brother and younger sister had moved to Alabama. Stephen had established himself in Conecuh County as a planter, and Sally had married a distant Boykin cousin and lived in Dallas County. Mary's mother, too, had settled in Portland, Alabama, though she paid each of her children long visits. With the support system of her own family far less frequently available, Mary began to take an active role in her husband's career, often serving as his secretary, and sometimes as his amanuensis. When her husband attended sessions of the state legislature in Columbia, Mary usually accompanied him. There, she hosted teas and dinners, renewed old friendships, and struck up new ones among South Carolina's political elite. There too she exercised her natural ability, born of her sharp intelligence and curiosity, for ferreting out information—rumors in the air—which could be of use to her husband.

Because they were so separated, the Miller children and their mother grew dependent on correspondence to maintain close touch. Each wrote long, chatty letters and grew adept at sketching characters and situations for the delight of the rest of the family, among whom the letters passed. Thus, Stephen wrote to Mary in 1850 of his escapades at a rehearsal for a "Tableau party" in which he was to take the part of the spinster aunt in *The Pickwick Papers*:

> First they made me get . . . into a splendid silk dress—which would not meet by half, & as I could not get my hands into the sleeves, they pinned it up & tied a long white string round the waist to hold it on—then a sack, Joseph or Jenny Lind (I dont know the names of such things) concealed all the irregularities of the fit—the head dress, two caps well pinned to my hair, with gold pins—hair whitened with chalk, face, ditto, arms & neck covered with jewelry to the amount one or two thousand dollars worth—(while all this was going on just imagine that you could hear the merry & ringing laughter, mine particularly loud & boisterous,) but the curtain is up & my toilette complete,—well it is over & I am back in the room to change—but before I had commenced some one raised the *fearfull* cry of 'fire' . . . & I forgetting, the spinster's dress jumped on a large blaze to put it out with my feet—in a second I, apparently to the others, was enveloped in flames—One lady forgetting my *character* & seeing the *caps* cried out, that, her Aunt was in the fire . . . the dress was ruined—all of the men agreed to take a drink to settle their nerves—we had a dance & then retired as I ought to do now, I've been writing for your ammusement two hours.[32]

For the three eldest Miller children, Mary, Stephen, and Kate, part of the fun of a thing was the challenge of getting it down on paper to amuse their mother and siblings, and to this end each cultivated an eye for the absurd. When Kate and David traveled north with Sally and two young friends in 1852, Kate wrote of her adventures on the boat to Wilmington to Mary, certain that her sister would share her laughter:

> In spite of the sea sickness we had a very amusing time—Sal & the girls joined the crowd on the floor—(as thick as pigs they were all packed) but I could not stand it—so contented myself with a *hard*

tiny Sofa up in one corner—where I could lie by drawing up &
holding on tight—but all through the night I could hear *my girls*
laughing & chatting away as tho' they were quite comfortable—
once a fat old lady rolled over Missie who called out in a stifled
voice "*oh* the delights of travelling" . . . We had *three* Brides along
whose public display of their felicity did not serve in any way as an
antidote for Sea Sickness—one told Sal the whole history of her
Courtship & Marriage—the last event took place but ten day's before—to which Sal very quietly answered "We thought it had been
a *very* late affair".[33]

Thus the *bon mot* was savored, Mary's closeness to her family was
preserved and strengthened, and her touch with the Old Southwest and the major cities of the Northeast was maintained, even
when she found it necessary to remain in Camden.

Although Frogvale was only six years old, the Chesnuts in 1854
built a far larger and more elegant house in Kirkwood, the fashionable northern section of Camden. Apparently because the new
home seemed so remote from the center of town, they named it
Kamchatka, for the Siberian peninsula by that name. The Kirkwood area, in the sloping terrain slightly north of downtown Camden, was considered particularly healthful. Its few houses were
stately, and Kamchatka quickly became one of the most elegant
homes in the neighborhood. Of a transitional style borrowing
from both Greek and Gothic Revival, the white frame house was
beautifully proportioned, with a broad piazza on three sides supported by simple eight-sided exterior columns. Visitors reached
the piazza by ascending double stairways; as Mulberry and many
neighboring homes had been, the main floor of the house was
built over an above-ground basement. Long graceful windows
opened every room to the breezes that played around the high
ground, and Mary could glance out in any direction and see hills
gently rolling away from her.

One reason for building a larger home was so the Chesnuts
would have plenty of room to entertain. To Mary, perhaps the
most bitter disappointment of her marriage was her failure to have
a child even though, as she later wrote in her Civil War journal,
sometimes "hope told a flattering tale." Almost certainly her childlessness had contributed to her despondency of 1848, for it was

during that year that her sister Kate gave birth to her first child. Her sisters and closest friends held out hope by telling her of other women who had finally achieved healthy pregnancies after years of waiting.[34] Now, in her early thirties, Mary began to indulge her very strong maternal instincts by "borrowing" children for extended visits—an arrangement that suited everyone. She loved having children visit, children loved equally well to stay with her, and, because she and James traveled frequently and in interesting circles, many of her friends and relatives felt that sending their children to Mary provided them with advantageous opportunities.

In Camden, Mary often cared for James's various nieces and nephews. Her favorite was Johnny Chesnut, the youngest son of James's older brother, John, who had died in 1839. Johnny had been three years old when James and Mary married in 1840, and though Mary felt little affection for his older brothers and sisters, in Johnny—who regarded his Uncle James as a father—she found a kindred spirit. As he approached young manhood in the mid-50s, he turned frequently to Mary for friendship, often both amusing and frustrating her by ignoring her advice. She admired his cool exterior and his independence of mind (qualities she found lacking in many of the Chesnut grandchildren) and watched over his budding love affairs with a sympathetic eye.

Sometimes she took Harriet and Mary Grant to Columbia to shop, a practice that disturbed their father somewhat. One of Mary Boykin Chesnut's mild rebellions against the staid dignity of the Chesnut family was her pleasure in urging her coachman to drive far faster than Colonel Chesnut's prescribed slow trot, and James's brother-in-law William Grant felt his daughters' lives were endangered by such reckless driving. More to her liking than the Grant girls were little Caroline Perkins, a niece of James's oldest sister, and Mary Withers, Mary's own cousin. She frequently traveled with Mary Withers, her namesake whom she had almost come to regard as a daughter; in 1856, for example, Mary Withers joined the Chesnuts at White Sulphur Springs, Virginia.[35]

But Mary's favorite charges were the children of Kate and David Williams. Serena had been born in 1848, Mary in 1850, and Miller in 1853. These children (with their brother David born in 1858 and sister Kate in 1860) Mary called her "little sweet Williams."

Whenever Kate and David Williams traveled, Mary Boykin Chesnut was the preferred person with whom to leave the children. In 1857 she kept the three oldest Williams children for a year while their parents were in Europe. As an adult, Mary Williams wrote about her stay with Aunty.

> When I was about seven years old our parents decided to go abroad for a year, and it was arranged we should stay with my Mother's sister, Mrs. Chesnut, who was our dearest Aunty . . . . Aunty was to meet us; and all that I recall of the parting was Mama's face buried in Enie's [Serena's] curls and calling for Miller and myself, who with the absolute heartlessness apparently a part of youth, had climbed upon a high pile of cotton bales and were amusing ourselves by gazing down with delight and merriment and trying to make Rachael, the under-nurse, see how very, very queer Aunty's face looked, as, with all her dear impulsive nature, she was weeping unrestrainedly and with her face all pucked up, and red and swollen from crying . . . . Happy and careless as ever children were, a torment and delight to our Aunt, and an endless source of anxiety and care to dear old Mammy. I so well remember that Aunty's one punishment for us if we were naughty was to forbid us having any cake for tea; and, as sure as that was the case, Mammy would come the next morning with her clean pocket handkerchief tied up in a bundle and, opening it out, offer us a bit of cake in a most nonchalant manner.[36]

Mary Chesnut would continue to be a second mother to the Williams children until her death, but occasional substitute motherhood could not entirely compensate for being childless herself, a fact about which she was extremely sensitive. In her revised Civil War journal, she would later write of a day in 1861, when "I did Mrs B a Kindness—I told those women [in Montgomery] that she was childless now—but that she had lost three children—I hated to leave her all alone—women have such a contempt for a childless wife—Now they will be all sympathy—and kindness. I took away 'her reproach among women.'" And in March, 1861, she would record: "Mrs Chesnut was bragging *to me* with exquisite taste—me a childless wretch of her twenty seven grandchildren & Col Chesnut a man who rarely wounds me—said to her '*You* have not been a *useless* woman in this world—because she had so many

children'—& what of me! God help me—no good have I done—
to myself or any one else—with the [power] I boast so of—the
power to make myself loved—where am I now—where are my
friends—I am allowed to have none." [37]

Perhaps because she had no children on whom to expend her
energies, Mary became absorbed in her husband's career. He had
been elected to the state senate in 1852 and served as its president
from 1856 to 1858. When in 1858 he won unanimous election to
the United States Senate, his wife was both gratified and excited.
She immediately accompanied her husband to Washington, and
launched wholeheartedly into the social side of national politics. [38]

The Chesnuts went to Washington expecting to fill a six-year
term. Expenses would be high, so they made arrangements to sell
Kamchatka. Although James's family was extremely wealthy, his
own funds were limited; until 1859 his father retained title to all
Chesnut lands, and James and Mary lived on James's law practice
and allowances made by Colonel Chesnut. Now Mary's beautiful
home was sold and her servants distributed; some went to Mulberry, some were hired out to the Camden Hotel, and some went
to James's plantation, the Hermitage, part of his father's estate
which the elder Chesnut would formally sell to his son in 1859,
but which James had been managing for over ten years. [39] In Washington, Mary set about the numerous tasks involved in establishing a new residence and changing living patterns.

One such task was the replenishment of her wardrobe—a serious undertaking in an era when, on a given day, fashionable
women frequently needed a morning dress, a dinner dress, an evening dress for tea, and a ball gown. Mary's approach to matters of
dress was relatively efficient; she loved beautiful clothes, but found
the details of dressing to perfection boring. Hence, she provided
herself with elegant dresses (often imported from Paris), left the
responsibility of her toilette to her maid, arranged her hair simply,
and hoped for the best. Accordingly, she wrote to a Philadelphia
dressmaker whom she and her sisters had patronized for years.
Though she rarely saved letters, Mary saved the dressmaker's answer, probably because she was delighted by its combination of
outspoken good sense, unasked-for advice, and friendly gossip:

Phil. Jany 7th 1859

DEAR MADAME

I am very much gratified that the order gave satisfaction and that the dress fitted well. The Point d'Paris capes I wrote you about have all been sold and I fear no more can be got . . . . Had I not better send you on subject to your approval two Point Alencons at $110 & 120 as they are always elegant and never go out of fashion. You need not pay for it untill Spring and it is just what a Senators wife ought to have—provided she thinks she can afford it. . . . We are now at the height of balls and parties and every thing elegant in Lace is bought up particularly in capes as some married ladies will not go bare neck whilst others are very prodigal in these members. All this depends early training and a good constitution . . . . Business is business and I dont wish to take up your time with gossip so forgive me as you and yours have been been old patrons for many years and thro all this I am yours faith fully

MARY M WHARTON[40]

Mary may well have worn some of the Alençon lace in April to the marriage of Mary Withers to Thomas Kirkland. Two years later Mary Boykin Chesnut would write: "When J C was made Senator—I was so engrossed by Mary Withers her recent engagement her future &c &c I scarcly cared for it—only thought it a bore as taking me from her—I had wished for it principally to take her to Washington." The Chesnuts returned to Camden for a wedding so private that there were only four guests besides themselves. Mary Withers Kirkland later recalled that the Chesnuts outspokenly regarded an April wedding as inconvenient: "Cousin James was most anxious that the wedding take place in March . . . . Cousin Mary thought [it] strange that the groom did not wish the wedding as soon as possible." Mary Chesnut seems to have been concerned and curious about the husband of her young friend; shortly afterward she paid a visit to the new bride: "The furniture was all covered and I recall Cousin Mary . . . insisted that the covers be taken off so she could see what was under them." It was what Mary herself would have called "a character touch," indicative of her unfailing curiosity and her happy insistence upon having her way.[41]

After the wedding, Mary returned to Washington and devoted herself to living as fully as possible. She frequently performed secretarial chores for her husband. It seems likely that she also assisted him with his speeches, and debated endlessly with him about the growing political tensions between North and South, and as the year 1859 passed, the implications of John Brown's raid, and the upcoming presidential elections.

Chesnut's politics reflected his personality; they were cool, reserved, and conservative. Like many southern statesmen who came from families of long-standing wealth and social position, he strongly believed that his role as public servant was just that: a sacred trust to be upheld even at personal sacrifice. He held to what he regarded as his own high ideals, and refused to curry public favor—a scruple later to be his political undoing. Now, as the controversy over states' rights and the institution of slavery reached fever pitch, he eloquently maintained the sovereignty of the southern states over their own internal affairs. His was an outspoken and—throughout the South—much admired rebuttal to Charles Sumner's attacks on slavery even though James Chesnut, Jr., had personally no great love for the system nor any deep conviction of its moral rightness. Chesnut was a skillful orator and quickly rose in prominence in the Senate.

His wife was instinctively and by training a far more practical politician. She loathed slavery. In fact, early in 1861, before the firing on Fort Sumter, she would write: "I wonder if it be a sin to think slavery a curse to any land—Sumner said not one word of this hated institution which is not true—men & women are punished when their masters & mistresses are brutes & not when they do wrong . . . . God forgive *us* that ours is a *monstrous* system & wrong & iniquity."[42] But despite her hatred of the social system her husband upheld in the Senate chamber, she wholeheartedly agreed with his view that the southern states must not be dictated to. Further, she set about to do whatever she could to cement his position in the controversy.

Her role was necessarily social. As the Chesnuts settled into the celebrated "Southern mess" at Brown's Hotel on Pennsylvania Avenue, Mary Boykin Chesnut soon earned a reputation as a "brilliant" conversationalist and a "literary" lady. She came to know well most of the southern politicians and their wives. Her days were filled with luncheons and outings; her nights devoted to the theater, an occasional lecture (she heard Fanny Kemble give a reading), and innumerable dinners. Because of her facility with French and German, she came to be thought of as one who had no doubt been educated abroad, and found herself a frequent guest at affairs honoring foreign dignitaries.[43] Once at the White House she was seated for dinner between President James Buchanan and a visitor from Spain, so that she might speak to the Spaniard in French and translate for the president. When she and the visitor became engrossed in conversation, the president bent over to remonstrate with his guest for monopolizing Mrs. Chesnut. Although she realized with amusement that her reputation as a linguist far exceeded her skill, Mrs. Chesnut had cause to be grateful, nonetheless, for she met ambassadors from numerous countries. She later recalled an absurd trip on a government barge with an official of the Japanese embassy—a jaunt on which conversation was at a minimum.[44]

James Chesnut appeared willing for his wife to manage his social obligations. He disliked large parties and often found reasons not to attend. On one hand his love of privacy earned him a reputation for impeccable morals in a town for which gossip was stock-in-trade. Rose O'Neal Greenhow, an unquestioned leader of Washington society (in 1861 she would be hailed throughout the South as a heroine for her activities as a spy), once jokingly told a mutual friend that James Chesnut, Jr., had been one of the few men in the District of Columbia to whom no scandal was attached—primarily because he never spoke to a woman. On the other hand, though, James's reluctance to attend social functions sometimes caused his wife embarrassment. A particularly irritating instance occurred when Chesnut excused himself from a dinner at the home of Secretary of Treasury Howell Cobb. Mary went anyway and found the experience of arriving alone humiliating enough to make her blush. (When she told her mother later, her mother wryly noted that anything that could make Mary blush was indeed a phenomenon.) Fortunately, Vice-president

John C. Breckinridge escorted her home.[45] Such moments produced tension between James and Mary at a time when everyone's nerves were taut anyway. In private, tempers occasionally flared between husband and wife.

Despite sporadic disharmony at home, Mary was having the time of her life. An important factor in her enjoyment of Washington was the chance to associate with other intelligent and accomplished women. In addition to Rose Greenhow and President Buchanan's niece and official hostess Harriet Lane (whom she had known casually for years), Mary now formed friendships with Charlotte Wigfall, a Charlestonian who was the wife of Texas' volatile senator Louis Wigfall; Virginia Clay, wife of Clement Clay, a senator from Alabama; and Senator Jefferson Davis's wife Varina. Though Mary Chesnut and Varina Davis would not become close friends until after secession, in Washington each developed a high regard for the other and enjoyed one another's company thoroughly. In deference to her mother-in-law's friendship with the Washington-Custis family, Mary called on Mary Custis Lee, wife of Colonel Robert E. Lee. She came to like the invalid Mrs. Lee very much, and struck up a real friendship with the Lee sons Custis and Rooney, and with Lee's nephew Fitzhugh. Robert E. Lee's brother Smith Lee quickly joined Mary's growing circle of friends and admirers, and she awarded him a permanent place in her estimation.

In 1859, during their stays in Washington, the Chesnuts remained in the hotel, but in January, 1860, they moved to a house at H and 10th streets. The arrangement suited James because it removed him from the never-ending socializing of a congressional mess. Mary approved the move because it enabled her to entertain more frequently. Entertainment was on a lavish scale. Mary indulged her love of good food by employing a skilled Frenchwoman as cook. One may surmise what must have constituted a formal dinner party from a description of a simple family meal at the Chesnuts' table written by one of South Carolina's former governors, John Manning, to his wife: "Dined in the evening with Mr Mrs Chesnut, who are comfortably situated in a house of their own, & gave me a very plain but nice dinner, Julien soup fish tenderloin of beef and mushrooms & veal larded with vegetables & green peas & salad. Ice cream & champaign & Madiera as concomitants." [46]

Manning, a friend of James Chesnut since boyhood, had become something of a friendly political rival. In 1861 he would indulge in a rather serious flirtation with Mary. Therefore his next comment on her to his wife is interesting: "Mrs C very talkative introducing great names in her discourse as if intimate with them & giving her husband sharp hits in a quite unprovoked way." Whether Manning's response to Mary at this time was precisely honest (four days later he wrote to his wife, "I have seen Mrs Chesnut only twice. She is full of gossip on the inside and of unneatness on the outside") or whether the attraction had already begun and he was attempting to persuade himself or his wife otherwise, Manning was quite wrong to imply that Mary was namedropping (or, more accurately, that she was name-dropping undeservedly). [47] She may well have been intentionally making the point to Manning that Chesnut, his rival, had become important in Washington circles. But she was, in fact, intimate with the most prominent members of Washington society, and she was enjoying that intimacy immensely.

Mary Boykin Chesnut's two years in Washington were broken by frequent extended trips, particularly when the Senate was not in session. She spent several weeks at White Sulphur Springs during the summer of 1859, as she had done for several years. In the late fall she journeyed to Flat Rock, North Carolina, where Kate Williams had just built a summer home, and from there traveled to Alabama with the entire Williams family. The occasion was a family reunion—the first time the four Miller children had been together with their mother for many years. Mary described the trip—a far cry from the elegance of Washington—in "We called her Kitty":

> We left the cars at Montgomery—or somewher[e] below it—took a hack—which broke down & did every thing disagreeable—We were packed in too compactly—for one was a baby—& the eldest not ten—I had not patience enough—& made things worse—finaly—all were slapped round—it began so suddenly like a clap of

thunder & ended as quickly—Mamie—the darling—nearly broke her heart. She sobbed—"it is Auntie—Mama let us go somewhere out of Aunties way—she worries children" I felt it to be true & was as meek & quiet as a mouse after the storm.

Mary found that travel through Alabama had not improved much in twenty years: "The first night we stopped at a place where they showed us a room—*for all*. & the Land lord made a man in the bed get up—& offer it to us which he did with great politeness—half asleep—& half undressed as he was—there was not even any talk of clean sheets." [48] The party left the rumpled bed alone, swept the floor, and spent the night on makeshift pallets of shawls and cloaks.

Once in Alabama, accommodations were better, but still considerably less comfortable than those to which Mary was accustomed. Her sister Sally had described brother Stephen Miller's summer home to her in a letter several years before: "Tebe's house here is large & airy & he keeps a first rate table . . . there is a fine place for bathing in 30 yards of the house, which is a great comfort in this climate, the house has five rooms in it just sealed not plastered . . . we have a pleasant breeze all the time from the water." [49] Mary was, of course, pleased to see all her relatives, particularly Sally's children. But she found the neighborhood dull and was certain it would be a dismal place to live.

The following summer Mary again spent a few weeks at the Virginia springs, and then made a trip to Philadelphia and Hoboken. Mary Stevens, the daughter of James's cousin Edwin Stevens, had spent the winter with her, and though she had been thrilled with the social whirl of Washington to which Cousin Mary introduced her, it was time to take the girl home. Mary Chesnut used the opportunity to shop and to pay her respects to numerous Chesnut relatives. In New Jersey she met Winfield Scott, general-in-chief of the Army, now in his mid-seventies. Entering into political debate with him, she defended South Carolina's threats of secession. Scott replied, "I know your little South Carolina—I lived there once. It is about as big as Long Island—and two thirds of the population are negroes—Are you mad?" [50] Although she did not know it, travel to the North would not again be possible for many years.

In the fall of 1860 Mary went south once more, this time with the Withers' son Randolph[51] (Tanny) in tow. With tensions high in the nation's capital as everyone awaited the results of the presidential election, Mary knew that the future was uncertain. It might be many months before she would be able to get away to see Kate, who was expecting her fifth child in a few weeks. Mary and Tanny Withers met David Williams and his daughter Serena (who had spent the year with her grandmother Miller) in Charleston and traveled to the Williams' new plantation home, Serenola, in north-central Florida near the heart of present-day Gainesville. On her arrival at Kate's, Mary witnessed a scene that moved her profoundly—and left her feeling very empty, very alone:

> When we arrived at Kates—it was late at night—That part of Florida is ugly. it has the same lonely dismal swamp owl hooting, dispairing, depressing effect—as Mississippi—Conecuh &c . . . Kate was in white & looked lovely—& was so tender & so glad to see me—& so disappointed Serena did not come. All at once Serena who had hid—flew around the corner of the Piazza—into her Mothers arms . . . I know what a man's love can be—for I saw it [my father's love for my mother] in Mississippi—here I saw a Mothers—she wept—& chattered—& kissed—& laughed aloud—& when the lamp was brought—I saw a face glorified by feeling the blazing grey eyes—twice their size & *black* with emotion &—I sat down as one in a trance—see what I had missed again—a natural bent for the feeling—I was choked up with—& nobody has ever wanted it—I would lavish it here & there to relieve outraged nature—only to make ingrates.[52]

Mary spent "two anxious weeks amid hammocks & everglades oppressed & miserable."[53] When she left Kate's in November, 1860, to return to Charleston, she had reached a turning point in her life. Twenty years of marriage to the cool, reserved James had by no means provided adequate outlet for a creative and frankly passionate nature. She was thirty-seven, a woman of discerning intellect and great charm, a woman of strong opinions, strong loves, strong hates, and very little to do that she considered useful. She needed something to absorb her utterly, to challenge her, to give added meaning to her life. It was on the train, just before she reached Fernandina, that the Withers boy tapped her on the shoulder and told her someone else in the car had just received a telegram: Lincoln had been elected. For the South and for Mary Boykin Chesnut it was a disastrous event, but it would prove just the catalyst she needed.

Mary Boykin Chesnut, portrait by Samuel Osgood, 1850s. On loan to National Portrait Gallery, Smithsonian Institution, by Serena VanRensselaer

Mary Boykin Chesnut, 1850s, painted from a daguerreotype.

Mary Chesnut said this picture, a carte de visite made in Charleston, 1861, made her look like a washerwoman.

James Chesnut, Jr. Portrait by
William Harrison Scarborough.

James Chesnut, Jr., 1861, carte de
visite photographed in Charleston
before the firing on Fort Sumter.

James Chesnut, Jr., late 1870s.

Mulberry, the Chesnut home,
three miles south of Camden,
South Carolina, where James
and Mary Chesnut began their
married life.

The staircase at Mulberry. Mary Chesnut's room on the third floor became her retreat.
ROBERT M. SMITH, JR., PHOTOGRAPHER

"The Chesnut Cottage," 1718 Hampton Street, Columbia, South Carolina. Jefferson Davis, the Chesnut's guest here in October, 1864, made a stirring address from the front porch.

Sarsfield, Camden, South Carolina, was Mary Chesnut's last home. The revised journal was written in its library, shuttered bay windows at left. The house was built with brick from outbuildings at Mulberry.

Mary Bowes Cox Chesnut (1775–1864), James
Chesnut, Jr.'s mother. Portrait by Gilbert Stuart.

James Chesnut, Sr. (1773–1866). Portrait by
Gilbert Stuart.

Mary Boykin Miller (1804–1885), Mary Boykin Chesnut's mother, photographed in her seventies.

Governor Stephen Decatur Miller (1788–1838), Mary Boykin Chesnut's father, artist unknown.

Charlotte Boykin Taylor (b. 1817, d. 1900), Mary Boykin Chesnut's beloved Aunt Charlotte, who cared for Mary in her last illness.

Burwell Boykin (b. *ca.* 1749, d. 1817), Mary Boykin Chesnut's maternal grandfather.

John Chesnut (1743–1818), James Chesnut, Jr.'s grandfather and first owner of Mulberry. Portrait by Gilbert Stuart.

Catherine Boykin Miller Williams (1827–1876), Mary Chesnut's beloved sister Kate. Portrait by Samuel Osgood.

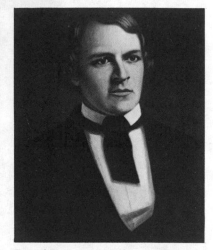

David Rogerson Williams II (1822–1907), husband of Kate Boykin and nephew of James Chesnut, Jr. He inherited Mulberry.

Mary Boykin Chesnut, childless, called her sister Kate's five children her "sweet Williams." Serena Chesnut Williams (1848–1876), age seven, portrait by Samuel Osgood. Mary Boykin Williams (1850–1931), age five, portrait by Samuel Osgood. Stephen Miller Williams (1853–1938), from a pencil drawing by his father. David Rogerson Williams III (1858–1928), also a pencil sketch by his father. Kate Miller Williams Kirkpatrick (1860–1954), the youngest of the "sweet Williams."

Serena Chesnut Williams as a young woman.

Mary Boykin Williams Harrison
Ames as a young woman. From
an old glass negative plate.

Jane North Pettigrew Williams (1855–1890), wife of Stephen Miller Williams.

Sarah Chesnut (1813–1889), Mary Boykin Chesnut's sister-in-law, "Miss Sally." Made from an old glass negative proof plate.

Mary Serena Chesnut Williams (1821–1887), sister of David Rogerson Williams II. She was Mary Boykin Chesnut's girlhood friend, a fellow student at Madame Talvande's school in Charleston.

Thomas Jefferson Withers (1804–1865), Mary Boykin Chesnut's uncle and her guardian after her father's death.

COURTESY SOUTH CAROLINIANA LIBRARY

Mary Withers Kirkland (1838–1925), daughter of Elizabeth Boykin Withers and Thomas Jefferson Withers.

John Laurence Manning (1816–1889), governor of South Carolina, 1852–1854, and father of Ellen Manning who married David R. Williams III, to whom Mary Boykin Chesnut left Sarsfield. John Manning, who carried on an extended flirtation with Mary Chesnut in Charleston in 1861, lived at Sarsfield with his daughter after Mary's death.

Jefferson Davis (1808–1889), portrait by John Robertson when Davis was fifty-five. This is Davis' only portrait painted from life during the Civil War.

COURTESY MUSEUM OF THE CONFEDERACY

Varina Howell Davis (1826–1906), miniature by John Wood Dodge, when Varina was twenty-three. Varina and Mary Chesnut, who became acquainted in Washington when their husbands were senators, remained friends all their lives.

COURTESY NATIONAL PORTRAIT GALLERY, SMITHSONIAN INSTITUTION

Francis Wilkinson Pickens
(1805–1869), governor of South
Carolina, 1860–1862, was a
political antagonist of James
Chesnut, Jr.

COURTESY SOUTH CAROLINIANA
LIBRARY

Lucy Petway Holcolmbe Pickens
(1832–1889), wife of Governor
Francis Pickens. Her face was
printed on Confederate currency.
She was regarded by Mary
Chesnut as a rival hostess in
Columbia and Charleston.

COURTESY SOUTH CAROLINIANA
LIBRARY, CHARLES GAY,
PHOTOGRAPHER

Sarah Buchanan Campbell "Buck" Preston (1842–1880), who with her sister Mary, visited Mary Boykin Chesnut often during the war.

General John Bell Hood (1831–1879) courted Buck Preston in Mary Boykin Chesnut's drawing room.

Dr. John Darby, General John Bell Hood's surgeon and a friend of Mary Boykin Chesnut. He married Buck Preston's sister, Mary.

Louisa Susanna Cheves McCord (1810–1879), an author, and friend of Mary Chesnut. During the war she administered a hospital on the grounds of South Carolina College.

Isabella D. Martin (1839–1913), Mary Boykin Chesnut's friend who, with Myrta Lockett Avary, edited the first publication of *A Diary from Dixie* in 1905.

Mary Boykin Chesnut's original journal, dated June 28, 1861, during the period when Mary found herself in the middle of a feud between the Jefferson Davises and the Louis Wigfalls. This entry describes a conversation with President Davis.

43

In Mrs Davis drawing room last night
the President took a seat by me on the sofa
where I sat.     He talked for nearly an
hour.        He laughed at our faith in our
own prowess.  We are like the British.
We think every Southerner equal
to three Yankees at least.  We will
have to be equivalent to a dozen ~~at~~
~~least~~ now.  After his experience of the
fighting qualities of Southerners in
Mexico he believes that we will
do all that can be done by pluck
and muscle.  endurance.  and
dogged courage.  dash - and red hot
patriotism &c -        And yet his
tone was not sanguine.  There was
a sad refrain - running through it -
all ◦ for one thing - either way -
~~He~~ thinks it will be a long war.
That floored me at once.  It has been
too long for me already.      Then he
said -        ~~Before the war came~~ we
would have many a bitter experience

Revised journal, entry dated June 28, 1861, corresponds to passage in photo-
graph of the original journal. In it Mary Chesnut expands her conversation
with President Davis.

FIVE     1861–1865

WHILE MARY BOYKIN CHESNUT was en route back to South Carolina, James Chesnut, Jr., resigned his seat in the United States Senate on November 10, 1860, in response to Lincoln's election. Mary spent only one night in Charleston, sleepless, listening to loud oratory in the room below hers, then proceeded to Camden. At Kingsville, she met her husband who was returning from Washington. If Chesnut stopped at Camden, it was only briefly, for he proceeded directly to Columbia to report on the political situation. Shortly after Mary arrived at Mulberry, she picked up a daybook she had started in Washington, and carefully recorded her husband's resignation—the first by a southern senator. Then she added a note that suggests she did not entirely agree with his action: "Alas I was in Florida I might not have been able to influence him—but I should have tried."[1]

Mary remained in Camden for the next several weeks, while James spent most of his time in Columbia, assisting in the organization of the South Carolina Secession Convention, to which he was duly elected. The convention convened in mid-December, and after voting unanimously to secede, appointed a committee, which included Chesnut, to draft an Ordinance of Secession. Because smallpox had broken out in Columbia, the convention adjourned to Charleston. Mary joined her husband there, and then went on to spend Christmas with friends and relatives at Combahee, near Beaufort, amid "Camelias as plentiful on the lawn as the Hawthorn in an English hedge." Immediately after Christmas, the party returned to Charleston, in time to hear the news that Major Robert Anderson had moved his garrison into Fort Sumter. South Carolina was galvanized with war fever. At sleepy Camden,

Mary Chesnut saw "unprecedented excitement. Minute men arming with immense blue cockades & red sashes soon with swords & gun marching & drilling."[2] By the first of February six more states had joined South Carolina, and the Chesnuts went on to Montgomery to a hastily called convention of seceded states.

The tense excitement that vibrated the very air of her world registered instantly on the delicate barometer which was Mary's emotional nature. Alternately hopeful and distraught, she arrived in Montgomery concerned about her sister Kate (who she knew was seriously ill following the birth of a child), unsure of what the future held, and afraid of what she saw from the start would be that most horrible of political upheavals: civil war. Her husband remained convinced that the formation of a Confederacy could be achieved without bloodshed, and at times Mary felt that he was blind to the realities around him.[3]

Before she got thoroughly settled in Montgomery—a relative matter at best, since the city was strained by the influx of convention delegates and offered poor accommodations—she took the opportunity to pay a quick visit to her mother in Conecuh. Conscious that history was being made and that her husband was in the center of the action, Mary decided to keep a daily journal of events. At her mother's, in mid-February, she wrote the first entry on a few loose pieces of paper. Back in Montgomery on February 25, 1861, she began to write regularly in a book bound in red leather. She was aware of the profound change that had been wrought in her life by the secession of South Carolina and the other states: "I cannot write in this book without thinking of the happy days [in Washington, a year before] when I sat & read & heard the scratching of my darling Mary Stevens pen as she scribbled her love nonsense in a red book like this."[4]

In Montgomery, Mary found herself caught up in a whirlwind of confusion and excitement. Rumors were rampant and everyone spent the days running from one meeting to the next, then visiting everyone else to hash over the latest gossip. Early on, Mary realized that keeping her journal was one way to reduce her busy days to manageable size, and to retain a strong measure of objectivity about the barrage of people and events that came into her life.

After a particularly hectic day, Mary wrote in March: "What nonsense I write here—however this journal is intended to be intirely *objective*. My subjective days are over—no more *silent* eating into my own heart—making my own misery when without these morbid phantasies I could be so happy." Then alluding to a quote she liked from Dryden, she went on: "I think this journal will be disadvantageous for me for I spend the time now like a spider spinning my own entrails instead of reading as my habit was at all spare moments."[5]

In fact, Mary didn't have many spare moments; she was busier than she had ever been, paying and receiving calls all day, entertaining almost every night in the drawing rooms of the Montgomery Hall hotel. On March 2, immediately after Varina Davis arrived in Montgomery, Mary went to see her. Mrs. Davis greeted Mary "with open arms," and the women talked for two hours. Obviously delighted to see her friend, Varina related all the news from Washington. "We discussed the world & his wife," Mary wrote later in the evening. "I could only get away by promissing to come back every day."

The friendship that Varina Davis and Mary Boykin Chesnut were now renewing would develop into a lifelong one. The two women had remarkably similar backgrounds, interests, and opinions. Varina, like Mary, came from a politically and socially prominent family. Her grandfather, Richard Howell, had served as governor of New Jersey, 1793–1801. (His daughter Sarah had stood at Trenton Bridge with Mary Cox Chesnut to strew flowers before General Washington as he rode to his inauguration.) As a girl, Varina had been well educated; she still read incessantly and loved a good literary debate. Both women were gregarious and enjoyed the social side of political life, though neither James Chesnut nor Jefferson Davis shared this enthusiasm. Both women took pleasure in matching wits with men, and cultivated comfortable relationships with the famous men of their day. Each possessed an irreverent sense of humor and a sharp tongue; neither was always successful at curbing her temper. Like Mary Chesnut, Varina—who was younger by three years—had married at seventeen, and had found her husband's family difficult to live with. Varina had so angered her brother-in-law Joseph Davis, head of the Davis family, that he had already drawn up one will for Jefferson Davis that severely limited her inheritance, and he would later refuse to leave Jefferson title to Brierfield for fear it would fall into Varina's hands. Understandably, Mrs. Chesnut and Mrs. Davis sought one another out frequently during the two weeks the new president's wife was in Montgomery, sometimes to let down their hair and exchange private news, sometimes at the levees which Varina Davis gave, graciously asking Mrs. Chesnut to assist her.[6]

By the middle of March, the Chesnuts made plans to return to South Carolina until May; there James would attend the constitution convention and Mary would go on to Florida to see for herself how Kate was doing. Pleased to get away from the inconveniences of hotel life—no carriage of her own, horrid food, and a family of unruly children in a nearby room, Mary was also glad to remove herself for a while from the political machinations around her. She had found the constant jockeying for position distasteful: "This war began a War of Secession it will end a War for the Succession of Places." Further, she noted a scapegoating of Davis with real alarm: "What a pity—these men have brought old hatreds & grudges—& spites from the old Union. Already we see they will willingly injure our cause to hurt Jeff Davis." As a city, Montgomery didn't appeal to her: "Everybody persists in opening conversation by saying—How do you like Montgomery—& I hidious Hypocrite—answer charmed."[7] But she was beginning to transform her intense loyalty to South Carolina into an equally intense patriotism for the new Confederacy.

The trip back to Camden, on dusty railroad cars, occasioned a particularly serious argument with her husband. She did not record in her diary what the fight was about, but she did flare into a temper and, during the day the party had to wait in Augusta for a connecting train, shut herself up in a hotel room, refusing "to accept overtures for peace & forgiveness." There she recorded her fury: "after my stormy youth—I did so hope for peace & tranquil domestic happiness—There is none for me in this world."[8] Whatever the source of her anger, it was exacerbated by the pain from an impacted tooth, and by a backache caused by the rough travel.

The luxuries of Mulberry, "pure white House linen—cream in coffee—& good coffee," and the rare beauty of a South Carolina countryside covered with a foot of snow, were a welcome relief. But Camden proved, as usual, unpleasant for Mary. The town was in an uproar over an impending duel; prominent citizens were dashing around trying to calm the two parties. Mary asked why they were not simply arrested, thus preventing needless death. James said he supposed Judge Withers, Mary's uncle, could make the arrests, but characteristically did nothing further. Mary, sick with a toothache and with blisters on her side and back from an inadvertent overapplication of chloroform ointment, took action. Enlisting the aid of her favorite Chesnut nephew, Johnny, she secretly sent for the judge to put a stop to the proceeding.[9] The Chesnuts remained in Camden only a week, during which Mary had the offending tooth pulled. Then they went to Charleston. With the help of her maid Betsy, Mary packed economically, taking only absolute necessities: clothes, a few books, and her journal.

The journal she was keeping would become transformed twenty years later into a book, but in its original form it was a sometimes cryptic work, crammed with names and brief phrases written hastily between visitors and dinners and receptions. In Montgomery, Columbia, Charleston, and Richmond she wrote in hotels or rented rooms—often in bed—sometimes skipping several days when life became frantically busy; in Camden she occasionally escaped to the schoolhouse on Mulberry Plantation to get away for a few hours from the hubbub of the house. So that she could write candidly, she kept her journal locked and allowed no one (not even her husband) to see it. Thus she could record her most private opinions about men and women: of South Carolina's Governor Pickens' appearance at a reception she could write "old Pick was there with a better wig—& his silly & affected wife"; she could call rude people "cattle," unattractive ones "fat & stupid" or "ugly as sin." After a dinner party, she could write "I can give a better dinner than that!"—a luxurious boast she would never allow herself in public.[10]

A typical entry simply listed and briefly characterized the people she had seen since she last wrote and included a phrase or two which would later remind her of an anecdote. Mary wisely made very little effort to separate the important from the trivial, but rather recorded everything that occurred to her as she was writing. Nor did she often pause, as she would later do frequently in her book—the revised journal—to reflect on the scene around her. From the outset, she was amassing material, notes to be used later. Though she enjoyed the social whirl in and for itself, she also seems to have attended many events with an eye toward what she might there see and hear which would later be of use. After a reception at the Confederate White House in Montgomery in March, she wrote: "found it all from having a head ache & ill humour—stale—flat—& unprofitable." [11]

Mary Boykin Chesnut's revised journal, first published as *A Diary From Dixie*, offers the reader an excellent and full account of the author's life during the Civil War and, more than that, it provides a carefully considered, skillfully written picture of the society in which Mrs. Chesnut lived. But even though *A Diary* makes a conscious—and usually successful—effort to portray the period 1861–1865 accurately, it is nevertheless the product of a woman who has had almost twenty years to sort out the events of those years and the meaning of the Civil War itself. Further, in her book, Mary has had time to control the picture she gives of herself, to leave out or deemphasize much of the emotional turmoil of these years. Thus the reader of a published edition of the revised journal cannot know for certain whether, for example, the author's antislavery sentiments are the result of hindsight or were, in fact, opinions held during the war years. The manuscript journals kept between 1861 and 1865, then, offer a rare opportunity to see the private Mrs. Chesnut before she had a chance to prepare an edited version of herself for the public.

Without extensive annotation and amplification, her manuscript journals that survive from the Civil War period tell us a great deal more about Mrs. Chesnut than they do about the war itself or the central figures in the Confederacy. They reveal an extremely complex and emotional personality, a woman capable of being totally subjective one moment and highly objective the next; an arrogant and ambitious woman who, alone with her thoughts, could and did feel abjectly humble; a woman quick to judge, but perfectly willing to change her mind. They reveal an active and wide-ranging intelligence—the kind of intelligence that delights in the thrust and parry of repartee and can, at the same time, easily grasp large political, psychological and moral issues.

Above all, these journals reveal a thoroughly feminine woman. With much justification, Mary Boykin Chesnut regarded herself as superior to most people she knew—male or female—but she thoroughly enjoyed using her femininity to exact admiration from the men around her even though, in a society venerating physical beauty, she had never been pretty. Early in the first volume of her journal she wrote, "I never was handsome—I wonder what my attraction was for men did fall in love with me wherever I went." On March 15, 1861, she wrote and then erased this statement: "I can make any body love me if I choose I would get tired of it." These private remarks appear out of context to be gratuitous and conceited, but there is abundant evidence throughout the Civil War journals that she was merely stating fact. From girlhood she had drawn men to her, and the power apparently did not diminish as she approached middle age. Men daily sought her out, sent her flowers, gave her presents, boasted of having conversations with her to their friends—all this far beyond that which mere politeness required in a courtly society. She seems to have been the central figure in any group, and she happily recorded evidence to that effect: "Dr Tom Taylor was saying how stiff it was at the reception yesterday until I got there—& I went in like a ray of warmth & sunshine—pretty good for a woman of my years," and "Mrs Elmore said she was afraid to meet me she heard so much of the charming Mrs Chesnut wonderful!" [12]

Nevertheless, Mary Boykin Chesnut was well aware that in charming her circle of admirers, she was nothing more or less than a superb player of a kind of universal parlor game: "Mr Joscelin—the poet says I look younger & better than I did in Washington I wonder if in the thousand compliments I hear there is one *grain* of truth." To real love affairs or even serious flirtations, Mrs. Chesnut remained aloof. Occasionally in the journals she records an instance of someone carrying intimacy too far: "I will not write to Trescott because he was too *frenchy* in some of his anecdotes to

me—& he writes frantically 'to know why I do not answer his letters—that Mr Chesnut is the most tyranical of men & prevents
my writing or I am the most ungrateful of women.' " [13]

Surely one reason Mary so enjoyed her male friends was because they annoyed her husband. In March, 1861, he became enraged over attentions paid her by the handsome former governor
John Manning. On the train to Charleston, Manning asked Mary
to save the seat beside her for a young lady and, after the train began to move, announced that *he* was the "young lady" in question. Thereafter, for over a week, he sought her out three or four
times a day, often breakfasting with her, taking her for morning
and afternoon walks on the Battery and paying evening calls.
James protested and, as Mary's father had once done because of
James Chesnut himself, forbade her to walk on the Battery with
gentlemen. Mary pertly recorded in her journal, "Is not all this
too ridiculous at my time of life." For several days, the more
James spluttered, the more Mary enjoyed the situation: "Is it not
too funny—& he is so *prosy*." Apparently, at the end of a week or
so, Mary decided that James had been tormented enough and put
an end to the flirtation, perhaps not without a parting shot at her
husband: "Breakfasted today with John Manning—Mr C res-
tive because I said I did not tell him every thing—then John Manning brought me a bunch of violets." The journals give no hint
that Mary regretted cutting off her relationship with Manning at
the time, but four months later she would write: "Mrs Johnson
[wife of General Joseph E. Johnston] says . . . John Manning
ask[ed] her—does Mrs C really speak well of me? the deceitful
wretch! he suspects every body! . . . John Manning knows I never
believed in him or trusted him—snake in the grass—*beautiful* as
he is. [14]

Such flirtations aside, there was only one man in Mary Chesnut's life: her husband. Scattered throughout her book of the
1880s, Mary has provided her reader with enough clues to amass a
good portrait of James Chesnut, but she allows us very little insight into the nature of her relationship with him. We are shown a
quiet, cool, reserved man who meets the world masked by unexceptionable manners: "The raggeder and more squalid the creature
the more polite and the softer Mr Chesnut grows." Among inti-

mate friends, though, he becomes an attractive figure—a man with a dry wit who can say to a dinner guest with perpetually dirty hands, "My dear fellow if you have such an aversion to water—why not grabble in a little clean sand." Chesnut dislikes controversy, preferring quietly to read history or to commune with his horses: "As long as he has a dollar left in the world it will go in horseflesh. If fate will leave him a fine horse to ride she can never utterly depress him otherwise." Even his enthusiasms are usually understated: "Late at night when we were seated alone . . . Mr C said—gravely—'This has been a very happy day.'"[15] A reading of Mary's book written in the 1880s reveals that she and her husband had opposite temperaments and that, though they often sought one another out for quiet companionship, Mary's need for excitement and society and her quick tongue frequently baffled and infuriated her husband. When they argued, James accused Mary of lacking self-control and Mary called her husband cold.

Throughout both her diaries and the revised journal, there are hints that Mary Chesnut's feelings for her husband were often confused. Of marriage she wrote: "Is it not as with any other co-partnership—say—travelling companions—Their future opinion of each other—'the happiness of the association depends entirely on what they really are—not what they felt or thought about each other before they had any possible way of acquiring accurate information—as to character—habits &c—Love makes it worse." She made a very clear distinction between love and its imitations: "In all my life how many persons have I seen in love—not a half dozen—And I am a tolerably close observer—a faithful watcher, have I been from my youth upwards—of men and manners."[16]

Of particular concern to her was the proper matching of partners in love or marriage, and her occasional disquisitions on the subject suggest that she may have regarded herself and her husband as poorly matched. Such disquisitions usually appear in response to her reading. Thus, having reread The Mill on the Floss she wrote; "I revolted at the sacrifice [made by Maggie]—Why give up Stephen Guest to her cousin—Love pays its own way—Maggie had the right divine to him—But then—right and wrong—

morality aside—Death is better for Maggie than a life with a *thin* soul like Stephen Guest. He was too small for her." And of Shakespeare she said: "What a time the sweethearts of that wretch— young Shakespeare must have had—What experiences of lifes delights he must have had before he evolved the Romeo and Juliet business from his own internal consciousness . . . . The poor creature that he left his second best bedstead to—came in second best all the time no doubt—and she hardly deserved more. Fancy people wondering that Shakespeare and his kind leave no progeny like themselves—Shakespeares children—were half his, only— the other half—was only the second best bedsteads." [17]

Such statements subtly reflect strains between James and Mary Chesnut, strains which were at least in part caused by forces beyond their control. The year 1861 was one for heroes. To Mary Boykin Chesnut, heroism meant the spotlight: honor, praise, attention—all things she longed for herself but could achieve only through her husband. And her husband, content to serve well and faithfully in the wings, could not oblige her. Throughout the war, he would be the fact-finder, the official observer, the carrier of news, the center of attention only when he was speaking of someone else's exploits. His role in the firing on Sumter presented a case in point.

The Chesnuts arrived in Charleston on March 25, and Mary instantly put the pains and aches that had plagued her in Camden out of her mind. Charleston was her favorite city, filled with people she had known from childhood and with shops and streets she had always loved. The city's population was swollen by newly mustered troops, convention delegates, and prominent South Carolinians who had arrived to be in the thick of whatever action was to come. Mrs. Chesnut's days were crowded with visits and visitors. April 3 was typical, and provides a good example of a complete diary entry:

> Sally R had a good time went to see old Miss Pinkney said Mr C's grandfather was very handsome—& had a picture of C C Pinkney like the one at Mulberry—met Mrs Carroll at the Allstons— had a charming time at the St Julien Ravenels—Sally R ran up twice to Quinby's for me—my likeness uglier than ever—called on

Louisa Hamilton & found Mrs Carson—came home barely in time for dinner—Dr Gibbes wanted to sit with Mrs Wigfall & me but I would not let him determined to undress & rest—but as soon as I was undone here comes Mrs Robertson then Mrs Richard Roper—then Mary Ford—then I may say Mrs Wigfall & I had a reception—The Cheves girls & Mr Langdon Cheves—Mrs D Hamilton—Captain J. R. Hamilton & Louisa—Mr. Edmund Rhett—to whom Mr Wigfall made a stump speech—Mr Hanckel—very pleasant man—Mr Hayne—Jack Cunningham Mr Sprate—Congo Sprate—Maxcy Gregg—Mr William Martin—Dr Gibbes &c &c such a merry time—I talked too much I fear but the people were so complimentary—To night we are to take tea at Mr Isaac Hayne—Mrs Pickens—formerly the lovely Lucy Holcom—called also—so affected—& me away—we are to meet her to night—Captain Harstien & Tom Huger were to take us to the forts to day—but came to say it was blowing great guns outside & so I was glad to post pone. I want rest—breakfasted with John Manning who made better jokes than usual—Mrs Robinson has come for me to pay bills.

Once, Mary paused after listing the friends and admirers who came to see her and added humorously, "a nice discriminating place Charleston is!!!"[18] To add to her feeling of well-being, news arrived that Kate was better so Mary would not need to make the uncomfortable trip to Florida.

The Chesnuts planned to return to Camden on April 9, but events centering on the fate of the Yankee garrison at Fort Sumter changed their plans. Mary had already packed to leave when John Manning came into the Mills House where he and the Chesnuts were staying and "in mock heroic style" announced, "Madame your country is invaded."[19] Six men-of-war were stationed just beyond Charleston Bay, and South Carolina regarded them as a hostile force. By afternoon, Chesnut had accepted a position as aide-de-camp on General P. G. T. Beauregard's staff.

Mary Chesnut began her entry of April 11 with the assertion that dinner had been a merry affair: "who could imagine *war* began today?" James Chesnut, clothed in a new uniform, resplendent with red sash and sword, had gone with Louis Wigfall to demand the surrender of the fort. The garrison refused. Chesnut, as Beauregard's aide, consulted President Davis by telegraph and then attempted to negotiate with Major Robert Anderson. When those efforts also failed, he ordered the first shots fired on the fort. At 4:30 on the morning of the 12th, Mary and Charlotte Wigfall heard cannon fire, dressed hurriedly, and rushed to the rooftop of the Mills House, where they watched the bursting shells in horror. The firing continued throughout the day, and by nightfall, Charleston was jubilant. No one had been hurt, and Mary recorded that "'tho' we hear the firing we feel so differently—because we feel that our merciful God has so far protected our men." When Anderson surrendered, Mary Chesnut called it a "great day." "I saw my husband carried by a mob to tell Gen Beauregard the news." But James's moment in the sun was brief indeed; it was Wigfall who had obtained the official surrender and Beauregard who had commanded the troops. Chesnut's work behind the scenes was forgotten by all but his wife.

For the next ten days excitement ran so high in Charleston that Mary had no time to write in her journal. War seemed a particularly glorious sort of game. A week was unofficially given over to celebration. Just before the firing, a friend had said to Mary that "the only feeling she had about the War was pity for those who could not get here." And Mary herself, after jotting down a few notes several days later, wrote "must try & remember every thing about that wonderful siege & write it as soon as I have leisure." [20]

Leisure was not forthcoming. Davis had called together his Provisional Congress, so the Chesnuts returned to Montgomery by April 27. There, once again, began the round of visits and conversations—with the Jefferson Davises, the Louis Wigfalls, the Robert Toombses, Confederate secretary of the navy Stephen Russell Mallory and his wife, and the first secretary of treasury, Christopher Memminger, and with Robert Barnwell Rhett, whose attacks on Davis in his Charleston paper, the *Mercury*, had already begun to infuriate Mary Chesnut. Once more she made a quick side trip to visit her mother, this time returning on a steamer grandly called the *Southern Republic*, but no less unpleasant for its new name. Three weeks after the Chesnuts arrived in Montgomery, they returned to Camden; Congress had voted to move the capital to Richmond, against James Chesnut's objections.

During May, the Chesnuts stayed at Sandy Hill, the family's summer retreat a few miles northeast of town. James appeared perfectly content to ride his horses and oversee the affairs of his plantation, but Mary responded with bitterness to the enforced solitude. She had not been an entire month in Camden since 1858, and now she found herself hopelessly frustrated. The townspeople seemed oblivious to the prospect of war, and equally oblivious to her own presence. The senior Chesnuts professed themselves thrilled at the return of James and Mary, and then promptly left for a visit to one of James's sisters. Her dear Johnny Chesnut departed for Virginia as a private, and Mary was simultaneously saddened by his absence, proud of his devil-may-care patriotism, and irked by the fact that he had ignored her earlier advice to raise a company and get into the fray as an officer. When Kate arrived with her children, Mary occupied herself for several days helping her sister get settled. But soon she began to notice slights—calls expected but never paid, remarks that seemed somewhat sarcastic or rude—directed against Kate and her two oldest daughters, Serena and Mary, and carefully recorded these, too, in her growing accounting of Camden's black marks.

In her revised journal of the 1880s, Mary's dissatisfaction with Camden life is focused on her mother-in-law and other family members at Mulberry, but in the wartime journals, this feeling is far more general. Almost everyone with whom Mary associated frequently was a near or distant relative, and most were wary of her. To a great extent, the fault was Mary's. The town was small, quiet, socially and politically conservative. Mary had undoubtedly alienated many of the women she knew by praising the culture and glamour of Saratoga, Newport, White Sulphur Springs, and Washington. Many of the usual topics of conversation were closed to her; she had no children and cared very little for fashion. The people she loved most dearly—her mother and her sister Kate—were there only rarely for visits. Mary Williams Witherspoon, once her closest friend, had become fanatically religious. And in the young girls like Mary Withers whom she had taken under her wing before the war and to whom she had grown—perhaps unwisely—extremely attached, she sensed a new formality; this formality was almost certainly a natural pulling away from childhood ties, but Mary Chesnut was hurt by it.[21] It seems likely, however, that her most serious handicap in Camden was her outspoken detestation of slavery—a decidedly improper viewpoint in the late 1850s and early 1860s.

Mary was not a likely person to espouse antislavery sentiments. Slavery had always been a part of her life as it had been of James's; the Boykins, Millers, and Chesnuts considered it a duty and a matter of honor and integrity to treat their slaves well and humanely. To avoid the danger of malaria and other illnesses prevalent in the hottest months, these families regularly moved slave children and mothers to summer plantations when the family went; it was customary for the same doctor to treat slaves and family members. Buying and selling slaves was uncommon; James Chesnut (who took four servants with him to war) had bought only one slave in his life—and had done so at the slave's request to prevent breaking up a family. Furthermore, Mary was frankly fond of being catered to, and was appreciative of the well-trained servants at Mulberry. And though she relished being waited on, she was not overly tolerant of blacks on the whole, considering them "dirty—slatternly—idle—ill smelling by nature," and adding, as most white southerners of the day would have, "when otherwise it is the exception."[22]

Nevertheless, Mary Boykin Chesnut had been unable since childhood to ignore the fact that slaves were human beings. The willingness of otherwise honorable men to own slaves was, for her, a profoundly disturbing hypocrisy—one over which she agonized throughout her life. A page of a daybook kept about 1880 contains this passage:

> Grandfather Boykin would not let his boys *find* any thing. Uncle Lem found an excelent knife in the Charleston road—Grandpa made him go & put it just where he found it &c &c. Now Governor Miller would not let his family *lose* any thing belonging to other people—above all public money. So—when he helped a nephew to gain his election for tax collector—& when he was set upon by robbers—& mauled & crushed & tied to a tree & robbed—he made the family make up the sum lost & say nothing of the robbers . . . . Yet

these rigidly honest veterans—were what Sumner called guilty of the sum of all iniquity—large slave owners—& without a misgiving as to its perfect righteousness—invincible ignorant . . . very kind to negroes in a general way—regarding them as little as the chairs & tables if they stood in *any body's way*.[23]

Mary had been taught by slaves and had, in turn, taught them. In Charleston she had watched Madame Talvande rear and educate a mulatto girl in a white society and had grown to love at least one of Madame's servants.[24] But the single most important element in her determination that slavery was wrong seems to have been her belief that the system of slavery undermined the sexual morality of southern men.

Frequently, both in the manuscript journals of the 1860s and the revised journal, Mary expressed disgust at the fact that white men could and did turn to their female slaves for sexual gratification. In Montgomery, Mary had seen the sale of a young mulatto girl who reminded her of one of her own servants, and had recorded her response in her diary: "South Carolina slave holder as I am my very soul sickened—it is too dreadful I tried to reason—this is not worse than the willing sale most women make of themselves in marriage—nor can the consequences be worse—The Bible authorizes marriage & slavery—poor women!—poor slaves!"[25]

Although she clearly linked slavery with marriage, and although she loathed the immorality slavery encouraged among slaveowners, the diaries contain no hint that James was involved sexually with any of his slaves. There seems little doubt that her primary case in point was her father-in-law, James Chesnut, Sr. In a passage in her journal that corresponds to the discussion of childless women quoted earlier, she ended her sentence about her father-in-law's pride in his twenty-seven grandchildren by saying, "*He did not count his children*!!" Now, at Sandy Hill, having called the legal wife of a southern planter "Leah" and the slave mistress "Rachael," she wrote: "Merciful God! forgive me if I *fail*—can I respect what is not respectable can I *honor* what is dishonorable—*Rachael*—& *her brood*—make this place a horrid nightmare to me."[26]

Mary Chesnut wanted desperately to end the nightmare—at

least temporarily—by following her husband, who left for Richmond in early June. Accordingly, she telegraphed Charlotte Wigfall to be on the lookout for suitable rooms, and as soon as Mrs. Wigfall found accommodations in the crowded Spotswood Hotel, Mary took her valuable silver to the bank for safekeeping and prepared for the journey. She had invited her young cousin Mary Boykin, daughter of her uncle Alexander Hamilton Boykin, to come along, and the two left Camden on June 24.

In Richmond they were met enthusiastically by Louis Wigfall and General Robert Garnett, and escorted with ceremony into the Spotswood, temporary headquarters of President and Mrs. Davis and dozens of Confederate dignitaries, among them the Garnetts, Wigfalls, L. Q. C. Lamar, and good friends from Columbia, the John S. Prestons. Mary Boykin Chesnut immediately found herself in the middle of a bitter quarrel between the Wigfalls and the Davises. Political disagreements between Davis and Wigfall had been picked up and intensified by their wives, once good friends. Because Mary Chesnut was close to both women, she was cornered by first one and then the other and regaled with tales of bad manners and abuse. Mary at first sympathized with Charlotte Wigfall—a friend of longer standing; by so doing, she provoked Varina Davis's anger. But even in the middle of all the wrangling, she was objective enough to find the whole matter both petty and dangerous: "They are so busy playing *court* here they forget the war *altogether*—these women!"[27] For a week or so, Mrs. Chesnut recorded slights and insults by Mrs. Davis in her journal—remarks she later erased or crossed out. And by early July, the two women had made a peace which strengthened as time passed.

James Chesnut was with Beauregard in western Virginia. Mary arranged a rendezvous with him at Fauquier White Sulphur Springs on July 6, but the visit lasted only a few days; James returned to his staff duties, and sent back a message that a battle was inevitable, and that it was no longer safe for Mary and her traveling companions to remain at the spa. Shortly after their return, Mary learned that fighting had broken out at Manassas Junction. For three days, Richmond waited anxiously for each scrap of news. Varina Davis and the other ladies at the Spotswood spent much of that time with Mary Chesnut, sometimes sitting until midnight worrying and wondering. On the 21st, Mrs. Davis came into Mary's room, kissed her, and told her that a victory had been won. But the women's excitement was tempered by news of the dead and wounded. And soon the sound of the "dead march" began as military funerals passed by Mary's window. It was a sound from which she would never again escape in Richmond, and which would haunt her for the rest of her life.

As the summer wore on, Mary Chesnut's life settled down into a routine of sorts. Days were spent in conversation—always with knitting at hand—and in frequent drives, sometimes to watch reviews of the troops. Visits to hospitals were almost a daily occurrence; at first, Mary took fruit and cheer to the wounded, then to the hundreds of soldiers who had fallen victim to various diseases that ravaged the southern armies. She made a friend of Miss Sally Tompkins, whose hospital work would earn her the only Confederate commission granted to a woman. President Davis was ill much of the summer, but when he was feeling well enough, he often sought out Mrs. Chesnut, claiming he liked her "style of chat." [28] Davis had call to approve of Mary, for she had become outspoken in her defense of the president at a time when there was growing acrimony from widespread disapproval of his administration. "Right or wrong," she wrote on August 12, "we must stand by our President & our generals—& stop fault finding."

As nearly as she could see, the war was being fought not on the battlefields, but in the newspapers. Particularly irritating to her was the report on Manassas by Colonel Joseph Kershaw, an old Camden friend: "Evidently from this report Hampton alone with 500 kept the whole army at bay & was just routed & repulsed & beaten when Joe Kershaw came up with Cash & Gen Kirby Smith & Olliver under his command returned the fight routed the Yankees—& would have followed into Washington but Beauregard forced him back—Oh my country men where is your *modesty* not to say decency." [29] Her husband, who declined to sing his own praises, was content to take his place quietly in the Provisional Congress. And though Jefferson Davis had offered Chesnut a choice of positions in the army, Chesnut had postponed making any decision. As the Congress adjourned at the end of August, his wife packed to return to Camden: "I am enjoying the noise & bustle of a city—that I so dearly love before the change takes me to my beloved country—The streets are as crammed as ever with uniforms & gay soldiers—but I *feel* the theatrical Joe Kershaw war is over—practical earnest bitter fighting begins." As she and her husband left Richmond, they were once again arguing—this time about whether James should go into the army. Exasperated, Mary simply wanted him to take action, any action. She noted wryly in her diary, "Jeff Davis ill & shut up—& none but noodles have the world in charge."[30]

Before the firing on Fort Sumter, when Mary first realized James was actually going to fight, she wrote: "I feel he is my all & I should go mad without him";[31] the cry would not be an odd one under the circumstances except for the fact that Mary erased it. The passion it expresses was something with which she was uneasy—it had no place in her marriage and, realizing that, she could not allow it to stand. In its place, she recorded almost daily concern that James was not receiving the appreciation and love due him from others: his family, his friends, his state.

Because she was a woman, Mary herself could not fight; nor could she hold office and thus direct the affairs of state which she followed so avidly. Her frustration at her own helplessness surfaces frequently in her journals: "Oh if I could put some of my reckless spirit into these discreet cautious lazy men" (April 27, 1861); "Beauregard is at Norfolk & if I was a man I should be there too!" (May 26, 1861); "if I was a *man* I would not doze & drink & drivel here [Camden] until the fight is over in Virginia" (May 30, 1861); "If Mr C takes a colonelcy I will go as *cook*—the men fare so badly" (August 26, 1861).

Unless James achieved a post of some importance, Mary felt herself doomed to view the war from behind the pillars of Mulberry. Therefore, she was extremely ambitious for her husband, who refused to lobby in his own behalf. Unlike most of his friends, he had balked at the idea of asking for a generalcy and scorned to campaign for his own election to the Confederate Senate. Mary was stymied. Frantic to be in the center of the "great revolution," she hoped that James would, without asking, be given an ambassadorship; barring that, she desperately wanted her husband to be elected senator: "I wish Mr Davis would send *me* to Paris—& so I should not *need* a South Carolina Legislature for anything else."[32] Journal entries from August to December reveal Mary fighting a losing battle with her own ambition:

> I am depressed today—Last night Mr Barnwell sat with me all the evening & the feeling against Davis is stronger than I expected in SC. . . . What if the same combination . . . which is against Davis likewise oppose J C—he must be left out of the next Senate! . . . I am trying to look *defeat* of my personal ambition in the face—So if it does come I can better bear it! & if it does not come the rebound will be so much more delightful.
>
> Mr C has let Mr Barnwell persuade him that he can be most use to the country in the Senate—& I dare not say—Go in the Army—because if anything happened what would I feel then—Why was I born so frightfully ambitious.
>
> Mr Chesnut came home today to say Slidell will be minister to France—so "all my pretty chickens at one fell swoop"
>
> Now if we are not reelected to the Senate! . . . pride must have a fall—perhaps I have not borne my honours meekly.[33]

Life in Camden was doing nothing to still Mary's frustration. Much of the time she was ill with a recurring fever she attributed to her hospital work in Richmond. Furthermore, she was beginning to be bothered seriously by a heart condition—later diagnosed as angina pectoris—which periodically flared up. On the 19th of September, she heard of the death of an aged cousin, Betsy Witherspoon, and soon news began to filter in that the old woman had been violently murdered in her bed by her house servants. While the family was trying to deal with this shock (Mary had nightmares for several days), a series of mild earthquakes hit Camden, followed by storms and a freshet that destroyed the corn crop. All the while her husband did nothing to further his election. "J C dashing aside letters & not answering them as if he was *heir* apparent to the throne of *the world* & his election certain!"[34]

Quietly, Mary answered some of the letters for him, entertained her nieces and nephews, and tried to devote herself to the war effort by working with the ladies' society in Camden. No one seemed to take such projects seriously, so Mary ripped up old curtains herself to make shirts for the soldiers, and set up her maid Molly in a butter-and-egg business. Hoping for the best, she wrote to Sally Tompkins asking her to find rooms in Richmond, but after a diligent search, Miss Tompkins replied that none were available. Inevitably, Mary's irritation at her husband's inactivity mounted: "*Now* when if ever man was stirred to the highest for his country & for his own future—he seems as utterly absorbed by Negro squable, hay stealing—cotton saving . . . . The only part of it that is not utterly horrible to me is the devotion to sick Negroes—If I had been a man in this great revolution—I should have either been killed at once or made a name & done some good for my country. Lord Nelson's motto would be mine—Victory or Westminster Abbey."[35]

Much to his own surprise, James Chesnut lost his Senate seat, largely because Mary's uncle, Alexander Hamilton Boykin, had mishandled his election. Mary's response was to pick herself up. She had shaken herself, "no bones broken no dislocation—but sore & stunned yet—*inward* bruises"; and to take stock: "Now let us look this thing in the *face*—this is an end of JC's political life." She spent the following day coming to grips with what was for her nothing less than a crushing personal defeat: "I have been busy all day reading old letters—what a meek humble little thing I was—how badly JC has played his cards to let me develop into the self sufficient thing I am now—for I think this last bitter drop was for *me*—he will care very little—but I had grown insufferable with my arrogance." True to form, James's reaction was mild: "JC says it was unexpected . . . he says it is moonshine to him [but] he is afraid it will annoy *me*."[36] *Annoy* was hardly the word.

Having refused to elect Chesnut senator, the South Carolina Secession Convention now appointed an executive council of five members to oversee the military and defense concerns of the state and named Chesnut head of the military department. Under his leadership, the council empowered itself to raise troops and impress slaves and supplies—thus enraging the governor, Francis Pickens, who had only one vote on the council and felt that he was being overstepped. Factions on both sides grew heated, and with each innovation that James Chesnut made, he received increased abuse from opposing political forces.

None of the journals Mary Chesnut kept during 1862, 1863, or 1864 have survived, and it is likely that for at least a part of that period (August, 1862–October, 1863) no journal was kept.[37] Thus what we know of her life through these years can be learned only from her book of the 1880s, based on the lost journals. She spent the first seven months of 1862 in Columbia while her husband served on the executive council. There, despite the controversy her husband's actions roused, she found herself surrounded by friends of long standing, most prominent among them the handsome and charming Preston family. When she was feeling well, Columbia offered much to occupy her. The beautiful Preston daughters, Sally Buchanan (Buck) and Mary, adopted her as confidante, chaperone, and friend, and charmed her with their literary discussions—they had been educated in France—as much as with their flirtations. Louisa McCord, busy establishing a hospital at the South Carolina College, sought her out every day or two, and Mary became actively involved in the effort to procure supplies and money for the sick and wounded in Richmond and Columbia. Fruit and flowers poured into her room, and invitations came for nearly every meal. But often, the old fever recurred, and Mary spent long periods of time sick or recovering from illness.

To recuperate, she was forced to go to Kate in Flat Rock in August, 1862; while there she wrote constantly to her husband, revealing her concern for him, her anger at the vilification his actions roused, and her frustration at being away from him and thus away from the center of the action: "If I could fight all Columbia anxieties I might be happy—but I *can't*—I see they talk of impeaching you for what I think you have done to save your country—'putting down distilleries—making arms & ammunition organizing the military—&c &c—' I wonder if they thought you would be like Pickens—a great old horse fly buzzing & fuming & fretting & doing nothing but hire & bribe newspaper people to write & abuse friends & enemies." As the situation in Columbia grew worse, Mary ventured to give her husband a bit of advice. "I think your friends in the Convention would gladly get rid of *you* (Executive Council) if they knew how, with out hurting your feelings! Why don't you resign and save them from their embarrassment. . . . Is it not rather inglorious work this great struggle . . And such a different fight going on in Virginia . . . let us try Jeff Davis awhile." [38] This advice was prompted by a real concern for her husband, but underlying that concern was a fear that Chesnut might be forced out of office.

In December, Mary finally got her wish; Davis sent Chesnut a commission as colonel and summoned him to Richmond as a personal aide. At the close of 1862 the Chesnuts went to Richmond. Shortly thereafter the daughters of their Columbia friends the Prestons came for an extended stay. Mary was thus caught up once more in the inner workings of Confederate society and involved with chaperoning two beautiful young girls. She entertained constantly. In Richmond the Chesnuts rented one floor of a house at 12th and Clay streets, near the White House of the Confederacy. Quarters were cramped; while the Preston girls were there, the dining room became a bedroom and even the stair landing was utilized when the drawing room overflowed with people. Visits back and forth between Varina Davis and Mary Boykin Chesnut were almost daily occurrences while Mary was in Richmond, and Buck and Mary Preston became friends with Maggie Howell, Varina's younger sister who lived with the Davises.

While he had held a place in the Provisional Congress, and later when James Chesnut served on the executive council in South Carolina, hundreds of people applied to Mary for favors, hoping she would speak with her husband on their behalf. "James Lowndes asked me if Mr C got up a regiment of cavalry to give him a *place* & he shall have it—if I have any *influence* Mr C says—why do not those young men come to *me* why all to you." In Richmond, because the Chesnuts were personal friends of the Davises, the supplications continued. At one point so many people called that Mary wrote: "no end of people *call*—I wish they would not— there is the expense of hack hire returning them." [39]

Occasional protestations notwithstanding, the six months from January to June 1863 were perhaps the most pleasant of the war years for Mrs. Chesnut. Although the war had become a weary reality and an inflation-wracked and overcrowded Richmond was, for most people, a city plagued by crises, Mary devoted herself wholeheartedly to garnering what pleasure she could from her days in the capital. Supplies arrived regularly from Mulberry, and James Chesnut's servant Lawrence and Mary's maid Molly contrived, given enough money, to procure the fresh foods and other luxuries to which Mary was accustomed. Thus the Chesnut household continued to be a place where pleasant people of good families—regardless of rank—could be sure of finding a sympathetic ear, good food, beautiful women, important men, and entertaining dialogue.

In the midst of all the merrymaking, Mary had two fascinating love affairs going on under her roof. Mary Preston had fallen in love with Mrs. Chesnut's friend John Darby, a surgeon attached to General John Bell Hood's division. Hood was in Richmond recovering from wounds sustained at Gettysburg, so Darby brought him to meet Mary Chesnut. Hood, usually shy in public, promptly fell head over heels in love with Buck Preston, whose circle of admirers already included several young men professing love for her. Mary Chesnut shepherded her young guests from dinners and teas at the Stanards and Randolphs to musicales arranged to meet visiting Frenchmen and Germans at the Davises. Once, when Varina was out of town, Jefferson Davis gave a breakfast for Mary and her guests: "He was so kind and so amiable and agreeable, we were all charmed, but Buck came away in a very ecstacy of loyalty." [40]

In June, Mary Chesnut went to visit her sister Kate in Flat Rock, and from there to Camden and Columbia. While she was staying at the Prestons, she received word that her mother was very ill in Alabama. She telegraphed James in Richmond, asking him to send Lawrence to travel with her. Her husband replied by forbidding her to make the trip at all; he feared that travel would make her ill. Mary ignored his injunction. In Alabama, after a miserable trip, she found her mother better than she had expected. But her sister Sally was crushed by the death within the week of two of her children, Mary and Kate. To see the sadness in the house was an ordeal for Mary, doubly so because there was nothing she could do to relieve her sister's grief.

Back in Richmond, she shook off the depression caused by her visit and entered once more into an unvarying round of social events. Now, though, the course of the war was not going well, and after Gettysburg it became more and more difficult to forget the situation outside the capital even for an evening. The Prestons had come to Richmond, and each daughter had brought a friend. Since Buck and Mary continued to regard Mrs. Chesnut's as head-quarters, the drawing room was still filled with young people gayly acting out their flirtations regardless of the tragic deaths about which they heard daily or the doom which seemed always to lurk just behind the doors. But more and more guests were wounded—visible reminders of stark reality. Hood lost a leg at Chickamauga, and afterwards moved slowly and painfully on crutches as he courted Buck. During the Christmas season, the Prussian Major Heros Von Borcke, wounded in the throat, and Alex Haskell, a Columbia friend who had lost an eye, came for visits. Mary Boykin Chesnut began to feel that a large part of her own personal role in the war lay in the very distractions and enter-tainments she and her friends so constantly contrived.

For James the round of parties seemed horribly heartless. When Mary returned one day in January, 1864, from a drive with General Hood, Maggie Howell, and Mary Preston, she found her husband in a bitter mood. "It has all gone wrong with our world. The loss of our private fortunes—the smallest part," she later wrote. "He intimates—with so much human—misery filling the very air—We might stay at home—and think." Mary's reply indicates she was fully aware of her own motivations: "And go mad? Catch me at it! A yawning—grave—piles of red earth thrown on one side—that is the only future I ever see . . . . It is awfully near—that thought of death—always—No—No—I will not stop and think."[41]

After the death of her mother-in-law in March, Mary Chesnut's activities were severely curtailed. James was deeply depressed and anxious to get back to South Carolina where he could be near his father. Accordingly, Davis promoted him to brigadier general and assigned him command of the South Carolina Reserves. As the Chesnuts made ready to go south, they were feted by friends sorry to see them go—not half so sorry, wrote Mary, as she was to leave. On the eve of their departure, she drove with the Lees, the Mallorys, Mrs. Robert Ould, and Maggie Howell to see an exchange of prisoners. After three and a half years of war, it was Mary's first view of Yankee soldiers, and she was fascinated by the excursion. As the party prepared to drive back to Richmond, they received word that one of the Davises' children, five-year-old Joe, had been killed in a fall from a piazza. Mary rushed Maggie Howell home, and sat for hours in the Davises' drawing room, listening to the president's steps above her as he walked up and down through the night. The child's funeral, and memories of the grief-stricken parents, marked a somber ending to the Chesnuts' years in Richmond.

Mary spent six weeks in Camden, proceeding to Columbia at the end of June. At first, she stayed with the Prestons, but by mid-July had managed to find a small cottage for rent close by. No sooner had she left her friends' mansion than the Prestons received word that their son, Willie, had been killed. This death, coming so soon on the heels of little Joe Davis', shocked Mary Boykin Chesnut, and seemed to sum up for her the horror of war.

> When I remember all—the true hearted—the light hearted—the gay and gallant boys—who have come laughing singing—dancing in my way—in the three years past—I have looked into their brave young eyes—And helped them—as I could every way—And then seen them no more forever—they lie stark—and cold—dead upon the battle field or mouldering away in hospitals or prisons—which is worse—I think if I consider the long array of those bright youths and loyal men—who have gone to their death almost before my very eyes—my heart might break too.
>
> Is any thing worth it? This fearful sacrifice—this awful penalty we pay for war?
>
> Willie Preston came to my house on Clay St. Richmond—just one year ago. He was worn out—he had had fever in the West. For once there was no laugh in his bonny blue eye—shaded like a girls with the longest tangled black lashes—"Mrs C—What a beastly hole—as the English would say—no Ice"—

—Indeed? Lawrence has discovered a mine of Ice across the "Noble Jeem's river . . . ." And I hastened away to return in a moment
with a Julip. A Mint Julip. cold within, and the outside of the gob-
let frosted with Ice.
—"*Dear* Mrs Chesnut—you have saved my life!" And the old
laugh came back. And the blue eyes—grew wide and deep in his
delight—Heaven's what a handsome fellow he was![42]

Much of Mary's time now was spent at Louisa McCord's hospital or at the Wayside Hospital run by Jane Cole Fisher. Having always been an early riser, she got up each morning at five o'clock
and drove to the Wayside Hospital, her carriage loaded with provisions. Early morning duty enabled her to have her afternoons
and evenings free, a necessity since the little cottage—as all Mrs.
Chesnut's residences, however temporary—soon became a sort of
perpetual open house for guests of every description. The city was
filled with generals and ragged troops; Sherman's capture of Atlanta hideously underscored the vulnerability of South Carolina.

Nevertheless, Varina Davis sent her sister Maggie Howell for a
long visit with Mrs. Chesnut. In Mrs. Davis' opinion, the girl
needed a taste of gaiety, or at least a brief respite from the gloom
of a city daily aware of the siege of Petersburg, just thirty miles
away, and from the domestic concerns of a household still in
mourning for one child and busy with caring for a new baby.
Varina Anne, or "Winnie," had been born in late June; although
she would later be called the Daughter of the Confederacy, the
Davis family had promptly pronounced her "Pie-cake" and Mrs.
Davis wrote to Mary that the infant had brought her solace and
even joy.

Maggie was still with the Chesnuts in Columbia when, in early
October, Jefferson Davis stayed with the Chesnuts briefly on his
way back to Richmond from a trip to inspect troops and consult
with Hood and other commanders in the field. The occasion was
one which challenged all Mary's instincts for hospitality. In rented
quarters, she felt her furnishings, appointments and larder all
needed sprucing up to receive the honored guest. The room he
would stay in was hastily refurnished with "mirrors of the first
Wade Hampton—prerevolutionary relics. Some fine old carpets

of ci devant Gov Miller curtains to match." [43] Neighbors sent elegant dishes to complement the Madeira and china Mary summoned from Mulberry.

Shortly after the president left, Kate arrived for a week, and then Mary Preston married John Darby, occasioning another round of dinners and parties. From Varina Davis came a letter of thanks for Mary's kindness to Maggie Howell and to her husband: "Thank you a thousand times my dear friend for your more than maternal kindness to my dear child—as to Mr Davis he thinks the best ham—the best Madeira, the best coffee, the best hostess in the world, rendered Columbia delightful to him, when he passed through." Varina went on to speak of her baby, and of the universal sadness in Richmond. In closing, she begged Mary Chesnut to write:

> Do write as often as you can, for added to my very sincere love for you, I have an enjoyment in your letters quite independent of friendly feeling. They are so charming in style. I always did insist the women who write letters in books do not do as well as those who have no books in which to put them, and therefore give vent to thoughts which critics might deride as trivial, but which are the more precious to those we love because it is our only means of conveying the inner life. So tell me of yourself. of your enjoyments—your cares—every thing.
>
> I cannot bear to think we shall grow further apart until you forget me.
>
> As ever your devoted friend. V. D. [44]

Maggie Howell stayed with Mary until the middle of November, 1864. No sooner had Maggie left than Kate's two eldest daughters, Serena and Mary, arrived for an indefinite stay. Although she occasionally groaned at this constant influx of other people's children, having young people around meant a great deal to her; not only was she fond of all these girls, but their presence also meant an increase in the number of callers and a constant source of amusement. For the girls themselves, visiting with Mrs. Chesnut meant a "taste of Society and life," [45] and an endless supply of interesting people and events. Mary Williams later recalled her visit to Aunty with great delight. She said of her arrival,

We reached our aunt's home and found Molly and Lennette waiting at the front door to receive us, telling us Aunty was on duty that day at the Wayside hospital, but would be in later on. We went to our rooms, and Enie decided to take a nap, and invited me to take myself off, as I was very restless . . . .

I looked at all the books in the room, gazed in turn out of each window, and finally threw myself on the bed; and, while lying there looking about, I spied a most extraordinary looking box standing up in one corner of a closet, the door of which was open. No sooner seen that it was seized and opened; and this time the yell I gave was so unearthly that Molly and Lenette flew up from the kitchen; and Enie from over the way and Aunty from the front piazza, where she was saying goodbye to a gentleman. They all came racing and running to see what was the matter, and the matter was that General Hood had ordered from England a new false leg and it had run the blockade by one of the W. C. Bee boats, and had been sent to my aunt's to await General Hood's orders, and there it stood and confessed me a Pauline Pry.[46]

As if all this activity were not enough to keep Mary Chesnut supremely busy, her journals of the war years and her revised journals indicate that she continued to read widely and voluminously. As Yankee blockades cut off supplies from Europe and the North, books and periodicals became difficult to acquire. Thereafter, Mary used any means of procuring reading matter she could think of, borrowing and exchanging books with whomever she could, and keeping up an extensive correspondence in the quest for specific titles. When Dr. John Darby went to England to acquire the artificial leg for General Hood that Mary Williams found, he brought back a large order of books for Mary Chesnut. Her best "source" in Richmond was the famous former editor of the *Southern Literary Messenger*, John R. Thompson, who rarely came to see her without a novel or a sheaf of periodicals, once bringing her a New York *Herald* only three days old.[47]

Mary read newspapers and magazines daily—usually including the Richmond *Examiner*, the New York *Herald* (whenever she could get it) and all Camden, Columbia, and Charleston papers. Early in the war, perhaps with an eye to observing various authors' firsthand accounts or treatments of earlier wars, she read

John Lothrop Motley's *The Rise of the Dutch Republic* and *History of the United Netherlands*, Sir Edward Creasy's *Decisive Battles*, and James Fenimore Cooper's naval history; she reread William Howard Russell's account of the British handling of the Indian mutiny of 1858, the Revolutionary memoirs of Sir Banastre Tarleton, Henry Lee, and William Moultrie, and Lord Rawdon's letters.[48] She mentions reading several essayists, among them Emerson, Charles Lamb, and Margaret Fuller Ossoli. With the Preston girls, she read German; when Mary Preston was attempting to translate Schiller's *Wallenstein*, Mrs. Chesnut could compare her friend's efforts with translations by Bulwer, Austin, Coleridge, and Carlyle.[49] During the war her reading in French included Balzac's *Cousin Bette*, Beaumarchais' works, as well as Scribe and many French plays. In 1864 she was asked to decide upon and translate a French play for some amateur theatricals.

Mary Chesnut frequently reread her favorite poets, and apparently was thoroughly familiar with many minor poets too:

> My girls thought themselves well read in modern poetry . . . .
> But little Hill [a daughter of Senator Benjamin H. Hill of Georgia who had asked Mary to keep an eye on his child] had Owen Meredith at her fingers ends—and they did not know him at all.
> —Dont you remember this—or that?—"
> —"Alas no—I have not read Owen Meredith.
> —"It is as well as it is"—I said—"I am not sorry—better for you to find out while you are young how much more other people know than you do—any thing my dears—[is] better than the awful self complacency of the Modern American girl"—I said not a word, of how small was the shame of not knowing Owen Meredith—But I sent to Camden at once for my copy—that they might keep up with the world.[50]

Clearly Mary knew Owen Meredith well, and had found him wanting.

Her taste was catholic, ranging from Shakespeare and Ben Jonson to the American humorists of the Old Southwest. But as had always been the case, her favorite works—perhaps because they offered her escape—remained novels: "How much of the pleasure of my life I owe those much reviled writers of fiction." It was in novels that she found life most clearly reflected: "Read Charlotte Temple—found the formal euphemistic language stiff & tiresome—'the pellucid drop' for a tear &c—but there is enough of nature in it to make it very readable."[51] Favorite authors during the war years were all English, including Dickens, Trollope, George Eliot, and, first and foremost, Thackeray.

> Thackeray is dead. I stumbled upon Vanity Fair—for myself . . . . I had been ill at the New York Hotel—and when left alone—I slipped down stairs and into a book store that I had noticed under the Hotel—for some thing to read.
>
> They gave me the first half. I can recall now the very kind of paper it was printed on—and the illustrations—as they took effect upon me—And yet when I raved of it—and was wild for the other half—there were people who said it was slow!! That he was evidently a coarse, dull, sneering writer—That he stript human nature bare—made it repulsive.[52]

Mary Chesnut read critically, demanding that fiction should indeed strip human nature bare. She felt fiction should meet certain standards, foremost among them being fidelity to life. Of Beverley Tucker's *The Partisan* she wrote: "Just such a rose water revolution—he imagines as we fancied we were to have." Fiction must also be memorable: "[A] test. two weeks ago I read [George Eliot's *Romola*] with intense interest. And already *her* Savonarola has faded from my mind." Interested in the relationship between author and work, she praised writers who wrote from firsthand experience: "Read Mrs Shelly's book [*The Last Man*]. The book stirred me. She wrote of things she knew." By the same token, she drew conclusions about authors from their works. Thus she concluded that Shakespeare, who knew so much about love and women, must have been a good lover. When told that George Eliot was living with a married man, she refused to believe it, and reread *Adam Bede* to make sure. "I cannot believe the woman who wrote it—'is a fallen woman'—'living in a happy state of high intellectual intercourse—and happy—contented immorality'—She could not be happy—Dinah—and the retribution that overtook Hetty—speak out—that she knows good from evil."[53]

Many of Mary Chesnut's favorite people were, like herself, devoted to literature; it was always a great pleasure for her to slip away from the general conversation at a social gathering for a good long discussion of writers and poets with R. M. T. Hunter or Paul Hamilton Hayne. But the people with whom she most frequently discussed literature were the girls and young women who gathered around her: Buck and Mary Preston; her nieces Serena and Mary; Mary Withers Kirkland and her friend Caroline Perkins; and Isabella Martin, who was a friend of the Preston girls and who had first known Mary Chesnut when Isabella's father, the Reverend William Martin, had served as pastor of the Methodist church in Camden in 1853 and 1854. These young women had all been well educated and to them Mary was an intellectual mentor as well as friend.

By the end of January, 1865, even reading had ceased to be a means of escaping the war. It had become evident that General William Tecumseh Sherman, whose army was on the coast of South Carolina, would move, but none knew whether to Charleston, Augusta, or Columbia. As people began to flee the city, Mary debated where best to go. James thought she should return to Camden, but at the last moment, when word came that Sherman had reached Branchville, South Carolina, she changed her mind and fled in the path of her friends the Reverend and Mrs. Martin and their daughter Isabella to Lincolnton, North Carolina. From there, she reasoned, she could quickly reach Richmond or Columbia, or if necessary, get to her sister at Flat Rock. She had been in Lincolnton only three days when she heard Columbia had been taken, but reliable news was nonexistent, and rumors flew thick and fast. "I do not care," she wrote on February 23, "ever to see another paper . . . . how I have wept this day! my poor heart is weary—& then how it poured—*rain* rain rain—& in it all I rushed down to Mrs Martin. I wanted so to get away . . . I am so utterly heart broken . . . to night Isabella calmly reads beside me—& I am quiet after the day's rampage—oh—my Heavenly father look down & pity us."

Now Mary tasted ruin. She had brought books with her— "Shakespeare—Moliere—Sir Thomas Browne Arabian nights in French—Pascal's letters"—but no food. What little money she had was worthless: "I am bodily comfortable—if somewhat din-gily lodged, and I daily part with my raiment for food. We find no one, who will exchange eatibles for Confederate money—So we are devouring our clothes." When James Chesnut came for a quick visit in early March, he left with her his last cent. Even now, her extensive family connections proved valuable. When she needed leather to make shoes ("else—I should have had to give up walk-ing"), she found a man who had leather to sell. Fortuitously, the man in question had been helped through college by Stephen De-catur Miller. "And then my uncle Charles Miller—married his aunt—and I listened in rapture—all this tended to leniency in the leather business—and I bore off the leather—gladly." [54]

In the middle of March her husband wrote that he had found three vacant rooms in Chester, South Carolina, so Mary moved once again. In April, Varina Davis, who had fled Richmond and was staying in Charlotte, wrote inviting Mary to come to her: "You will receive such a loving welcome." But the very day the letter arrived, Senator Clement Clay dashed up the stairs to an-nounce Lee's surrender. Now, as if Mary Boykin Chesnut were herself the magnet, the old friends were drawn through Chester, and once again she kept open house. The Preston girls, also in ex-ile, came to stay. "My dining room is given up to them—and we camp on the landing—with our one table and six chairs." There were no beds, so everyone slept on the floor. "Night and day this landing and these steps are crowded with the Elite of the Con-federacy—going and coming—and when night comes . . . more beds are made on the floor of the landing place . . . The whole house is a bivouac." [55] General Preston came, and General Hood, her nephew Johnny Chesnut, Governor Milledge L. Bonham (who had replaced Francis Pickens), the Wigfalls, and finally, ex-hausted and despondent, Varina Davis and her children Maggie, Little Jeff, Billy, and Pie-Cake—going they knew not where.

After Sherman had completed his devastating march through the Carolinas, Mary Boykin Chesnut returned with her husband to Camden. The excitement of the past four years, the maneuver-ing for favor and position, the never-ending rounds of entertain-ing, the political and literary gossip, the hospital work, the emotional highs and lows, the uncertainty were over. General Chesnut and his wife arrived home quite literally penniless: "In crossing the Wateree at Chesnuts ferry we had not a cent to pay the ferry man—silver being required."[56]

Though Mulberry was still standing, it had been badly damaged and pillaged by a raiding party which followed in the wake of Sherman. Far worse in terms of the family finances, all the Chesnut cotton had been destroyed. Mary Cox Chesnut's death had badly shaken old Colonel Chesnut, now ninety-three, "in a deplorable state blind—feeble—fretful—miserable." The old colonel was the monarch of nothing but land in 1865. His stocks and bonds had been converted into worthless Confederate securities, and his estates were riddled with debts incurred in part for the support during the war of his more than five hundred slaves—now free. All of the Chesnuts' former slaves stayed on the property and agreed to work the summer crops, but Mary had no illusions that they would remain: "My negroes—now free citizens of the U.S.A.—are more humble & affectionate & anxious to be allowed to remain as they are than the outside world—the readers of Mrs Stowe could ever conceive—not one expressed the slightest pleasure at the *sudden* freedom—but they will all *go* after a while—if they can better their condition—JC hires them—the violent emotional offers to live & die with him pleases JC—whether they are like lovers vows made to be broken or not."[57] During the summer months of 1865 the only hard cash coming into the house was that earned by Mary's maid Molly who, staked by Mary early in the war, managed a butter-and-egg business on shares.

Mary continued to write in her journal regularly through the summer. Her entries reveal she was badly depressed and physically ill. The illness she called "gastric fever," probably contracted in 1861 in the course of hospital work in Richmond, had flared up throughout the remaining four years, causing headache, fever, and severe stomach pain. To relieve the symptoms, she sometimes took opiates, though she disliked doing so; in the first several months of 1865 she was accidentally given near fatal overdoses of opium and morphine at least twice. Back in Camden, her health seemed closely allied with her emotional state, and when she

became overly upset, she fell ill: "No mails any where—so no letters written or received no newspapers—no safety valves of any
kind—so to day—I had a violent fit of hysterics—JC called shut
the door—& seized me—frightened to death—soothing me as if I
was dying—I was ill enough & *wish I had* died."[58]

Camden seemed no more congenial to Mary Chesnut now than
it had been in 1861. Many of her friends and acquaintances, seeking to explain their situation and to adjust to it, reviled the Confederate government, Jefferson Davis, and all the generals who
had failed finally to win victory. James's niece Harriet Grant
whom Mary, much to her own dismay, despised, wished the
Yankees would hurry up and hang Davis so that her fiancé could
come home and she could get married. Mary's disgust with Harriet increased daily; by July, Harriet became "Hecate" in the
journal.[59]

Walks and drives around Camden brought back vivid memories
of her youth. She visited Kamchatka. "I felt so touched & subdued
in my own old parlours—where I had danced & sung & *acted* &
been happy & miserable as life is chequered." Although she was
only forty-two, she wrote, "I am sick at heart—I thank God I am
*old*—& can not have my life so much longer embittered by this
agony."[60]

In the first years of the war, her dislike of Camden had caused
her to chafe at inactivity and long to get back to the excitement of
wartime Richmond and Columbia. Now, there was no excitement; in any case the Chesnuts had no financial resources and considerable responsibilities. James Chesnut was the sole support of a
host of relatives including his older sister Sally and his autocratic
father. There were perhaps fifteen or twenty house servants—
some old and infirm—who had to be supported. And there was
fear—fear that the uneducated blacks would be incited to riot and
destruction, and fear that James Chesnut would be arrested and
imprisoned for his role in Confederate service.[61]

In her revised journal, Mary summed up her situation suc-
cinctly by "quoting" her husband: "If there was no such word as
subjugation, no debts—no poverty—no negro mobs backed by
Yankees— If all things were well—you would shiver and feel

benumbed—he went on pointing at me—in an oratorical attitude—Your sentence is pronounced—*Camden for life.*" On days when she felt strong and energetic, Mary Boykin Chesnut could almost look "forward to making a home & striving to work in the new state of things" for her husband and for her nephew Johnny Chesnut. But when things seemed hopelessly bleak, she despaired: "I write myself now The wife of Damocles—for the sword seems suspended by a glittering hair—ready to fall & crush me." [62]

SIX     1865–1876

NATURE WAS BOUNTIFUL in the late spring and early summer of 1865; vegetable gardens overflowed with produce in Camden, and most people were no longer actually hungry.[1] As the year wore on, Mary Boykin Chesnut's depression began to lift. It was characteristic of her to grieve deeply, intensely, for a time; but it was also like her to laugh "at every body friend or foe,"[2] as she herself phrased it, to meet adversity head on, at least in public. Aware of both sides of her nature, she had once recorded in her Civil War journal: "I wonder if other women shed as bitter tears as I—they *scald* my cheeks—& blister my heart. Yet Edward Boykin wondered & marvelled at my elasticity—was I always so bright & happy—did ever woman possess such a disposition—life was one continued festival &c &c—& Bonham last winter *shortly* said it was a *bore* to see any one always in a good humour" much they know of me—or my power to hide trouble."[3] Now her natural good spirits healed her in spite of herself, and she began once again to take control of her life.

Mary and James had settled for the time being at Bloomsbury, James Chesnut, Sr.'s house in Camden. Therefore, they could not escape noticing daily that Yankee troops garrisoned the town, reminding them that they were a conquered and subjugated people. But the old colonel grew terribly homesick for Mulberry, so in the fall his son and daughter-in-law moved back to the country home to begin repairing its damage and to make the old gentleman's last days as happy as possible. On February 17, 1866, he died. Finally—too late—James Chesnut, Jr., fell heir to the Chesnut fortunes. His father's will, of which James was executor, plunged

Mary and James even further into debt. Written in February, 1864, the will specified that his entire planting interest could not be divided and was to remain in the hands of his executors until all debts against the estate had been discharged. The old colonel had refused to believe that defeat was inevitable for the South; in his will, he bequeathed over four hundred slaves by name to various family members. Concerned for the welfare of the women of the family (his daughters Sarah Chesnut and Mary Chesnut Reynolds and his granddaughters Mary and Harriet Grant, Mary Witherspoon, and the daughters of his eldest son, John), James Chesnut, Sr., stipulated that his son James would, at his death, support these women in part by paying the $16,000 bond he had signed in 1859 for the Hermitage plantation. Mulberry and Sandy Hill were now James's, but there were no cash funds to operate any of the plantations. The administration of the estate was obviously going to be extremely complicated; therefore James applied in March for the appointment of five commissioners to assist him. By October it had become clear that the will simply could not be carried out as written, and he petitioned for the permission of the probate court to sell some of the property to pay debts.[4]

Thus James and Mary found themselves in a "curious transition state" in 1866. James, who had devoted his life to law and politics, now owned several plantations and was administering several more; Mary, shut off from myriad friends of the war years, was hard pressed to amass money for stamps and envelopes to send letters to those friends. To Johnny she wrote: "I can find just these two envelopes . . . wherewith to buy more I have but ten cents current greenbacks of this model republic."[5] In a long letter to her old friend Virginia Clay, she described her life:

> We live miles from any body. Some times do not see a white face for weeks—the coloured ones hang on like grim death. We will have to run a way from their persistent devotion—we are free to desert them now I hope. In point of fact their conduct to us has been beyond all praise.
>
> We are lonely & healthy here—where neither life nor death seems to matter a great deal. We read a quantity but such a blow as we have survived does make one necessarily a little stupid the rest

of their lives. We have ample room for our two small selves. Noble trees not yet taken from us unpardoned sinners . . . . Our hearts turn to the vicarious victim [Jefferson Davis] there [in Fortress Monroe]. Ourselves in the shadiest of retired nooks—hoping to be forgotten by all but friends such as *You*. What are they up to now! Another revolution. for what? We are dead. in the grave they would torment us still. A tiger might be satisfied with the ruin wrought in this blooming paradise—but we will change the subject. I shall never again take the *stump*, a private station is the post of honour . . . . Among the shifts of honest poverty I sell old books & buy new . . . . New reading old authors. happy land happy homes—where foremost among the list of necessary house hold utensils ranks Sharpe's rifle & colts revolver . . . . [T]here are nights here with the moonlight, cold & ghastly. & the whippoorwills, & the screech owls alone disturbing the silence when I could tear my hair & cry aloud for all that is past & gone. I lived once opposite an officer's hospital in Richmond. & I dream now of the everlasting dead march & muffled drum—& empty saddle & the led war horse—to me the saddest of all human pageants—& it was a happy day then when an hour's interval came between acts of it. But dear friend I suppose we want all the strength & endurance of our hearts for the future they seem bent upon piling on the agony. We must not grow weak by vain pinings for the past . . . . We are in such a curious transition state . . . . I am glad "our seediness" is exhibited only to the speechless trees—& barren sands.[6]

As it became evident that Reconstruction was going to be a harsh experience for former Confederate generals and large slaveholders, James considered alternatives to remaining in South Carolina, but no opportunity seemed sufficiently attractive to justify relocation. To Johnny Chesnut he wrote, "Still utterly at sea as to future—see no haven where we would be—at rest."[7]

James and Mary Chesnut, whose marriage had been strained and sometimes stormy during the early years of the war, had become more tender toward one another as the war drew to a close, and they began to realize how little else they had to depend on. In her 1866 letter to Virginia Clay, Mary had written that though James, as a "companion in Exile" was not exactly "a gay & sportive companion," nevertheless "woe draws hearts together as weal

never can." And when, in the summer of 1867, James sent his wife
and her mother to Virginia in hopes that the mountain air would
be easier on Mary than the hot, humid weather in Camden, his
letters to her attested to his real devotion and concern:

> Solitary & disconsolate I write at your own little table with your
> person full in my mind's eye—and your self, whom alone I love on
> Earth, deep in my heart. You can not imagine how anxious, & how
> full of self reproaches I am about you. Still I have always intended
> for the best. And in now permitting you to leave me, I trust it will
> result altogether in your good. That the summer's sojourn, how-
> ever, may be beneficial to you, it is absolutely necessary that you
> should be tranquil, & endeavour to keep down all mental perturba-
> tions. Take the brightest view of every thing, and cultivate re-
> ligiously every kindly feeling. Further, don't laugh at my lecture—
> & give me another in return.[8]

Other families were in worse financial straits than the Chesnuts.
Mary's sister Kate and her husband had been forced to sell their
Florida plantation and go with their two youngest children, David
and Kate, to Flat Rock, North Carolina, to decide what course to
take. They had spent Christmas, 1865, at Mulberry and left Miller
in Camden with Mary and James. Under Mary's watchful eye,
Serena and Mary Williams were sent to school in Charleston.[9]
Having Miller with her gave Mary a new interest in living—at
long last, she had a child whom she loved dearly for more than
just a visit.

The Williamses, who returned for Christmas at Mulberry in
1866 and 1867, eventually determined to move to Virginia; Miller
was to stay with his aunt and uncle until he left to attend Virginia
Military Institute in 1869, and by about 1868 his brother David
came, too, to attend school in Camden and live with "Aunty."
Years later, when David was grown and serving as a civil engineer
in California, he wrote to his aunt, saying: "You know I often
wonder which it is I miss so much, those nice long talks we used
to have in which I got all the information I ever had, or Aunty's
coming into the dining room with a huge bowl of *milk* and talking
to me while I eat my dinner . . . . Downstairs Aunty did every

thing for me . . . . In the street, was Uncle Jimmie to look after me and ever ready to give me good counsel and help."[10] In Miller and David, and in her beloved nephew Johnny—the "cool Captain"—Mary Boykin Chesnut saw hope for the future of her South. But Johnny died in June, 1868, and she felt his death to be a tragic waste—a blow as severe as any she had yet sustained. She had said of him in 1865,

> John must have his great grandfather's taste—he loves every thing handsome & extravagant—generous with an instinct to every thing that the highest breeding & nicest sense of Honour would dictate . . . . he has behaved . . . like a simple hearted gentleman—he went in without a word he stuck to his country's cause—fought on gallantly through every thing—starvation—dirt—snow—heat— battle was almost the pastime of those four years privation & agony—not one word about promotion—& was found there—when every colour was struck—stands there now ready to stake life & limb once more—his fine Estate gone—sacrificed in vain—we had thousands of such!—*with a hundred* thousand we could not have been beaten.[11]

Throughout this period, many of the Chesnuts' closest friends were equally at sea about the future. A serious concern was the situation of Jefferson Davis—imprisoned in Fortress Monroe— and his family. Much correspondence passed between Mary and Varina Davis, Maggie Howell, and Burton Harrison, Davis' secretary during the war. Mary visited with Varina in Charleston in February, 1867, and entertained Maggie Howell briefly later that year. The Prestons had gone to Europe, but there found themselves in such serious need of cash that John Preston wrote to James Chesnut asking that Chesnut pay him a small debt incurred by Mary and Kate Williams for clothes which the Prestons had sent from Paris. Isabella Martin, the Preston daughters' close friend, wrote frequently to Mary, passing along news and gossip and describing the small school she had established in Columbia to help support herself and her family.[12]

Having kept a diary throughout the Civil War, Mary Boykin Chesnut had grown accustomed to writing regularly, a habit that provided her with an emotional and intellectual outlet and enabled her to escape domestic concerns for a time when she retreated to her third-floor library at Mulberry, long a haven to her. Further, she had now amassed a great deal of material of historical significance pertaining to the Confederacy, and had in hand at least twelve volumes of her journals.[13] During the war years she had periodically reread these journals, sometimes inserting a phrase or two, sometimes crossing out or erasing a passage; and whenever she found herself back at Mulberry or Sandy Hill, she spent time going through old letters and papers, saving a few, destroying most of them. In the years immediately after the war, she turned to this task again, preserving or copying over letters and documents that could later be used in a revision of the journal.[14] Her husband had also amassed a considerable archive of documents pertaining to the Confederacy, and it seems likely that Mary went through these papers, too, noting letters or reports that might supplement her own journal materials.

In the process of reimmersing herself in the papers, journals, letters, and daybooks she had saved, Mary occasionally found herself composing essays, often in response to speeches or articles she read in the newspapers. Such essays were not a new development. She had recorded in a journal entry in 1861, "I wrote a critique for the papers yesterday of Brady's & Wilsons speeches—but I did not find my self very *clever*. It read very flat—my sentences were too long & too intricate—& the ideas spun out—I could not compress & condense & intensify as I can do talking." Again in October of that year she had written, "commenced an abusive & denunciating letter of the Mercury which I stopped." Fragments of a book review and brief disquisitions on slavery preserved in her papers probably date from this period immediately after the war.[15] Mary never polished any of these writings for publication; they seem to have been essentially intellectual exercises or, at times, safety valves to relieve her outrage at the indignities South Carolina suffered in the northern press.

Nevertheless, Mary Chesnut, like many women of her class throughout the South, needed money and saw in her writing the possibility of realizing a small income. Several of her friends

(William Gilmore Simms, John R. Thompson, Robert Josselyn, Paul Hamilton Hayne, Sue King, Louisa McCord, and Margaret Martin among them) were established writers of greater or lesser repute, and she was acquainted with the editors of most journals and newspapers in the state. Accordingly, she began to regard herself as a potential writer of some kind. She had little respect for writers of sentimental fiction, and she knew that she had no talent for poetry. The journal materials were still too immediate for her to bring any objectivity to bear on them; furthermore, they were replete with frank assessments of many people with whom her husband was still tied politically or financially. Thus Mary Boykin Chesnut determined that she would try her hand professionally at a skill she had been developing since childhood: translation. She started to translate in earnest, perhaps beginning with the tales of Émile Souvestre, some of which she had read during the war.[16]

Understandably, there was little time for Mary to write. James Chesnut's political interests involved him quickly in efforts to alleviate the worst aspects of conditions in postwar South Carolina, and Mary continued to concern herself with his affairs, taking care of correspondence and entertaining visitors as of old. Chesnut served as president of an ineffectual 1867 state convention protesting the establishment of military rule in South Carolina, and the following year he was a delegate to the Democratic National Convention which nominated Horatio Seymour of New York to oppose Ulysses S. Grant. In 1870 he served as delegate to the state Democratic convention. Though Chesnut remained disenfranchised until the late 1870s, he kept up a broad correspondence and traveled widely in an effort to alert politicians outside the South to problems in South Carolina.[17]

In addition to political interests, Mary was also perhaps more involved in family affairs than she had ever been. Miller and David Williams were living with her, and she was actively concerned with the relocation of the Williams family to Staunton, Virginia. In the fall of 1869 she visited the Williamses in Staunton and then went on to Baltimore to attend the wedding of her niece Mary Williams to Thomas B. Harrison. From the close of the war, she shared the task of keeping plantation accounts with her husband,

and was herself in charge of managing the household, including the cottage industries that supplied the Chesnut plantations with such items as cloth and clothing, garden vegetables, and dairy products. Now she paid her former slaves and servants with medicines, clothing, and supplies on a barter system and occasionally lent them small amounts of money, always keeping strict accounts.[18]

By 1870 Mary Chesnut despaired of ever having enough ready cash to purchase on a regular basis the books and periodicals so necessary to her. When she finally bought, for $7.50, a copy of Hippolyte Adolphe Taine's *History of English Literature*, which she called "the best book of the century of its kind," she wrote to a friend: "I have wanted it of all things but have been daunted by the price." She organized a book cooperative whose members each contributed what they could. By pooling resources, the book club was able to subscribe to many of the reviews and journals Mary so loved to read, among them the *Saturday Review*, the *Living Age*, *Appleton's Journal*, *L'Express des Modes*, *Blackwood's Edinburgh Magazine* and *Harper's Monthly Magazine*, and to buy current best sellers and works of literature and history. Mary operated the book club herself, sending along books to other members as soon as she had finished them. Whether or not the club was still in official operation by 1873 is doubtful, but by then the informal exchange of books was a routine matter. In March, 1873, for example, she sent a selection of schoolbooks to her friend Mary Withers Kirkland, who, as a war widow, was attempting to oversee the education of her young children. A note included with the books read, in part: "I got such a scare by Appleton's bill—I shall not send for any thing soon. Gladstones Faraday I am still reading—a beautiful English Edition—Mr C is at 'Huxley's Mans place in Nature'—both of which will go next Sunday to you. I will *read* any body to death who keeps up with my untiring gallop—Dont you think?"[19] An unexpected bonus of the club was the opportunity it afforded to exchange ideas about what she was reading. Half the fun of receiving the long-awaited Taine was being able to pass along to Mary Withers Kirkland her opinions—which in themselves attested to her broad knowledge of literature. On her fiftieth birthday, March 31, 1873, she wrote to her old friend:

> I have read Taine—*through* & faithfully—my enthusiasm some what moderated—still it is a wonderful book—cant see the propriety of making it a school text book . . . he is so untrue to our ideas as to men or things *morals* or *taste*—I should not like any one to take him as authority—I should like to talk him over with you— fortunately I was as familiar with his frenchman that he kept at his elbow as never failing referee in all cases—La Bruyere—Montaigne—Moliere—Balzac &c &c—as I am with his English— Think of any mortal preferring Alfred de Musset to Shakespeare Fancy a man finding Addison common place & vulgar—Milton as faulty as any—&c &c—It would take me ten sheets to say my mind on the subject.[20]

By any measure, the Chesnuts were not poverty stricken during this period. Their farming and plantation interests provided them with abundant food, and their other requirements were few. James had an annual legacy from his mother and earned some money through legal fees; Mary had small but regular amounts of money coming in from her butter-and-egg business. Nevertheless, before the war, James had been heir to one of the largest fortunes in the South—an estate now burdened by seemingly insurmountable debts that James had been forced to increase in order to procure capital for the rebuilding of the Chesnut plantations.

Mary's expense accounts of the early 1870s reveal her careful attention to every penny. In the summer of 1870, for example, she took a trip to Richmond, White Sulphur Springs, and Staunton, keeping a record of her expenditures. Upon her return she wrote, "arrived at home 10th September without one cent of the $400 I took." Unfortunately, the Chesnuts were not free of unexpected expenses. Having visited her sister in the summer of 1870, she was forced to return to Staunton the following December and January because her mother had become seriously ill on a visit there. On March 7, 1871, Mary noted in her account book, "am the owner of 30 cent." At about this time, she purchased a sewing machine for $25 and set several of her servants to making garments. The account book devotes two pages to listing and estimating the retail cost of each garment made by the new sewing machine. Apparently Mary, who regarded herself as frugal, felt that her husband was entirely too casual about money matters. Between December, 1870, and January, 1871, she experimented "to see if he knows when he is robbed," carefully noting in her account book: "Taken from Mr C's pocket $9 in all to be returned when he asks for it."[21]

Between 1871 and 1874 James Chesnut traveled extensively. He was serving as chairman of the executive committee to a statewide taxpayers' convention convened in 1871 and again in 1874 to investigate fraud perpetrated by the Reconstruction government of the state. Thus, much of the day-to-day business of planting and farming devolved upon Mary. She seems to have handled her role with some success, for by the fall of 1872, the Chesnuts were making plans to build their third Camden home.

The building of the new house was by no means an unnecessary expenditure in the Chesnuts' view. The maintenance and upkeep of a house the size of Mulberry constituted an extravagance for their small household. But far more important, James was concerned about Mary's future. His father's will stipulated that at James's death, the Chesnut plantations would pass to one of the Chesnut grandsons. In the event of James's death, then, Mary would be homeless—forced to live on the sufferance of her Chesnut relatives. It seemed to both Mary and James preferable that Mary have a home of her own, and the new house was to be Mary's alone. In October, 1872, title to land in Camden was deeded to Mary Boykin Chesnut by John Doby Kennedy.[22] A Charleston architect was hired to draw up estimates and plans, and in 1873 Sarsfield was constructed. To hold construction costs to a minimum, the Chesnuts tore down the large two-story brick kitchen behind Mulberry and used the bricks to build their townhouse. Mary must have been intimately involved with the plans for the house which stood on fifty acres and was modeled after a Norman villa. Probably because of her heart condition, which had continued to trouble her periodically, her bedroom and library were both on the first floor; they were rooms of which she heartily approved, and in later years she boasted in letters to Varina

Davis and Virginia Clay of her "handsome brick home" and the "splendid library" with its "bay window—filled with Confed tropheys [and] books." [23]

Settling into the new home, Mary Boykin Chesnut might well have breathed a sigh of relief. Miller had gone to college and David, fifteen, no longer required careful supervision. At fifty Mary had survived for the time being the dreaded task of rebuilding a life for herself and her family after the war. And she had her beloved library—a room in which she would spend more and more time as the years passed, sitting bespectacled in the soft light of a treasured brass lamp "which enables me to work all day & then drink strong tea & read half the night." [24]

Perhaps in the process of moving, rearranging, and sorting through old letters and journals once more, Mary began to think seriously about her past, her youth, and the changes she had seen in her lifetime. She had in her possession her father's papers and she may have contemplated writing a sketch of Stephen Decatur Miller, for she asked her mother to tell her anecdotes about him that she, as a child, would not have known. But such memoirs were not likely to earn money, so she continued with her efforts at translation, and sent a sample to Isabella Martin and Mary Preston Darby in Columbia for an opinion. Isabella's reply urged her to try her hand at fiction: "The Goatherd is very fine indeed . . . . I have scarcely ever seen a better translation why don't you go on? You once get your name up & the money is secure—If you could get the Galaxy or some paper like that to employ you the thing is done—but why dont you write something original? if not a book sketches?" [25]

Isabella's suggestion was certainly not the original inspiration for Mary's interest in fiction writing. In 1861 she had recorded in her journal, "the scribbling mania is strong upon me—have an insane idea in my brain to write a *tale* for Dr Gibbes weekly literary paper." [26] But she had disregarded the whim and had made no such attempt. Now, with her renewed interest in her family and her own past, she began writing in earnest. Early drafts of two short novels, which she seems to have worked on more or less simultaneously, date from this period. One, a largely autobiographical story centering on her trips to Mississippi and her schoolgirl days at Madame Talvande's school in Charleston, she entitled "Two Years of My Life." After completing a first draft of this, she sent it to her sister Kate for comment. (She would later, perhaps in 1877 or 1878, revise "Two Years" thoroughly; it will be discussed at some length in Chapter VII herein.) The other was a war novel, "The Captain and the Colonel."

As her maiden effort at fiction, "The Captain and the Colonel" was an extremely ambitious project: a kind of *Vanity Fair* of the Confederacy, concerned mainly with one family, but which also deals—often satirically—with a number of social themes the author regarded as crucial to the understanding of her time and region. Thus, "The Captain and the Colonel" may be regarded as Mary Chesnut's first sustained effort to use the materials she had amassed and the observations she had made and recorded in her journal during the Civil War. As a devoted reader and admirer of novels, she must have thought of this novel as a vehicle that would enable her to tell her story of the war in fictional form, thereby not only engaging her readers, but also avoiding the enmity that would inevitably result from publication of her candid diaries.

According to an account in the revised Civil War journal, the novel was first conceived on New Year's Eve, 1863:

> The last night of the old year. Gloria Mundi sent me a cup of strong, *good* coffee—I drank two cups—and so I did not sleep a wink.
> Like a fool I passed my whole life in review—and bitter memories maddened me quite—Then came a happy thought. I mapped out a story of the war—The plot came to hand for it was true. Johnny is the hero—Light dragoon and heavy swell. I will call it *FF's* [*First Families*]—for it is FFs—both of So Ca—and Va—It is to be a war story—and the filling out of the skeleton is the pleasantest way, to put myself to sleep.[27]

If this statement is true (and we cannot be certain because the corresponding wartime journal for this period no longer exists) then surely Johnny's death in 1868 made the idea of a novel focusing on a Johnny-like character all the more attractive. For by dying young and unmarried, Johnny was in a sense arrested in time as "the cool Captain" of the war journals.

Other characters in "The Captain and the Colonel" are also based in part on people Mary knew, but aside from the fact that she had lived through the war that forms the backdrop, there is no real sense in which the novel can be said to be autobiographical. Perhaps the fact that Mary was also working at about the same time on "Two Years of My Life," concerned very directly with her own childhood experiences, made the idea of another autobiographical novel unattractive to her. Each major character in "The Captain and the Colonel" is a fictional creation in his own right, but endowed with a composite of the mannerisms, habits, and bits of personal history of a number of people Mary Boykin Chesnut had known.

The novel centers on the Effingham family [a name that plays on *FF's*] of Eff hall, large South Carolina planters, and their neighbors and friends. Frank Effingham, the nominal head of the household, has died before the action proper of the novel opens, but Chapters I and II are devoted to describing his entrapment into marriage by Joanna Hardhead of New York and the last year of that marriage before his death. Frank, an eminently proper and honorable man, is utterly weak-willed and seems to be almost a caricature of those qualities in James Chesnut, Jr., which Mary both admired and was most annoyed by. Joanna, nicknamed "Regina," has the Dutch ancestry of Mary Boykin Chesnut's mother-in-law, Mary Cox Chesnut, but she too is in part a caricature of the author's perception of herself:

> He thought her a trifle too stout, and too loud, and at times he fancied she was too clever; but he smiled as persistently when she was wrong as when she was right. He rarely spoke ill of any one; and even after a domestic storm that might have shaken the serenity of an angel, he was as unruffled, as calm, and as benign as ever, a true philosopher, self complete and brave, never taking the world into his confidence. That slight smile of his might be caused by his own blunders, or by the noise and folly of others. No one knew. After years of a life in which he stood aside, a mere looker on, he grew inert; even given to self indulgence at table.

He was a literary glutton, devouring all that came in his way, good or bad. If the new book, so anxiously looked for failed him, so much the better, for had he not the old, in his library to fall back upon, he said—cheerfully.

In season and out of it, he spoke of Regina always in terms of loftiest praise; oftenest when she had been doing something which jarred his nerves to the uttermost.

He was a charming person. She was pleasant too, nay brilliant, when her temper was not crossed; but sneering and snarling; when resisted or contradicted in the slightest degree. Their hospitality was enjoyed by all who could attain unto it.

Cavillers said: (there are such in every community), "That Mrs. Effingham, violent, high-handed, imperious always; nay sometimes almost vulgar in her outbursts; had a human heart in her bosom; but the quiescent, self sufficing, dignified, and polished gentleman—where was his?" [28]

At Frank's death, Joanna Effingham is left with three daughters: Margaret, Susan, and Emily. These three girls have distinctly individual fictional personalities, and none of them is clearly modeled on anyone; yet the three girls of marriageable age call to mind Mary Chesnut's frequent chaperonage of the Preston girls and her nieces Serena and Mary Williams throughout the war. Indeed, many of the events and details of the Effingham daughters' lives are borrowed from real-life flirtations which Buck and Mary Preston and the Williams girls carried on under Mary Chesnut's eye: Emily is given a horse by one of her suitors just as John Chesnut had given a horse to Serena in 1866; Emily wears her true love's signet ring throughout the war as Mary Preston had worn John Darby's; Susan rushes out into the snow to talk to Johnny just as Buck Preston had actually done in Richmond, and so on. Joanna Effingham's overseer and trusted advisor, Mr. Tame, holds many of the same sentiments as the Chesnuts' own overseer, Adam Team. [29]

Only one major character in the novel can truly be said to have a real life counterpart: Dr. Charles Johannis, usually called Johnny, of the neighboring plantation of Johannisberg. Dr. Johannis possesses a European medical degree, but in most other respects he is based closely on James Chesnut's nephew John, the youngest son of James's older brother John who died in 1839. Johnny Chesnut had been born in 1837, and had spent much of his life at Cool Spring, just north of Camden, in a plantation home built in 1834 or 1835 by John and Ellen Whitaker Chesnut. Johnny's mother died in 1851. Although two older brothers had attended West Point,[30] Johnny chose instead to go to Princeton, following in the footsteps of his grandfather, James Chesnut, Sr., and his uncle, who assumed a parental role toward the child. Unsuccessful at Princeton, in part because of poor health, he graduated from South Carolina College. When the war began, Johnny, twenty-four, enlisted as a private under Maxcy Gregg; after Gregg's regiment disbanded in 1861, Johnny joined the cavalry unit named for Mary Chesnut's uncle, A. H. Boykin: Boykin's Rangers. During the war Johnny rose to the rank of captain, frequently serving with J. E. B. Stuart. In 1865 he returned to Camden and found his home burned, his plantation and his fortune ruined, but both the original and revised Civil War journals attest that his response—at least on the surface—was light hearted; he continued to court beautiful women (including Serena Williams) and to propose picnics and dances. He died intestate on June 15, 1868; when his personal effects were sold, they amounted to about $500.[31]

Mary Chesnut's sketch of her nephew in the revised Civil War journal points up many parallels between him and his fictional counterpart:

> Johnny . . . does not care for books . . . . He comes, pulling his long blonde moustache, irresolutely as if he hoped to be advised not to read it—"Aunt Mary—will I like this thing?" . . . He keeps his face so absolutely devoid of Expression—Except upon rare occasions one knows nothing of any thoughts or feelings of his. He knows nothing of politics—and cares less.
>
> Roughing it in Camp instead of killing him as we thought it would, has made him, comparatively strong and hardy. He rides like an Arab and loves his horses in the same way. He is devoted to what he calls "good Eating" and he will have it.
>
> I think he is happiest when he sends one of his fine horses, to some girl . . . who is worthy to ride such a horse. She must be beau[ti]ful and graceful . . . . Strange to say he has not one jot of personal vanity. Being so silent, one does not suspect him of being

a close observer—but he is—always taking notes—And he is a keen and merciless, caustic and cruel critic of men and manners— above all things he waits and watches for the short comings of women—

I do not think he has an idea what we are fighting about—and he does not want to know . . . . He enjoys life thoroughly—He loves dancing as well as riding and fighting—swimming horses jumping fences—or fox hunting. He sneers at women—being now a few years over twenty—And he has been idiotically in love with one woman all his life. Her presence brings a hectic flush in his pale face, as clear and distinct as a girls—But that subject is tabooed, for of course she loved another.[32]

Dr. Johannis' love of beautiful horses, beautiful women, fine food, and fine Madeira, his cynical mind masked by apparent in- difference, and his unrequited love for Emily Effingham, all recall John Chesnut. Like John, Dr. Johannis prefers to wear clothes from Paris and prides himself on his small hands—his only vanity. John Chesnut is described in the revised journal as a soft-hearted slaveowner who, after having had two Negroes arrested for sell- ing whiskey, visited them in jail and gave them money wherewith to run away.[33] In "The Captain and the Colonel," Dr. Johannis is likewise lax:

"Johnny's perfectly appointed Establishment is an inscrutable fact to our dear Mother. According to all rule of right reasoning it ought to be otherwise . . . .

"She can not forgive him. With all her genius for organization— her law and order mania; he does quite as well without any. No- body takes care of his little negroes—and they grin and grow like young monkeys, and increase and multiply beyond ours. Ours who are cared for like young princes. He has no army of semp- stresses and yet his people look as tidy and comfortable as ours . . . . It is Mamma's despair."[34]

And yet John Chesnut and Dr. Johannis are by no means identi- cal. Like other characters in the novel, Johannis is, in the final anal- ysis, a fictional creation; his relationship to the Effingham family, his love for Emily, and his eventual marriage to Margaret are crea- tions of Mary Chesnut's imagination. For all of her characters, the author has simply taken types she knew well and placed them in various conventional or standard fictional situations to see how they would react. The end result—the novel as a whole—is not very satisfying, but many of her characterizations are sound and well handled, particularly when we consider that Mary Boykin Chesnut, now over fifty, was just beginning to teach herself to write.

The plot of "The Captain and the Colonel" is, at best, contrived; at its worst it is sometimes incomprehensible. The widowed Joanna Effingham has three daughters to marry off. Margaret, the eldest, has her mother's competence in music and art and her mother's intelligence, but lacks both the will and the integrity of her parent. The next daughter, Susan, is regarded by all as a featherbrain, given to rambling monologues spiced with quotations—usually inappropriate. Susan is the reporter, the gossip of the family, blithely telling everyone exactly what she has seen and heard and precisely what she thinks, untempered by tact or discretion. In reality, though, Susan misses very little and is, because of her genuine friendliness, universally loved by all but her mother. The youngest daughter, Emily, is perfect: intelligent, honorable, strong willed, charming, demure; she is the heroine of the work, the flower of southern womanhood. The Effinghams' closest friend and neighbor is young Dr. Johannis, a bachelor who has as a houseguest a handsome Kentuckian he had come to know in Paris, Robert Collingwood. We never learn much about Collingwood's background except that he, like Johannis and the Effinghams, is suitably rich and cultured. Johannis has loved Emily since she was a child, but because she is just seventeen, when the novel opens, he has kept his love hidden; only Emily has discerned his passion for her, and it is a passion she cannot return because she regards him as an older brother.

When Collingwood arrives on the scene, he and Emily fall in love at first sight. Unfortunately, Margaret, Emily's oldest sister, also loves Collingwood and thinks her love is reciprocated. When she discovers otherwise, she is furious, and in a fit of unthinking rage, steals a note from Emily to Collingwood and hides it in the lining of a small leather bag. Johannis "delivers" Emily's letter to her lover, but Collingwood finds the envelope empty. Interpreting this as an inexplicable insult, he leaves South Carolina and joins General John Hunt Morgan's cavalry as an officer. Johnny, crushed that Emily has fallen in love with his best friend, also goes off to fight—recklessly, of course, for he has nothing to live for. Well over half the action of the novel takes place before the war actually begins, and yet, as in Thackeray's *Vanity Fair*, war is a metaphor central to the love stories in the work; Mrs. Effingham thinks of her matchmaking as a series of campaigns. After she has forbidden Emily's marriage, for example: "When the smoke of the battle field had blown away, Mrs. Effingham, felt she had used her great guns in vain. Victory had not perched upon her banners. The foe was in motion all along the line. To herself—she was constantly saying, 'To think a child of mine could be so insolent—so insubordinate. But I will conquer her yet.'"[35]

At the end of Chapter X, Johnny leaves for the war. Then with no transition whatsoever, Chapter XI opens in Richmond. Three years have passed, and Mrs. Effingham is now serving as director of a Confederate hospital. At one of the president's receptions, Emily and Collingwood again meet. Love has grown even stronger between these two, though neither has known the other's whereabouts. The problem of the missing letter finally comes to the surface, but Collingwood accuses Johannis of stealing it, and the two men fight a duel in which Johnny is wounded. Horrified at the situation, Collingwood again joins General Morgan. Margaret nurses Johnny back to health and precipitously marries him. Susan confesses to Emily that she has secretly married the husband of Annita, the Effingham's second daughter who died before the opening events of the novel.

As Chapter XV begins, all parties are once again back at Eff-hall—again without the slightest transition—discussing the end of the war and the experiences, both tragic and funny, through which they and their neighbors have gone. When a servant who has found the mysteriously lost leather bag enters, Margaret confesses that she has been haunted by her knowledge of her own guilt, but Johannis, now her husband, becomes cold at the discovery of her treachery. Collingwood returns and is to be married at once to Emily. The last pages of the novel are devoted to two letters explaining all to Mrs. Effingham: one, from Emily, describes Collingwood's rescue of Margaret, who has attempted suicide by jumping from the boat on which Emily and Collingwood are sailing; the second, from Johannis, assures Mrs. Effingham that Margaret will be all right and records his determination to be a more understanding husband in the future.

By far the weakest element in "The Captain and the Colonel" is its plot, and Mary Boykin Chesnut handles the story line as if it were a nuisance to be dispatched in as few words as possible. Most events take place offstage and are simply announced by the characters—for example, Susan's return to South Carolina in the midst of war and her secret marriage to her dead sister Annita's widower. This event is potentially dramatic, but the reader learns about it only after the fact, from one of Susan's rambling conversations. Susan's marriage is nothing more than an effort on the author's part to tie up a loose end and provide a resolution for Susan—in this case, an entirely artificial one that adds an unnecessary complication of plot.

Furthermore, many minor characters are introduced, but few are developed in any way or have any real role in the story. Sometimes a character is discussed in great detail without any preparation for his entrance on the scene. In Chapter XIV, Joanna tells her daughters a long and poignant story of "young Paul" and "Lennox." After several pages, she finishes by saying, "I have dwelt upon these two because you know them."[36] Clearly, the author wished to have Joanna relate some of her experiences at the hospital, but did not go back to an earlier point in the novel to establish Paul and Lennox as members of the Effingham circle.

Closely related to Mary Chesnut's inability to advance her plot smoothly is the dearth of narrative and descriptive passages in the novel. The author, in this apprentice work, does not tell her reader all he needs to know to make sense of the story. At the end of Chapter X, for example, we are told that as part of the war effort, Joanna "chose for her self a position she was eminently fitted to fill with credit and usefulness; namely the head of one of our largest Hospitals," but we are not told that the hospital is in Richmond, and that the entire Effingham family will move to Virginia for the duration of the war. The "Mrs. Davis" whose drawing room is the setting of Chapter XI is, in fact, Varina Davis in the Confederate White House in Richmond, but unless the reader realizes this immediately, he cannot avoid being confused for several pages.

As this instance indicates, Mary Chesnut rarely attempts to set a scene. The reader is given few clues as to the physical appearances of places or people; the author assumes Eff hall, Confederate Richmond, Varina Davis' drawing room are completely familiar to the reader. In fact, in one of the very few descriptive passages in the novel, the author writes: "The house was roomy, quaint, and comfortable. The live oaks, the shrubbery . . . gave the local coloring; *within doors there was of course little difference between ladies' surroundings there, and those of ladies every where else over the world.*"[37] Because, in Mrs. Chesnut's view, "ladies' surroundings" differ so little from one home or one city to another, she sees no need to describe them. Perhaps it simply did not occur in 1875 to the woman who had lived through the Civil War, and had spent countless hours in Varina Davis' drawing room, that her reader would require careful orientation.

As a piece of fiction, then, "The Captain and the Colonel" fails in many crucial ways. Nevertheless, it deserves a careful reading, for in it we can discern an intelligent mind brought to bear on a society, exploring and presenting themes central to that society. Of equal importance is the extent to which we can see Mary Boykin Chesnut experimenting with the kinds of characterization, technique, and style she would later use with such a sure hand in her revised Civil War journal.

Most of the themes (among them society's overemphasis on pedigree, the relationships between blacks and whites, the stupidity of dueling, and varied attitudes about honor and patriotism) with which the author is concerned are presented didactically. Rather than depicting interaction between slaves and masters, for example, the author has the Effingham daughters converse on several occasions *about* slavery. Similarly, Joanna and Emily discuss dueling; and Joanna, Mr. Tame, and Johnny talk about their neighbors' reactions to war as it becomes inevitable.

But one theme in "The Captain and the Colonel" is implicit, developed through the relationships between characters: the role of the woman as parent, as child, and as adult. The characters of Joanna, her sister Annie, and the Effingham daughters show us a variety of roles the nineteenth-century southern woman could fill, and further affirm that adult women, given the opportunity, inevitably grow and change. That the author accomplishes this end within the confines of a stereotyped and contrived plot, which she often handles so awkwardly, represents a notable achievement.

The most interesting and successful character in the novel is Joanna Hardhead Effingham, the "autocrat," first contrasted with her more feminine sister Annie:

> She [Joanna] took rank however as a superior person because of her proficiency in Music, and her excellent painting in water colors. Then she spoke French fluently, she read Italian and Spanish with ease. She had always a new language on the stocks. Before they had been a week at home, she discovered a German Professor, and arranged a class for him; of which she was *facile princeps*. He pathetically inquired why her sister, the "beautiful lady mit de blue eye, and mit de fair hair" did not join them?
>
> Annie firmly declined to do this. She thought her education completed; she had so much more English at her command than she ever used. Her rosebud mouth and her violet eyes, spoke for her with a thousand tongues. She was mutely aware of that; even when those eyes were shaded by their long tangled lashes, they cast a spell no words of hers were likely to heighten and she knew it.
>
> Joanna had absorbed the intellect and the strength of the family. Annie was only lovely and good; to the last she was a mere baby in her sister's hands. [38]

Joanna, lacking the long lashes and sweet charms of her sister, determines to achieve success through organization and discipline. She organizes her sister into marriage, organizes her father's business affairs after his death, and organizes Frank Effingham into marrying her. Once on his plantation, "Queen Joanna did not abdicate; she had conquered new realms. She took possession of her house promptly, but she relieved her husband of the care of his plantation by degrees; and her management was perfect." Upon the birth of her first child, she inquires of a neighbor, "At what age do you begin to discipline a child?"[39] As the novel opens, she has already forced one daughter, Annita, into a disastrous marriage and, though the girl died less than a year later, is sure she had only done her "duty." Since Frank's death, she has been successfully operating both family and plantation on the principle of discipline, and sees no reason to change her system.

Her daughters, having all grown up under the tyrant's thumb, have each devised a method of living peacefully within their mother's iron rule. Annita, who shared both the beauty of her Aunt Annie and the weakness of her father, submitted completely—and died. Margaret has forced herself, on the surface, to become as organized and competent as her mother. Susan has retreated into silliness, a role in which she can successfully ignore her mother's coldness and slights. Emily has become quiet—allowing her mother to suppose she agrees with her on every topic but in fact reserving private opinions and fostering her own inner strength. Each of the surviving daughters has responded to strict discipline by longing to be free to run her own life.

Joanna represents the woman of intelligence and ability who, with a limited scope for her talents, turns to managing the lives of those around her. With the advent of war, she lends her administrative abilities and her cool head to hospital work, and there, finally, she finds she has a heart. The constant sickness and pain and death she witnesses mellow her and enable her, finally, to acknowledge her own emotional needs. She is not weakened, but rather enriched by the experience. Margaret, on the other hand, joins her mother in the hospital not because she truly wishes to contribute to the war effort, but because she feels it her "duty." She is not mature enough to withstand the pressure, and breaks under the strain, becoming shrewish and cynical. Susan, hurt by the death of her young lover, hardens and gives up hope of ever loving or being loved deeply. She arranges a marriage for herself that will assure her material well-being. Already endowed with many virtues, Emily changes less than any of the other characters, but she does learn patience and forgiveness. At the end of the novel, she and Collingwood are the only young characters for

whom the future is hopeful. All the rest—Susan, Margaret, Johannis—are trapped in marriages that, at best, they can only
endure.

To present these characters, Mary Boykin Chesnut has used
two basic techniques to good advantage: she had set up parallel
characters and situations, and she has managed to present lifelike
dialogue. Parallels, though never explicitly stated, abound in "The
Captain and the Colonel." Joanna's management of her sister Annie's marriage to a fool foreshadows her insistence on her daughter
Annita's marriage to a similar man. Joanna had entrapped Frank
Effingham into marriage by sending him a letter that he, as a man
of honor, could not refuse to interpret as a demand for marriage.
The letter, the only thing in her life Joanna is ashamed of, touches
off the events leading up to the novel's opening: her marriage, her
daughter Annita's marriage and death, and Frank's own death.
Margaret, very much her mother's daughter, also commits one
shameful act, again associated with a letter, but where Joanna had
the power to blot the letter to Frank from her consciousness, Margaret becomes obsessed with her theft of Emily's letter. Mary
Boykin Chesnut uses the response of each woman to her own act
of dishonesty as a telling way to contrast the two characters. Similarly, Emily's response to her mother's strength of will contrasts
clearly with her Aunt Annie's and her sister Annita's earlier re-
sponses, and serves to illustrate Emily's strong character and her
intelligence.

Occasional minor touches also parallel to good effect. In the
first chapter, for example, Joanna and Frank discuss a seal of his
family arms which bears a skylark. To Frank, who regards social
ancestor mongering as ridiculous, a skylark seal is an ironic ac-
couterment; to Joanna, it represents everything to which she as-
pires—wealth, good family, prominent social position. Later in
the novel, Emily wears Collingwood's seal ring, which also de-
picts a skylark—this time a symbol of real love. Such paralleling
would later be one of Mary Boykin Chesnut's major devices in her
revised Civil War journal, used there to heighten, to point up elements she wished to emphasize.

But it is in her use of dialogue that Mary Chesnut excels in "The

Captain and the Colonel," and though her efforts to create realistic conversations are sometimes clumsy in this novel, by the time she was revising the Civil War journal in earnest in 1881, she had mastered the technique. As Dickens, one of her favorite authors, had done so brilliantly, she lets her characters define themselves by their speech. The reader can gain an instant understanding of Susan, for example, by reading only one of her many monologues. The description of Collingwood is representative:

> "Ah!" said Susan. "You know they were ever so long in Paris together. And in New Orleans last winter. Johnny calls him a guitaring fellow, because he sings divinely. But he does a quantity of other things. I know this—he did something or other while they were abroad. But Johnny is so ridiculously discreet—I could not make head nor tail of it. This I remember—it was very amusing. There was the duel with the little creole who led the German— No—Mr. Collingwood led, and a fractious little New Orleans Frenchman quarrelled with him. That was the laughable story. Ask Johnny to tell you. He swims beautifully and saved somebody—up some where. That's the wager. Oh on Red River—such frightful names—Nachitoches—it sounded like that. That was South. But the boat race—and he was stroke whatever that is. He seems to be always some where. Like Johnny after being abroad he takes his time about going home. I have made it all as short as I could to leave any sense in it. Johnny wound up with this: 'He is such a pleasant tempered fellow—that is the best of him.' "[40]

In the same way, the drone of the meaningless gossip of a drawing room—the kind of gossip that abounds in the revised Civil War journal—is suggested by one speech of a "military magpie" gushing in Emily's ear at Varina Davis's reception. And just as Susan's monologue quoted above succeeds in conveying a great deal of information to the reader, so the "military magpie" reveals several facts about Collingwood's military career.

> "That group in the centre of the room—they have chosen a conspicuous place truly. Let me point them out to you. They are the four magnificant Kentucky generals. Look at Breckinridge—and Gnl. Preston! And yet they say we have degenerated on this side of the water—bodily, and mentally. If that kind of thing goes on—

after a while the average will be seven feet out there. Here comes another. Did you ever see him before? He is splendid—Eh? He is young Collingwood—Colonel I see by his stars. They say Albert Sydney Johnston gave him a letter asking for his promotion—gallantry in action—you saw an account of it in the Examiner. The President never fails to honor drafts from that quarter.

"There are no end of romantic tales about him. No wonder—with that face, and that figure! There is a young lady in the case—she jilted him. She must be hard to please. He has been in prison and he escaped—with wonderful adventures. He has been desperately wounded; I see he has saved his legs and his arms. A letter from Sydney Johnston—a fellow might keep that as a patent of nobility—to show his children.[41]

Mary Boykin Chesnut was learning how to use conversation to convey information, character, and mood simultaneously. Often, particularly when she was portraying general discussion, she made no effort to identify speakers. The effect is of rapid-fire conversation in which individuals merge into an undifferentiated chorus whose gossip illuminates characters and incidents, a chorus that comments upon the society of which it is a part. It is an effect that later gives verisimilitude to many conversations in the revised Civil War journal—conversations Mary Chesnut fashioned using the materials of her journals and her memory, but formed and shaped by her imagination.

Rarely does she interrupt a dialogue with narrative clarifications or insertions. Rather she handles speech almost as if she were a dramatist—and with a minimum of stage directions. When Robert Collingwood comes to ask for Emily's hand, we do not learn until the last line of Joanna's indignant reply that she has rung for her servant and has been waiting impatiently for his arrival:

"Your extraordinary behavior in this house! I see you forever dangling after one of my daughters, and you are here to ask permission to marry another! It is an insult to my understanding—to my penetration, and my prudence—indeed to my watchful over sight as a Mother . . . . Should one of these children disobey me, and marry without my consent, she can be cut off from her inheritance. You do not know, probably, that I have absolute control of my husband's property."

"No—Madam—I did not know it, but I am very glad to hear it. It clears my way amazingly. Miss Emily Effingham does not think of me as you do."

"My children think as I choose them to think. Scipio you were slow in answering the bell. Show the gentleman the door."[42]

The formality and controlled dignity of Joanna's dressing-down of Collingwood illustrates the cold exterior she exhibits to the world, and her summons to Scipio points up equally well both her administrative ability and her instinctive understanding of the psychological power she wields. Because the author has avoided inserting explanatory intrusions, the reader is here shown an outsider's view of Joanna, which will be nicely balanced later in the novel by Joanna's candid and intimate conversations with her daughters during and after the war.

That realistic dialogue is something the author worked hard to achieve may be seen from the revisions she made on the manuscript page, particularly early in the novel. Often the pattern of revision moves from third person objective narrative to third person reporting of a character's words or thoughts to direct quotation. A striking example of Mary Chesnut's effort to avoid stilted dialogue is the conversation between Frank and Joanna in which Frank is discussing his beloved Annita's hapless marriage. In the original manuscript version, Frank quotes his son-in-law as asking which portrait on the wall is that of Eugenie, and continues: " '—I mean the Empress Eugénie you know—' he said—taking a more striking attitude.—'Neither—one was your wife—the other my sister Mrs Von Enden—they are more beautiful than your Empress—she has small eyes—My girls beautiful eyes— were large—soft—wide open—glorious Southern eyes—Do you not remember?' "[43]

Frank is obviously agitated here, and by revising his speech, Mrs. Chesnut intensifies her portrayal of that agitation: "My God—Annie and Annita—and he prates of his Empress. She has small eyes they say. Look there—large—soft—wide open—glorious Southern eyes—Have you forgotten?"[44] The revised conversation makes less objective sense ("one was your wife—the other my sister Mrs Von Enden" becomes "My God—Annie and

Annita"), but it is more successful than the earlier version at portraying the workings of Frank's mind.

In the process of revising her novel, Mary Chesnut was attempting to define character more sharply, but she was also experimenting to find a comfortable personal style. Extensive revisions are evident on more than half of the manuscript pages. A tireless tinkerer with words, she frequently changed wording three or four times. On a scrap of paper in one of her daybooks, for example, we can see her trying several versions of a single sentence: "The cavalry [raced about & brought the news] were the ears & the feet of an army brought all the news—The artillery [all] made the noise—the Infantry did the fighting—and a Genl or so [grabbed the] ~~got all the~~ glory. was covered with glory. pocketted the glory."[45] This sentence as it finally appears in "The Captain and the Colonel" has been revised once again: "Collingwood repeated what the soldier out west said to Gnl. Morgan. 'That the cavalry raced around and brought the news. The artillery made the noise—and the Infantry did the fighting. And they gave all the glory to a General.'" And the sentence would be changed still further for inclusion in the revised Civil War journal.[46]

The style she was working toward, the style in which she would finally revise her Civil War journal, is witty and compressed, colloquial, and richly metaphorical. And despite its flaws, "The Captain and the Colonel" contains many passages where Mary Chesnut writes with admirable precision. When Susan announces, for example, that Johannis and Collingwood are about to fight a duel, Joanna Effingham orders her daughters to send for a doctor and departs in a carriage to put a stop to the proceeding: "'Get on the box with Dawson [she says to her servant]. We have had enough of such stuff.' Mrs. Effingham was at home again in a surprisingly short time. She met a furniture cart, escorted by John Wilson and Dr. Gailliard. The wounded man was therein. She captured the whole party."[47] No words are wasted here. The statement "She captured the whole party" conveys with perfect clarity the extent to which Joanna considers herself superior to the duelists and in command of the entire situation. Again, toward the end of the novel, Susan tells of the death in childbirth of her best friend only hours after the woman had learned of her husband's death on a battlefield: "'Mrs. Sebbes and I sat up all night trying to keep that poor little baby warm—with hot flannels—and as near as we could get to the stove. It was of no use. It died before day. And so they were all buried together——. These chairs are very hard and uncomfortable,' cried Susan. 'How I miss my rocking chair! And the room is so close.' She went near a window—where every pane was broken." [48] Here, Mary records Susan's grief dramatically and places it within the context of universal desolation.

Mary Boykin Chesnut seems to have laid "The Captain and the Colonel" aside about 1875. Having by then completed a hasty revised draft of Chapters XVIII and XIX, the chapters that deal with the aftermath of war, she apparently reached a decision as inevitable as it was wise. The novel was simply not nearly so interesting as the material on which it was based—the Civil War journals themselves. The war journals contained, at least in embryo, all that the novel aspired to: historical interest, poignant love affairs, a wide range of characters. It had now been ten years since the last entry was made. Mary Chesnut herself had gained objectivity. In the process of writing the novel, she was able to see certain themes emerging from the diary material which she thought could be brought out with minor revisions. Furthermore, having visualized the ending of the novel, she could appreciate the inherent structure which the war itself had imposed on the journals: the quiet of a prewar society broken only by flirtations and outings, followed by a cataclysmic war, and ended finally by a return to the same quiet society—now so much changed, so much diminished, but with family and community ties somehow strengthened.

As Mary contemplated revising the Civil War journals, she very likely regarded the project as a relatively simple one. She had only to expand words and phrases into sentences, eliminate trivia, and copy the whole in good form. Accordingly, she launched into the revision intending, apparently, to use the actual diaries as a rough draft of the finished product. By spring, 1876, she had edited, smoothed considerably, and recopied entries from February, 1861, through at least November, 1864. [49] But the task was proving far more complicated than she had originally envisioned. As she worked, she could not have failed to realize the need to expand some incidents considerably, to eliminate others, and to rearrange or consolidate information and conversations. Her work on "The Captain and the Colonel" and the first draft of "Two Years of My Life" had provided practice in delineating character through dialogue and had given her the invaluable experience of creating a narrative voice, an authorial persona who was in many respects the real Mary Boykin Chesnut but who was also considerably more detached, more wry, cooler than Mary herself had been during the war.

Clearly, Mary was dissatisfied with this first major effort to revise the journals. A simple revision which did no more than smooth the original journal simply could not produce the important, expanded, and structured work she was beginning to visualize. Mary discussed the revision with her husband, and obviously allowed him to read some portions of it, for in 1876 on a visit to Richmond he in turn discussed the work-in-progress with R. M. T. Hunter, his close friend of the Washington and Richmond years. In a letter to Chesnut several weeks later, Hunter wrote: "Pray present me most kindly to Mrs Chesnut and tell her I am very anxious to see her 'history of her own times'—If published just now by a So Ca lady, such a work might make the world a little too hot to hold her but the day is coming when it will do good. Amusement I am sure it would always afford." [50] The following week, Hunter wrote again, adding: "You must tell Mrs Chesnut for me that I should be delighted to read her book, I should turn over its pages with more pleasure I believe than the writings of Lady Mary Wortley—But you say it is a little too spicy—If so it would be better not to publish for as Grant said 'let us have peace' . . . . It would make my time much pleasanter if you & Mrs Chesnut were still residing here . . . . Much has past since I saw her last upon which I should like to hear her comments." [51]

No evidence exists that Mary Boykin Chesnut worked further on her Civil War journal per se until 1881. Other projects and a series of family problems intervened, and perhaps the advice of people like R. M. T. Hunter had its effect: the time was not yet right for such a book. But occasionally during the next five years, Mary would sketch out a brief essay—often in the purple pencil she habitually used for notes and very rough drafts—which she later inserted so smoothly into the revised journal that it read as if the author, pausing in 1861 or 1863 to reflect on the scene around her, had simply jotted down her thoughts of the moment on a certain topic.[52]

That Mary Chesnut had, by 1876, ceased work temporarily on her journal and other large-scale projects was largely due to the fact that the Chesnuts were forced to meet a series of crises that began in 1875 with a period of severe financial stress. Possibly the expense of building Sarsfield had proved greater than Mary and James anticipated. The debts upon the old colonel's estate had not yet been discharged. Too, James Chesnut may have wished to amass more capital in order to make improvements or restore planting equipment for the lands under his operation. Whatever the reason, negotiations were begun with William Corcoran, the Washington art dealer, to sell a portrait by Gilbert Stuart of George Washington and two Stuart portraits of Mary Cox Chesnut and James Chesnut, Sr. Furthermore, James sought a loan from his Charleston factors, J. M. Caldwell and Sons, and offered as security the legacy from his mother of $2,000 with interest per year. In a letter to Caldwell, he added that if the legacy was not sufficient, he was also willing to assign "my life Estate in the Mulberry plantation containing about three thousand acress [sic] which my father left me in his will. This last however has not yet come to me in as much as there are yet debts due by the Estate to be paid—& besides that it will be subject to other claims."[53]

Financial pressures were severe enough that Mary Boykin Chesnut made a will in December, 1875, which was carefully worded. Were she to leave her property—Sarsfield was hers—to her husband, she feared it might be seized for debts. To outmaneuver James's creditors, she left her home to Kate's husband, David Williams, to be held in trust "for the benefit of my husband":

> In as much as the creditors present and future of my husband James Chesnut have no claim either legal or Equitable to my Separate property or any interests or rights therein, and in as much as I have

the right legal and moral to dispose of the same, in such manner, and upon such conditions as I may see fit, I desire and direct that if the said creditors of my said husband shall seek or in any way attempt to disturb or dispossess my said husband of any part of my said Estate or to subject it to the payment of his Debts then and in that case my said Estate shall vest absolutely in my said Trustee David R. Williams to him and his heirs forever.[54]

In the midst of money worries, sometime in June, 1875, James managed to allow himself to be gored by a bull, probably from the rear. The accident was no laughing matter; he was severely injured, and bedridden for several weeks. But news of his plight— the reserved, dignified general overtaken in such an undignified way—elicited funny correspondence from his friend General John S. Preston and from Isabella Martin, whose letter read in part: "I never knew anything greater than the excitement the General's accident created I hope he is entirely over it now . . . . I hope he will bear in mind 'The ills that come in full Around a man that meddles with a horned bull' and let the critters alone in future." Because of his own forced inactivity and because of his deep affection for his nephew, James became impatient for Miller Williams' return. Accordingly, Miller returned to Camden in the fall of 1875, to assist his uncle with plantation affairs.[55]

No sooner had the general regained his health than family troubles began to worry Mary. Her aunt, Charlotte Boykin Taylor, whom she had admired and loved so much as a child, was now widowed and penniless, so Mary repeatedly wrote urging her to come live at Sarsfield. Charlotte's son Tom was having difficulty finding a suitable job, and he, too, was invited to come to Camden. Seldom out of her thoughts, Mary's relatives were of immense concern to her; in the fall of 1875 she wrote to Kate, her favorite sister and dearest friend, "I dont live here in my loneliness but where you (all) are."[56] Thus, when Kate died on April 17, 1876, her older sister was stunned.

Kate and Mary had been devoted to each other since childhood. Sent to school together in Camden and later in Charleston, they were one another's only family away from home. After Mary's marriage, the friendship grew even closer as Mary and James introduced Kate to Columbia and Charleston society. Because Kate married David Williams, James Chesnut's nephew only slightly younger than himself, the two families had ample opportunity to be together at Chesnut family gatherings. The Williams children seemed to Mary almost her own. During the war years, it was to each other that Kate and Mary turned in times of emotional crisis or illness. Now, Kate's death propelled Mary into a state of depression which, characteristically, she sought to relieve by writing.

One project that absorbed her for a time was a commencement oration that her husband had been invited to deliver at Princeton in June. Mary helped James compose the speech and wrote out the copy from which the printed oration was set. Princeton's president, James McCosh, urged Chesnut to use the opportunity as a "powerful means of binding the North and South more closely."[57] Chesnut responded by speaking on freedom and civil liberty, voicing what was, in effect, both a warning and a measured plea to wake up to the dangers of Reconstruction. The speech closes with an analysis of the relative value of past to present worth quoting; some of the analogies in the final paragraphs sound very much as if Mary Boykin Chesnut wrote them.

> One portion of our race has ever been restless, energetic, enthusiastic, and heedless . . . . To these novelty has ever presented itself with irresistible charm. It is the pabulum of their mental existence, the fuel without which their minds would smoulder into lifeless ashes.
>
> In this day they constitute a large and powerful class—and perhaps it is well—for it may prevent the surcharged air bred in stagnant pools from settling down as a stiffling incubus on the life of society. But they present also an element of danger, and unless wisely restrained do as often work injury as wholesome change. They undervalue the past, and are regardless of its experiences . . . .
>
> Besides this, there is a class of ancient gentlemen—among whom is often seen the smooth brow, and ruddy cheek of youth—who wrap themselves up in the venerable vestments of antiquity, and upon whose polished armor the light of new revelations falls as harmless and unheating as the moon's soft beams on the gilded dome. To whom the mere sound of change, whether implying solid progress, or dangerous innovation, comes alike as the knell of death . . . .

But, gentlemen, there is still another class, upon whom rests the world's hope; and in which are found the men of real progress, who recognize the force of the law of change, and seek the guidance of its true philosophy. They neither undervalue the past, nor ignore the claims of the present.[58]

Whether James or Mary Chesnut drafted this passage is unimportant; it states a theme that Mary had already flirted with in "The Captain and the Colonel" and which she would later dramatize repeatedly throughout her revised Civil War journal. During the remainder of 1876, she grappled with the problem of the relationship of past to present in a number of ways.

In April, 1876, a series of articles entitled "Old Times in Camden, Pen Pictures of the Past" began to appear in the *Kershaw Gazette*. The articles written by Colonel William M. Shannon attempted to sketch Camden's history and to pay tribute to its worthiest citizens. The first several articles in the series enraged Mary Boykin Chesnut. Already distraught by Kate's death and having long been antagonistic toward much of what Camden represented, she resented Shannon's emphasis on the importance of the Kershaw family in the founding of the town.

In his account, Shannon made it clear that the citizens of Camden were indebted first and foremost to Joseph Kershaw and his brothers. One entire article was devoted to these men, lavishing praise in the best tradition of small-town newspaper rhetoric of the nineteenth century. Calling Confederate General Joseph Brevard Kershaw "our favorite citizen," Shannon ended his sketch of the Kershaws by saying:

> We have devoted more space to this family than we can in these sketches devote to any other. This may be properly excused as the success, the tone, and the prosperity of this community are more indebted to this than to any other family, as high as the achievements have been of others. Time and opportunity were afforded the founders of the family here, and well did they seize and improve them. In the private walks of life they have been most exemplary; in society, genial and accomplished; in patriotism, abreast of the foremost; and in honors, neither time nor change had diminished.[59]

Relegated to a subsequent article in which a number of old Camden families were treated, Shannon's discussion of the Chesnuts was, by comparison, perfunctory. Mary Boykin Chesnut, always highly sensitive to Camden's treatment of herself and her husband, was in no mood to ignore what she felt to be a public slight. Instead, she seized upon the Shannon articles (which were much praised in the community) as something on which to focus all the bitterness and unhappiness she felt as a result of Kate's death, and wrote draft after draft of an almost vitriolic rebuttal.

Of these drafts, forty-three manuscript pages survive, and though they cannot be pieced together to make a complete draft but rather represent fragments of miscellaneous attempts to handle her material, they do provide clues to her state of mind at this period, and contain many reminiscences of biographical interest.[60]

Mary Chesnut seems to have responded to the Shannon articles first, as had long been a habit, by writing a private essay for her eyes alone. A portion of this essay reads:

> It all applies to Wm Shannon but I have not time to write it & this to his stalking horse Joe Kershaw—
>
> None but himself can be his parallel. This is the greatest elephant in the world, except himself—I must write all the scandals Aunt Betsey [Withers] told me—
>
> Chesnuts were perfectly self satisfied—& never did I hear in that house anything but good of anybody—they beamed & the[y] shone on the righteous & the unrighteous alike—Mrs Chesnut said her Mother & Grandmothers maxim was never to speak unless you spoke well of persons—& as she found silence impossible she graciously praised every body  She believed scandal so little—she actually at once (it seemed) dismissed it from her mind—My folks were different—they praised the good as those they liked or like frank Heathens hated their enemies—& if they knew of wrong doers—the were zealous in expressing their disgust—so they told me of old Joseph Kershaw leaving his wife to her Punch & going in happy immorality to abide in solitude at the Hermitage—They told me that old Adam McWillie was a cruel brute who rolled his negroes down hills in barrels spiked with nails—They told me that old Arthur Cunningham owed his negroes fifty dollars for meat & clothes—and was called "Dirty bottom" because he put rubbish at the bottom of his cans to sell more—That John Kershaw married a

Miss DuBose who was an imbecile to be near the Champion estate—& that after the downfall of the first Kershaw his sons drank
& lived unclean lives.

Having gotten all of her anger out on paper, she apparently decided to write to the editor of the *Kershaw Gazette* and accordingly
drafted and redrafted a long letter. It seems unlikely that she seriously intended publication; throughout these drafts, her language is sarcastic and her tone scornful. After describing Colonel
Chesnut, for example, she writes: "But this I know—with what a
chuckle of delight this old monarch of Mulbery Lord of no prob-
lematical Isle—but of all he surveyed from the bridge down to his
house, would have received the Shannon's tidings of great joy—
that Chesnuts Cantys—McRa's Brevards—Boykins Whitakers—
ever played second fiddle at any time or in any way to his quakers
or Kershaws."[61]

Several pages among these manuscript fragments appear to be
part of a formal essay entitled "Let *Sleeping dogs* lie," a further rebuttal of Shannon's articles. (The pun on "lie" in the title had earlier been used in "The Captain and the Colonel.")[62] One draft of
this essay begins:

> We have an author among us—an esteemed citizen commonly
> known as the writer of articles which have got the name for them-
> selves some how—with a laughter loving public as Fine flattery—
>   Just now for his own glory—for the pious desire to laud & mag-
> nify his grand children & may be to turn an honest penny by writ-
> ing for the newspapers:
>   The long bow is drawn not to shoot folly as it flies—but to fire a
> train of pyrotecknic for the mighty dead—the old Kershaws &
> quakers . . . .
>   We cant honour the dishonorable or love the unloveable—or re-
> spect the disreputable—& the truth of history must be vindicated—
> as the children say They began it—& now as we were blessed with
> Mothers & Aunts who knew the past century we mean to tell all—
> except where it is too bad to soil our paper with—
>   . . . Neither the Canteys—Chesnuts—nor McRa's have em-
> ployed me to write them up—they can take care of themselves.

Finally, a single page among this material suggests that Mary
Boykin Chesnut at one point contemplated writing a parody of

the Shannon articles entitled "Memoirs of P. P. Clerk of this Parish," so that she could "review" the spurious work: "Advertisement. The original of the following Treatise consisted of two large volumes in folio—which might justly be entitled, *The importance of a Man to himself.* But, as it can be of very little importance to any ~~one else~~ body besides, I have contented myself to give only this short abstract of it. As a taste of the true *Spirit* of Memoir writing.—In the name of the Lord—Amen—I P. P.—by the Grace of God clerk of this Parish, writeth this History:"[63]

Unfortunately, no other pages of P. P.'s memoir survive, and its author apparently put her various attacks on Shannon aside. They had served their immediate purpose. Mary had been able to escape for a time her own grief by lashing out—however privately—at William Shannon who undoubtedly stood as surrogate for Camden itself in her mind. But they served another purpose too. When, in the early 1880s she once again began to revise the Civil War journals, she returned to these drafts and mined them for phrases and anecdotes. Old Adam McWillie, who rolled his slaves down hills in nail-studded hogsheads, escaped exposure in 1876, but he found his way into her revised Civil War journal.[64]

In writing down *her* view of Camden and its history, in the process of recording some of her own reminiscences, Mary found her interest in the history of her family and her region rekindled. Within the next few months, it was her own memories about which she wrote most often. One long manuscript memoir appears to have been written to Kate's children, her "little Sweet Williams," in memory of their mother. Because it contains so much biographical information, this memoir which begins "We called her Kitty" has already been quoted at length in earlier chapters. Although it bears the date June 14, the opening pages of the manuscript seem to be copied from an earlier draft, and the entire memoir (which is missing one or more pages at the end) shows signs of having been planned and perhaps outlined prior to its composition. Focusing on Kate, "We called her Kitty" often veers from the subject at hand to record the author's own past, and reveals Mary to be still very much depressed in June. One passage, which has been lined through, reads, "I often feel I had a quantity of love nobody seem[ed] particularly to want & I was always thrusting it out to" and then breaks off. Manuscript fragments written in late July, 1876,[65] which discuss her half-brother, Elias Dick Miller, and childhood memories of her father and brother Stephen also seem to be addressed to someone, for they contain phrases like "Be it also remembered."

It is likely that no one besides herself saw any of these writings during her lifetime. They all remained with her papers, and no copies have survived among the papers of various members of the Williams family. A few years later, Mary would write in a day-book, "I write for my own amusement and for nobody's profit—there!" Nevertheless, in all of her 1876 writings (the Shannon re-buttals, "We called her Kitty" and the Elias Dick Miller memoir), no matter how private the material, Mary Boykin Chesnut was writing for an audience. Having completed numerous transla-tions, one apprentice novel and a first draft of another, having made her first major attempt to revise her Civil War journal, she no longer was able to write for her eyes alone as she had done in the journals kept during the war. For the rest of her life even diary-type entries in her daybook show her to be conscious of style, content, and structure.[66]

By the fall of 1876, political events in South Carolina had come to a head. The Chesnuts' lifelong friend, General Wade Hampton, had been nominated for governor in an effort to overthrow the Reconstruction government. The campaigning—in which James Chesnut played a conspicuous part—involved numerous riots, often accompanied by bloodshed.[67] The excitement of the forth-coming election might well have been precisely the tonic Mary Chesnut needed to dispel her lingering depression. And perhaps it did so in August and early September. But on September 16, her oldest niece, Serena, died suddenly. This second death in five months affected Mary so severely that she fell seriously ill. A letter from Serena's sister Mary, written one month later, suggests that the state of her health had alarmed the entire family.

MY DEAR AUNTY,

This mornings mail brought the last half of a letter from you send on the first if you please. It is very hard on me getting only one half of any of your letters I think. I had a letter from Grandmother a day or so ago—asking about you very anxiously and wanting to know if she could come to you if you would like it. I wrote her you were very much debilitated and worked to death that you wrote you were better, as to how you were, as to her going, I thought she better stay where she was till after the elections and then wait till you wrote for her because you could tell better than I the state of affairs. If you are strong enough write to her about yourself for she is frightened about you—and her letter is one long string of questions about "My own Mary" "my first child" etc and then in her end she says I mustnt feel hurt because she writes of you but that she really loves me too—so I am not hurt this time but I am not going to [be] pushed into background all the time by the "first Mary" so I wrote her. But my own old Aunty I hope you are better and stronger.[68]

Hampton's victory in the election was contested so strongly by Republican Governor Daniel H. Chamberlain that for several days South Carolina had two legislatures, each claiming to be the duly elected government of the state. The problem of dual governments would not be resolved until April, 1877, when federal troops were at last withdrawn. Nevertheless, after a dramatic series of political maneuverings, Hampton was inaugurated on December 7. Ten days later, in a letter to her nephew, Miller, who was visiting friends, Mary commented on the inauguration: "Only time for a line—had the Doctor again here to day he finds me better . . . now Hampton is innaugurated we have the highest hopes— Dum spiro, spero  Mrs H . . . writes H is a happy Gnl—All right at Mulbery . . . ."[69] Before he sealed the letter for mailing, James Chesnut added a postscript to Miller: "Come back as soon as you conveniently can. All is not so well as Aunty indicates."

FROM THE AUTUMN OF 1876 until her death ten years later, Mary Boykin Chesnut was never again entirely well. Her heart condition became increasingly troublesome, she may also have had a chronic lung ailment of some sort, and she seems to have been particularly susceptible to minor diseases such as colds and intestinal flu.[1] Thus, in the last decade of her life, she was frequently unable to travel, and became more and more confined to Sarsfield in Camden. Despite illness, however, she remained as busy as ever, gardening, supervising her dairying enterprise at Sarsfield, and, whenever health permitted, entertaining James's friends and her own. At Mulberry, planting was now largely handled by her nephew Miller, but she kept a close eye on Miller's progress. In the hours when she could retreat from domestic duties, she maintained an active correspondence with friends and absent family members and, as usual, read at an untiring pace. Above all, she wrote voluminously. Between 1877 and 1881, she thoroughly revised her autobiographical novel "Two Years of My Life," completed at least one draft of another novel, and continued to work at translation.

Perhaps the first writing project during this five-year period was a biographical sketch of her husband. About 1877 James Chesnut had received a form letter from W. W. Butler, a son of Confederate General M. C. Butler. Butler asked for material for a brief essay to be included in a proposed collection of "Sketches of the Lives of the Leading and Prominent Men of our State, from 1861 to 1865 inclusive." Apparently, James turned the project over to Mary, for it was she who wrote a twenty-two-page manuscript draft outlining James's career, as Butler had requested.[2]

The sketch represents an interesting attempt on Mary Boykin Chesnut's part to write in a relatively formal style. In the sketch, although she is casual about certain facts (she says, for example, that James graduated from Princeton in 1837 when in fact he had done so in 1835, and she neglects to give his exact birthdate), she conscientiously provides historical context for her statements, even when such context is not strictly relevant: "James Chesnut, a sketch of whose life you desire, was born in Camden South Carolina; and at a marked period of the nation's history; January 1815, while our transatlantic world was still wild with rejoicing over Jackson's famous victory at New Orleans." Throughout the sketch, we see its author placing her husband and family in a public perspective rather than revealing a private view. Of her father-in-law, she offers her reader no trace of the autocratic personality or courtly manners which figure so prominently in her revised Civil War journal, but rather uses the old Colonel as a device to show the enormous political and social changes of the last century:

> No man had a larger stake in the country. He was a rebel from the great nullification party who so long ruled the state, and he remained a union man until the secession of South Carolina left him no choice.
>
> Born a subject of George III he had renounced his allegiance and cast in his lot with the Independent states of America. He had taken the oath to South Carolina—to the Confederate States—and when over ninety years old, blind and dispairing there was yet another change. He was asked to take the oath, or to renew his allegiance to the U.S.A. He gave it grimly, saying "surely this must be the last."

Particularly interesting to the reader of *A Diary From Dixie* is Mrs. Chesnut's assessment of her husband after the war:

> When all was over, he returned as did his forefathers, to a desolate home, he had pledged all—and he had lost, there was nothing more to be said.
>
> He was rich still in lands to be taxed à merci et à misericorde. A country gentleman with an hereditary Estate, which he could neither live upon, make profitable nor sell. . . .
>
> In the dark decade of his country's history, his cultured and philosophic spirit found solace still. There was pure air, large rooms,

quiet nights, and literary leisure by day. With his great power of reasoning, his accomplishments and learning he is, as he always was, inclined to stand back, and let the world flow by him.

His friends urge upon him the necessity of recording what he has personally known in these last forty years of American life.

He has amassed documents and letters invaluable as material for "memoires pour servir". His style is clear and correct and he has the gift of telling his story so as to interest all hearers.

"His vision takes a wide range, and he is cool and dispassionate. From his first entry into life he was never so lost in his admiration of one object as to overlook all the rest.

His faults lie in the opposite extreme: his perception of the universal weakens that of the particular."

From such a character, his dealings with the freedmen left upon his Estate may be inferred. He is just and liberal. Mercy so far getting the upperhand of Justice, as in a pecuniary point of view to be his ruin.

To wind up this brief monograph we quote the words of a friendly critic when he revisited Nassau Hall, after almost the interval of a lifetime.

"Gen Chesnut has received the highest honors South Carolina can give. And his name is as stainless as when he who bears it bade farewell to the classic shades of Princeton more than forty years ago."

After completing the sketch, Mary Boykin Chesnut may have sent a fair copy to Butler for inclusion in his proposed book. The book was never published, however, and it is certainly possible that the sketch of Chesnut was never submitted. In any case, the brief exercise suggested to Mary the idea of writing a full-scale life of her husband, and from time to time, she jotted down notes intended, eventually, to be worked into a biography.[3]

Sometime in 1877 or 1878, Mary Boykin Chesnut returned to her largely autobiographical novel, "Two Years of My Life," which she had written in 1874 or 1875, at about the same time she was working on "The Captain and the Colonel." After completing a first or second draft of "Two Years" she had sent it to her sister Kate for comment, and Kate had responded with suggestions for its expansion and improvement. Mary put the novel aside and, between 1875 and 1877, turned to work on her Civil War journal and other writings. Now she again picked up "Two Years" and reworked it thoroughly. She had, in 1875, read and enjoyed Trollope's *The Way We Live Now*.[4] Pleased with the implications of Trollope's title for her own work, she now changed its title from "Two Years of My Life" to "Two Years—or The Way We Lived Then."

"Two Years" is a vastly different kind of novel from "The Captain and the Colonel"; in some respects, it is less successful; in others, far superior. "The Captain and the Colonel" is a third-person narrative, which, though it draws upon Mary Boykin Chesnut's friends and acquaintances as well as her own experiences, nevertheless sustains, however shakily, a fictional plot. "Two Years," on the other hand, is told in the first person, and attempts to blend the actual events of the author's life with a dramatic tale of frontier intrigue and vendetta. This weaving of real with imaginary is often strained, and towards the end of the novel, Mary comes close to abandoning any fictional plot and eventually ends her novel in the third person.

Unfortunately, several chapters from the first half of the novel have been lost, and it is therefore difficult to discuss the plot of "Two Years" with any certainty. But the manuscript that survives tells a lively story of a young girl, Helen Newtown, who is removed from Madame Talvande's boarding school in Charleston and taken with her family to a cotton plantation in Mississippi. Once in Mississippi, she becomes involved in a series of dramatic and exciting adventures in which a young Princeton graduate with whom she has fallen in love in Charleston also figures. After she returns to Madame Talvande's, she learns of her father's death and goes back to Mississippi with her mother to sell the plantation. At the end of the novel, Helen marries her lover. In short, the basic outline of the novel covers the period in Mary Boykin Chesnut's own life from 1836 to 1840.

We know from the information contained in "We called her Kitty" that many incidents in "Two Years" are based very closely on fact. On the other hand, there can be no question that the author intended her work to be read as fiction. Just as in "The Captain and the Colonel" she had attempted to present several truths about the South and the Confederacy in palatable form, so in "Two Years," she is attempting to entertain and interest her reader in order to teach him about life in the 1830s—the wide differences between an established and traditional society in Charleston and the primitive conditions that pertained in the Deep South states then emerging from frontier status. The emphasis of the author of "Two Years" is never on explaining herself or recreating her initiation into adulthood as is often the case in autobiographical novels, but rather on making an era come alive which had, by 1877, faded into the dim past, obscured by the cataclysmic events of the Civil War and Reconstruction. Helen Newtown, the narrator, exists in the novel not as an introspective voice but as an observer, a storyteller, and a preserver.

In "The Captain and the Colonel," Mary Boykin Chesnut had made a conscious attempt to write realistic dialogue, but had paid very little attention to setting and description. In "Two Years," description becomes far more important, and the author frequently blends dialogue with narrative passages quite skillfully. The novel opens in the middle of an argument. With no apparent scene-setting, Mary Chesnut manages to convey all the reader needs to know in a few lines of dialogue:

> "Why are you dragging me away? I don't want to be buried in a Mississippi swamp. I do want so very much to stay here."
> "Why ask? When you must see what a nice arrangement it is? The girls must have a Governess. Your father likes us all to be together. Besides it is economical. People are beginning to object to large boarding schools—. Then your father's mind is made up—."
> "Really and truly? That is the amount of it? Why did he change his mind so suddenly? Yesterday, I was to be left as always before, with Madame; to day—I must be carried off by force to the Grindstone! I wish you could hear Kitty describe her."
> "I wish you could see your own discontented face. You must learn to make the best of things. You will find this world does not arrange itself exactly to suit you. Now don't say another word. You must go with us." [5]

By the end of this conversation, the reader has been introduced to a whole family, complete with governess, on the eve of a trip to Mississippi, and has made the acquaintance of a strong mother whose patience has worn thin, and of a proud and impudent daughter. Mrs. Newtown's closing remark, "You must learn to make the best of things. You will find this world does not arrange itself exactly to suit you," states a major theme of the novel.

In the next few pages of Chapter I, Helen Newtown describes her family, modeled very directly on the Miller family in 1836; Frank (called Dan) is based on her brother Stephen; Constance or "Kitty" on her sister Catherine (also called "Kitty"); and Harriet or "Tatty" on her sister Sarah. Also introduced is a maid named Fanny, and though many other servants who figure in "Two Years" had real-life counterparts, no evidence exists that Fanny is based on Mary Boykin Chesnut's own childhood maid. As nearly as can be determined, the trip in a landau to Mississippi is patterned on the trip Mary had taken in 1836, with some incidents drawn from the trip to Alabama, which she later took with her sister Kate and the Williams family in 1859.

On the trip, Helen amuses herself by daydreaming, inventing romantic stories in which she is always the heroine, always beloved by a dashing hero: "We had 'Corinne' with us—which I could translate with the aid of a dictionary. Then I would shut my eyes—for gorgeous day dreams, and arrange the fortunes of An American Sappho. At fifteen a girl is rather shy of such intense love as Phaon created—so I soon fell in with a more congenial style of heroine—Joan of Arc. With her for awhile I performed heroic and patriotic feats—always saving my Country at full speed on the most beautiful of horses." The adventures Helen invents for herself are thoroughly sentimental and sensational.

> But I have always found it easier to concentrate all the energy of my imagination on a hero—and to make him a military conqueror. As a heroine, I found myself a burden. For variety's sake, when I selected a civilian as my jeune premier, I had speedily to endow him with a gold mine, or a coal mine, in more difficult circumstances I did not shrink from diamond mines, so that I might enable him to strike at once a heroic attitude, as bridegroom and millionaire. If I

had ample time given me—I made him a genius—or made him invent some miraculous thing for the benefit of humanity.

At first it was easier. I fell into the regular "Novel" plan of killing
off more or less tragically all of his rich relations; but that seemed
hard hearted. And as I held in my hand the wealth of the Earth and
the sky and the water, I concluded to leave his fortune unstained by
kindred gore.

Some times I went in for love in a cottage; but that was before I
had seen or lived in the three room log house on the plantation.

Some times I left for Europe in a coach and six, where I had innumerable adventures with every body I had ever read of and
equally thrilling ones, with purely imaginary characters. I rescued
every body from suffering; and by my astounding sweetness and
my persuasive tongue alone, I turned all wrong doers from their
evil ways.[6]

Helen's imaginings (probably accurate reflections of Mary Boykin
Chesnut's own at fifteen) seem wildly improbable, but she is soon
plunged into an adventure as wild as any she could have invented,
and with an ending every bit as romantic.

This adventure begins with the advent of the Newtowns' governess, Mrs. Grindstone—an entirely fictional and wonderfully
funny character whom the author takes care to describe in detail:

Our Governess was tall and stout. I thought her old—I dare say
she was fifty, but one's ideas of age vary so—perhaps she was
younger. Of these facts I am certain; she had a brown leathery com-
plexion—with large ears—so large indeed that Dan who had no respect for persons in authority—compared them to Peter Plummer's
flying woman's—who slept upon one of hers—and covered with
the other. Her eyes were deep black—and she had dark rings under
them. Her shaggy eyebrows hung lowering. And yet the expression of her eye was kindly. She had a good straight nose. The black
line of eyebrows, and the nose formed a perfect cross in the centre
of her face. A broad, flat mouth and beautiful teeth. Her cheeks
hung flabbily, and her hair was so thin, that she had it cut short like
a man's, and parted at the side. Indeed she came near being that unusual creature a bald woman. Her upper lip, more than shaded,
gave her a somewhat masculine appearance. And my young partners at the dancing school would have been too happy for such a

moustache, those poor little fellows who had only of late mounted long tail coats.[7]

Mrs. Grindstone, so masculine in appearance, is a fluttering, feminine creature and has been terrified by her trip in a stagecoach: "Mrs. Grindstone seated herself—the chair creaked and groaned as if appealing loudly against the weight that was put upon it. She said gloomily, 'Thank God—I am now under a man's protection. Women ought not to travel alone in these wilds. Poor helpless creatures that we are! Does your father go armed?'" In the stagecoach, Mrs. Grindstone has been mistaken for a murderer, Colonel Blueskin, whom she closely resembles, and who is being stalked by the Hamlins, sons of Blueskin's victim. A man employed by the Hamlins to track down Blueskin has chanced to ride the same stage as Mrs. Grindstone, and accuses her of being the murderer in disguise. But also in the stage is Sydney Howard, Helen Newtown's lover who, unknown to Helen, has followed her west. Unaware that Helen knows Sydney, Mrs. Grindstone describes his gentlemanly defense of her: "I could put Mr. Howard in my pocket—but he sat by me as my protector—he is so slight and slim—he was quiet—yet bold as a lion—I asked him if he was armed. 'No,' he answered, 'Never wore arms in my life.' 'Poor boy,' I said. 'You had better go home.' And in that row he was as rash and reckless as if he had cannons at his command."[8]

Some of the finest writing in the novel centers on the Blueskin-Hamlin feud. Mary Boykin Chesnut creates these entirely fictional sequences with a fine comic flair. As Helen and Mrs. Grindstone listen through the wall of an inn, for example, they hear a scrap of conversation between the passengers of the stagecoach:

> "I am dead sure it is old Blueskin—I could swear to his ears. I mean to tell the Hamlins."
>
> "Let him alone Mr. Dickson," said a voice which sent the blood in a shower to my face. "It is only his drunken pertinacity."
>
> "Say another word like that and I'll rouse the country. We will soon scare up old Blueskin for he is in this house."
>
> "Thou God seest me," cried Mrs. Grindstone on her knees—with her hands clasped piteously.

It is particularly unfortunate, therefore, that the portion of the novel that is missing (Chapters IV through V) is precisely the portion which develops this material. By the end of Chapter III, Mrs. Grindstone has allowed herself to become too terrified to remain on the Mississippi plantation. After she departs, "disguised to the utmost and doubly—nay trebly veiled," Mr. Newtown remarks: "That poor old Governess in spite of her dark upper lip is womanly in the extreme. She is all nervous fidgets and hysterical fears. She had some cause of alarm that she kept to herself. The drunken fool whose very name she did not know, made too deep and abiding an impression." [9] The next two chapters are missing; hints scattered throughout the remainder of the novel suggest that the events of the missing chapters concern the villagers Helen meets in Mississippi. The heroine has attended at least one country dance, and has attracted some rather comic suitors. At the end of Chapter III, Sydney has not yet officially revealed his presence to the Newtown family. Presumably he does so, for he and Mr. Newtown act in concert in an affair sparked by the Blueskin-Hamlin feud, which apparently involves the death of a Mississippi shopkeeper, Mr. Dickson. Chapters V through VIII detail the trip made by Helen and her father back towards civilization, and include an episode in which Helen's life is endangered by a runaway team of horses; she is, of course, rescued by the ever-present Sydney Howard. By Chapter IX, Sydney is preparing to accompany his sister Madelaine (who is Helen's best friend) to Europe for two years. Mr. Newtown has extracted a promise from Sydney that he will make no attempt to communicate with Helen, but the young lovers have exchanged rings, and have vowed to remain true to one another.

The real events of Mary Boykin Chesnut's life at this time are no help in reconstructing the missing portion of the novel, for the author has invented the Hamlin-Blueskin feud, and has so thoroughly adapted real events that they become entirely fictional in character. There is, for example, no evidence that James Chesnut ever went to Mississippi prior to his marriage. Chesnut did go to Europe, but for only six months, not for the two years of the novel. And Mary Serena Chesnut Williams, James's niece on whom Madelaine Howard is based, did not accompany her uncle to Europe.

Chapter IX provides a transition between the two halves of "Two Years"; Helen and her father journey from Mississippi to Charleston, from the somewhat barbarous and primitive environment of an as yet uncivilized world to the proper and cultured world of Charleston. Chapters X, XI, and the opening pages of XII detail Helen's life at Madame Talvandé's, and are given over in large part to description. For almost three chapters, the shaky story line of the novel is abandoned in favor of an essaylike picture of the boarding school, and in this case, Mary Boykin Chesnut has remained faithful to fact and memory. Even when the author includes dialogue, she does so to recreate an atmosphere rather than to advance the plot:

> Friday was "piece day." That is every one had a selected piece to recite or declaim. This thing every body prepared in an audible voice. I arrived on Thursday, and on Friday morning as I entered the smaller schoolroom—a splendid brunette, was standing on a desk in a striking attitude. She stretched out her right arm toward me.
> "The breath of submission I breathe not,
> The sword that I draw, I'll sheathe not"—[10] a sudden break down—a spring on the floor and a search in the desk for her Campbell's poems.
> A faint little voice at my elbow piped up.
> "And fire they cried
> And then *I cried* Oh Lord what shall I do!"
> "Oh! Haggard Queen to Athens
> Dost thou guide—guide—thy chariot—steeped—steeped— in what? Kindred gore.[11] What a dunder head I am." "Take the book and hear me." "Don't you see you don't know a word of it." . . . As the door was opened came in stentorian tones—from the private parlor—"Row, brothers row"[12]—with a ting, ting, of guitar and accompanying the deep voiced old man the shrill singing of a child.
> "Oh for mercy sake let us get out of this row." And we go toward the drawing room to wait until Miss Anne's advent shall still

the tempest. As we approach the door which is wide open—a mighty crash—four hands come down at once on the Piano in a stunning "duet."

"From Scylla into Charybdis."

"Do you suppose Bedlam is worse than this."

"It is because you have just come—in a day or so you will not mind any more than we do." [13]

By far the most vivid characterizations in the novel are those of her teachers—the fictional Mrs. Grindstone as well as her real teachers, Miss Stella and Madame Talvande. Mary Boykin Chesnut's portrait of Madame Talvande is as fine as any writing she ever did. In it the best elements of her prose in the revised Civil War journal are evident; the author's objective eye, her keen observation, her sense of humor, her appreciation for the complexity of character, her compression:

Madame, the Tyrant of Legare St. was of an excellent French family driven in to Charleston by stress of weather, that is driven out of San Domingo . . . .

She was small, but beautifully formed, her hands and feet were models both as to size and shape. We had opportunities of regarding her from various points of view. Different rooms in the house looked down upon her dressing room. So in warm weather, when open windows were a necessity, we saw her in absolute dishabille; her head tied up in a red bandana and her torn and soiled dressing gown flying in the breeze, slippers down at the heel, or kicked off.

At ten every day she descended upon us in the school room. She advanced with airy grace and rapid pace; smiling, bowing, curtsying, flirting a gossamer handkerchief redolent of Cologne. The sombre widow's cap strings floating at right angles, did not disturb, the cheerfulness of the general effect. On cold days she wore a boa, a fur lined cloak and even her tiny shoes were lined with fur.

She was quite regal in appearance seated on her throne; she took off her gloves, waved her handkerchief aloft—and business began in earnest.

Once a dead hawk was brought in and thrown upon a table in the Hall. Later in the evening, the hawk having come to life, to our amazement walked into the drawing room. He was ruffled, and bloody, as he staggered across, unsteadily on his feet. Heavens!

how well I remember the keen and bitter expression of that eye. Reproach, rage, indignation, hatred, scorn, vengeance, it was all there.

Madam's eye was the counterpart of that broken winged Hawk's eye; it was the fiercest I have ever seen in a mortal head. She had the faculty of inspiring terror, and by that power she ruled us absolutely.[14]

Here Helen, the romantic narrator of the first half of "Two Years," has all but disappeared. In her place is the narrator of the revised Civil War journal, Mary Boykin Chesnut herself, intelligent, discerning, worldly wise and amused:

Madame was indeed an awe inspiring person. It was agreed on all hands that her temper was fiendish.

Upon mature reflection I have come to think there was method in her madness. She kept her tantrums as people keep a loud-barking dog, more to scare than to hurt—and to be untied only at regular hours. Dreadful as she was in the school room, in the drawing room, she was as pleasant tempered, as amiable, nay as fascinating a woman of the world as heart could wish. She was too well bred to unmuzzle the growler there.[15]

Rarely, in her description of Madame, does the author employ dialogue, but when she does so, it is to good effect. As with Susan's monologues in "The Captain and the Colonel," Mary Chesnut uses dialogue to reveal character:

Once she smilingly laid aside her wraps and stood up to fill a vacant place in a Cotillion.

We saw dancing then. And we understood why Terpsichore was called the "Muse of the many twinkling feet."[16] She flew; barely touching the floor with the tips of her toes. She held her dress high, and her tiny foot was poised and pointed higher still in air, as she prepared to dart away.

Her face was radiant with delight, and self approval, as of a good thing well done.

"Why do you stare? Have you never seen a lady dance before?"

"No! Nenaine! not like you."

"You lazy, awkward, heavy footed clods—an old woman can shame you."[17]

One very interesting aspect of Mary Boykin Chesnut's chapters describing Madame Talvande's school is the care taken by the author to sketch the black servants, and to stress the individuality of each one. In "The Captain and the Colonel," she had provided no descriptions of blacks; they do figure in the war novel, but usually in dialogue passages inserted at a late stage, where they were presented as humorous, stereotyped figures. In "Two Years," blacks are always accorded descriptions as full as white characters, and the tone the author uses in discussing them is indistinguishable from that used to sketch whites:

> Maum Jute was always slip shod, and you could hear her flip flop in regular cadences when she did not object to her whereabouts being known. When on any predatory expedition she went bare foot—and was noiseless as a cat. She wore a Linsey Woolsey gown, always sufficiently unbuttoned to reveal the absence of all undergarments—and so short as to show the entire contour of those old husky legs set in the middle of her feet. Her much soiled red handkerchief, which she wore as a turban, was always out of plumb. It hung over one ear—or over her forehead, or was pushed back as far as it would go; for when spoken to, her first movement was to scratch her head, and to shove her head gear out of place; it was always toppling, but never fell.[18]

Here, Maum Jute, like Mrs. Grindstone, is a comic figure—but a sympathetic one, and distinctly individual.

Not until the middle of Chapter XII does the author return to her story, and she does so awkwardly. Once more the narrative voice becomes clearly that of young Helen Newtown, as she picks up the threads of her plot: "Do you fancy I have forgotten my dearest friend of last year? I am neither false nor fickle. For a time Madelaine wrote with surprising regularity. Her life was a very busy one. She was taking lessons in every thing; and at the same time going every where, to see every thing."

"Going over, aboard ship, they encountered a family called Hamlin; concerning whom, it was hinted to her, she might write me as much as she pleased."[19] In Europe, Madelaine and Sydney Howard fall in with the Hamlin brothers—hitherto unseen in the novel. The older brother (like John Chesnut in 1839) is ill and dies;

the younger marries Madelaine and also soon dies. This complication of plot is only that; the author makes no further use of the story: "The shadow of him [Mr. Hamlin], and his name will cause trouble once more in these pages—but in the flesh we will never see him more." Madelaine reappears only briefly at the end of the novel, with no reference to her romantic and tragic adventures in Europe. Clearly, Mary Boykin Chesnut is simply trying, as she had done often in "The Captain and the Colonel," to tie up loose ends as quickly as possible.[20]

As with the final few chapters of "The Captain and the Colonel," the end of "Two Years" is often quite confused. For example, an incident in the drawing room of the Planters' Hotel, where Mrs. Newtown and her youngest daughter are staying, introduces an unidentified beau. At first the reader suspects he is, in fact, Sydney Howard, but subsequent events preclude this possibility. Whatever the mysterious suitor's identity, he is immediately dropped and never reappears. All hands discuss another handsome man, this time at the races, who likewise turns out not to be Sydney, and plays no further part in the plot. Mary Boykin Chesnut assigns Chapter XIV to Helen's learning of her father's death, but the chapter is only slightly more than one page long. With no transition, Chapter XV finds Helen and her mother back in Mississippi and follows closely Mrs. Chesnut's outline of her second Mississippi trip in "We called her Kitty." But Fanny, who has previously been shown to be in Charleston with Mrs. Newtown, is now said to have been, for the last year, "mother" to her infant sister and occupied night and day with the care of the baby in Mississippi. Mary Chesnut finishes her story of the mystery behind the Blueskin-Hamlin feud quickly, using the same device she had employed at the end of "The Captain and the Colonel": a letter. Sydney writes to Helen revealing what he has accidentally discovered about the secret past of Colonel Blueskin who is, in reality, Mrs. Grindstone's look-alike brother.

The final chapter of the novel describes Helen's wedding. Curiously, the narrative is now in the third person. No explanation is offered as to how or when Helen has returned to South Carolina, nor is the reader privy to any conversation between Sydney and

Helen. Such an ending to a work that has, in the preceding chapters, been predominantly humorous and objective in tone, jars the reader. And yet this last chapter has a palpable impact that the rest of the novel does not. Mary Boykin Chesnut's picture of her heroine's wedding seems to be a very personal, subjective one. Helen goes through the motions of her role as bride in a dreamlike state, which is so convincing that it is difficult to avoid concluding that here the author is describing herself:

> The Bride left alone looked down; utterly without interest; subdued by the numbness, and deadness of mind and body which always overtook her at the supreme moments of her life . . . .
>
> A man standing near the gay party below, caught sight of this slim figure in white; he gently pushed aside the crowd who were blocking the stair way.
>
> He sprang up three steps at a time.
>
> She saw him coming, as in a dream . . . . She was calmly watching the white gloved hand, as at each upward bound it grasped the railing.[21]

Thus the novel ends on a tentative note. The romance has concluded successfully, but, for the moment at least, romance and adventure are over; in their place are calm and waiting. James Chesnut, Jr.'s courtship of Mary Miller had had just such a conclusion, forty years earlier.

Reading "Two Years" is a confusing experience; fine, clearly realized passages are interspersed with sections that are hopelessly jumbled. At times the author seems to be thoroughly engaged in her tale. At other times, she appears merely to be trudging and jolting along, much as her heroine, Helen, jolts along in a succession of stagecoaches. If one judges by the novel itself, Mary Boykin Chesnut simply lost interest in the project.

1878, the year in which "Two Years" was probably set aside, was a year of political activity in South Carolina, and of change in the Chesnut household. Almost certainly, 1878 was a year in which Mary had less time and inclination to shut herself up in her library and write than she had had the preceding year. On February 28, 1878, her nephew, S. Miller Williams, married Jane North Pettigrew of North Carolina.[22] The bride, related to the Petigrus of Charleston, was twenty-two, and impressed Mary at first as a bit insipid. In later years, though, particularly after the birth of Jane and Miller's first child in February, 1879, Mary would come to feel quite close to the younger woman, eventually writing to Jane more frequently than to Miller.

Now Miller brought Jane to live in Camden, probably at Mulberry, and by late summer it was evident that there was to be a baby born in the winter. It must have been with considerable anxiety, therefore, that Mary watched her nephew prepare for a duel in late August with W. Bogan Cash of Cheraw, a college friend of Miller's. Bogan Cash seems to have been a young man of rash temperament, for he would fight a second duel four months later with James Cantey and, in 1880, would serve as second to his father, E. B. C. Cash, in a famous and tragic duel with Colonel William M. Shannon. Miller and Bogan apparently quarreled over a racehorse named Prussian, but the exact nature of the argument is unknown. In any case, a duel was fought at ten paces at high noon on August 29, just across the North Carolina state line. Though both men were "of massive physique, and . . . should have presented ample marks to each other," each missed his adversary.[23] Tradition holds that Miller's young wife moulded the bullets for her husband's pistol. Miller's duel and the one that followed between Bogan Cash and Cantey so disturbed Camden society that General Joseph B. Kershaw—whom Shannon had praised as Camden's first citizen—organized an Anti-Duelling Society.

It is reasonable to assume that Mary Boykin Chesnut viewed these proceedings with profound disapproval. She regarded dueling as stupid and, in "The Captain and the Colonel," had included a duel between Dr. Johannis and Robert Collingwood which cast both men's roles in the affair in an ungentlemanly light. She had seen enough unavoidable bloodshed to shudder at the thought of needless killing. Further, she must have feared that Jane and the unborn baby might well be left unprotected. In light of this speculation, it is interesting that she never referred to the duel in any writing which has survived. About 1878 she began to use as a daybook a bound volume of blank pages entitled *Index Rerum*, which had probably been in the Chesnut library since the 1850's, but though the *Index Rerum* contains many diarylike entries, none refers to the duel.[24]

Because she rarely dated entries in the *Index Rerum*, and because it is made up of a hodge-podge of utterly miscellaneous types of notes and quotations, this last daybook of Mary Chesnut is more tantalizing than useful in an examination of her life. Nevertheless, it is worth pausing here to comment briefly upon it. The volume was published in 1850 as an aid to people, like Mary, fond of collecting interesting quotations on a wide variety of topics but unable to organize those quotations. A preface suggests that such excerpts should be organized alphabetically by key word or subject, and each page is headed by two key letters (Ba, Be, Bi, Bo, Bu, for example). A few entries in the volumes appear to attempt to follow the system, and these entries might have been made at any time after 1850.

But about 1878 Mary began to use the volume as a handy place to record facts or general observations she wished to remember, or simply to paste in newspaper clippings, and she used the book in this fashion until her death. Since many pages had already been written on, she made no effort to follow chronological order, but simply wrote in the book apparently at random. One of the earliest dated entries is that of September 18, 1878, in which she describes a political rally where "Every thing was better than the speaking—they were long enough—these speeches—but very dull." Few entries provide the twentieth-century scholar with any biographical facts, but many of them offer isolated insights into Mary Chesnut's wit. One undated entry, for example, follows a small newspaper clipping on rising campaign costs: "It seems the party of 'high moral ideas' require vast amounts of money to carry an election—Col Ingersoll—Rev Henry Ward Beecher—Senator Conckling—Ex President Grant each requires to be paid for the patriotic efforts they make, by speeches, to save the country . . . . Here we do not pay our speakers. for the reason perhaps that we have no money—if we had it—we might judiciously use it to induce them to hold their tongues." Another probably began with her intention to record an apt quotation, which then reminded her of another similar quote. Finally she embroidered extemporaneously on the theme:

> Life is a series of moments & Emotions—Mr Kase
> Life is a series of absurdities—Broad Church—
> Life is a Solemn Mystery
> Life is a damned Nuisance—
> Life is matter, which under certain conditions not yet fully understood has become self conscious—
> Life is a preface to eternity—
> A preface we can't skip—& generally dedicated to the wrong person—[25]

Some pages in the *Index Rerum* daybook contain brief quotations, revealing that Mary was still reading widely; she quotes, for example, William Dean Howells, and Edward Fitzgerald's translation of *The Rubaiyat of Omar Khayyam*. Still other pages mention the death of old friends: among them Mary Preston Darby's husband, Dr. John Darby, on whose life some incidents in "The Captain and the Colonel" had been based, or General John Bell Hood, who figures so largely in the revised Civil War journal, both of whom died in 1879. Page 10 of one draft of "The Captain and the Colonel" is pasted into the daybook, most likely because Mrs. Chesnut liked the remark it recorded of the anonymous "Irishman": "I am not one of your self made men—Thank God—I had a father and a mother." Perhaps the most interesting aspect of the *Index Rerum* daybook is what it does *not* show. Mary Boykin Chesnut, by 1878, lacked the incentive or the need to keep a journal as she had done during the Civil War. Though she occasionally included a dated entry, she did so to record information or material which she felt might potentially be useful in some way—to her proposed biography of James Chesnut, Jr., to her fiction, or to the revision of the war journal.

Few details are known about Mary's health during these years; no reference to it is made in any of the *Index Rerum* entries. And yet she was certainly ill much of the time. A letter from a friend of James Chesnut in November, 1879, reads in part, "Recollecting her [Mary] in the healthy and cheerful days of her life, I feel very deeply for her now that she has been such a patient sufferer of several long years." Nevertheless, she was well enough to accompany her husband to Baltimore (and, most likely, Romney, West Virginia, where the Williams family now lived) in the fall of 1879 on a visit to her niece, Mary Williams Harrison.[26] The Chesnuts returned to Camden for Christmas—the first Christmas with Jane and Miller's new baby Serena, now ten months old.

Despite chronic illness, Mary was to write voluminously for the next five years. In late June, 1880, she apparently wrote to the editor of the Charleston *News and Courier*, Francis Warrington Dawson, offering to send him for publication a translation of a "novelette" by Aleksander Pushkin, for Dawson replied on July 2 that he would welcome the translation and would "publish it, as soon as received, in either the Sunday News or the Weekly News."[27] If the novelette was ever submitted, it was not published. It seems likely that Mary Boykin Chesnut worked on the translation (of which no draft survives), but set it aside to concentrate on a more interesting venture: a third novel with the working title of "Manassas."

Only ten pages of one draft of this third novel survive, but these pages are numbered 411–419 (with two consecutive pages numbered 415), indicating that the complete novel was at least half again as long as either "The Captain and the Colonel," or "Two Years—or The Way We Lived Then."[28] A cover sheet with these ten pages has the words "Manassas rough copy" canceled, and "Susie Effingh" written above them, perhaps indicating that Mrs. Chesnut at some point changed the working title from "Manassas" to "Susie Effingham."

Needless to say, it is impossible to speculate about the novel as a whole from the evidence offered by ten pages toward the end of it. Nevertheless, we can draw some conclusions about "Manassas" from the ten pages we do have, which comprise part of a conversation among a group of young people. Like "Two Years," the novel is told in the first person by a Miss Newtown, whose two younger sisters, Kitty and Tatty, also participate in the conversation. However, as in "The Captain and the Colonel," the three sisters enjoy teasing their mother, née Miss Helena Hartringer (a name reminiscent of Miss Joanna Hartkopf in "The Captain and the Colonel"). The brief excerpt we have does not contain any clues as to the time of the action, though the title "Manassas" sets the novel, like "The Captain and the Colonel," during the Civil War.

Most of the ten-page segment relates an anecdote in the past, prior to Mrs. Newtown's marriage, when she was a beautiful *demoiselle à marier*. Just as Joanna Hardhead and her sister Annie had been rivals for the same man in "The Captain and the Colonel," so Helena Hartringer and her cousin Susan, an heiress, were both beloved by the same man, a wealthy landowner similar to Dr. Johannis, who possessed a beautiful estate named Eldorado, but who, because of his impossibly high standards, was notoriously unlucky in love. The anecdote is narrated by one of the young people present: Tom, the unlucky man's nephew.

> ——"Miss Susan was angelically kind. but Miss Helena was mighty pretty. In his heart he liked Helena a *leettle* the best; but his mind told in the long run Susan would be the best match. So it kept him going criss-cross—not straight forward at all. . . . My uncle called to see Susan—prepared to risk his fate. He had a box of new clothes from Philadelphia—and that gave him courage. . . . There were two drawing rooms opening into one another by folding doors. And in the first one he found Susan—carrying on what he called a Pianoforte arrangement. She strumming—he, (the man who was there before him,) turning the leaves over her shoulder. But he got a glimpse of Helena curled up at the other end of room number two, on a sofa. His heart gave a leap. Heaven had given him a hint.
> So he plunged in—he sat down before Helena with his back to the foe, and in passionate accents poured forth his soul—
> ——"And all the time we thought it was Susan!" remarked the besieged damsel most coolly.
> ——"Look in the glass and see the reason—It is you—You—your own loved self—"
> ——"What did she say" inquired Kitty.
> ——"No—No" and with a vim. He fled, but arresting his too hasty steps—on the slippery stair case—he remembered the card he had hid in his sleve and he went back to play it. So he popped again—adding "would a trip to Europe, induce you to reconsider, your savage decision."

——"No—No—No"—

——"Dont flurry yourself—Miss Hartringer. Rest assured that I will never trouble you again.

——"No trouble at all" said Miss Helena calmly and politely.

——"Will you solemnly promise never to divulge a word of this painful interview.

——"Oh. I never do—about this kind of thing."

——"Your cousin in there at the Piano. That fellow has gone at last—Do you think she will have me?"

——"Try her—by all means— Your hand is in—go in and win"—

——"Did Susan have him?" asked Tatty breathlessly.

——"Did you not hear he is an old Bachelor still—goosey—he fell between two stools . . . .

Like that of "The Captain and the Colonel," the tone of at least this fragment of the novel is that of a comedy of manners. And yet the presence of the Newtown family, fictional counterparts of Mary Boykin Chesnut's own, suggests that other parts of "Manassas" may have drawn more heavily on the material in "Two Years" than this segment does.

Unfortunately, aside from the ten-page fragment, no evidence whatsoever exists to shed additional light on what was obviously a third major effort at fiction. Mrs. Chesnut was astonishingly close-mouthed about her writing, and never once mentioned her work in fiction in any of the journals, daybooks, or letters that have survived; she regarded her fiction as an extremely private matter. Certainly, she found such writing pleasurable and interesting, for it is unlikely that she would have written three novels had she not enjoyed doing so. But in addition to the pleasure they gave, her experiments with fiction had taught her a great deal. The late revisions of "Two Years—or The Way We Lived Then" and the fragment of "Manassas" are both written with a sure hand. Mary Chesnut had, by the time she was revising "Two Years," developed a crisp, identifiable style with which she was comfortable; she had learned to write realistic dialogue and compressed, vivid character sketches. Whether or not she realized it consciously, she had completed her apprenticeship.

Nevertheless, in her fiction, Mary Boykin Chesnut had been unsuccessful at constructing plots. It was real dramas that fascinated her, not imaginary ones, and she no doubt realized that she wrote her best about people she knew and events which she herself had experienced. Almost certainly, she ceased to write fiction by 1881, though she may have hoped to return to it at some later date. In 1881, the year Mrs. Chesnut—who had called herself "old" in 1865—was fifty-eight, she undertook a different kind of task, a monumental project, the project which had been urging itself upon her more or less constantly since the end of the war. She bought a large supply of scratch pads and began a full-scale revision of the Civil War journal.

IT IS FOR THE WORK she did during three of the last five years of her life that Mary Boykin Chesnut is remembered at all, for between late 1881 and 1884 she substantially completed an expansion and revision of her Civil War journals—twenty years after they had been written. In the early 1880s, Mrs. Chesnut wrote drafts of the book totaling nearly a million words. When circumstances forced her to cease working on it, she had finished not a final draft, but rather a version from which, with the care and judicious editing she intended to give it, a final fair copy could be made. Though she had attempted to draft the first passages of the journal several times, she had not yet written an opening that suited her, nor had she determined precisely how to end the work.[1] By December, 1884, her husband's last illness necessitated setting the journal project aside for a time, and Mary herself died before she could pick it up again. But she had, in three years, essentially completed a work which is in many respects the most remarkable first hand account of the Confederacy ever written. More important perhaps, it is a creative work in a very real sense. In the revised Civil War journal, the author takes real events and real persons and, by using the fictional techniques she had taught herself, gives them life and places them in a complex, multidimensional society.

When Mary Boykin Chesnut first set out to revise the journal in 1875, she had apparently underestimated both the scope and the magnitude of the task. That first effort at revision had consisted of little more than polishing her actual war-time diaries—expanding phrases into sentences, smoothing prose, and so on. After working with her material for some months, she had set the entire project aside and turned, instead, to occasional pieces, to translations, and to fiction. Now in 1881, she had a much better sense of what she wished to do, but she also realized how little time there was in any given day to do it.

Life at Sarsfield had changed somewhat since 1875. At least through 1881, Miller and Jane Williams and their growing family remained in Camden and visited almost daily with the Chesnuts. Serena, born on February 7, 1879, had been christened that March; Mary Boykin Chesnut stood as the baby's godmother, and proudly recorded the fact in her daybook. A year later, in June 1880, another daughter was born, but survived less than a day. And in November, 1881, the Williams' first son, Charles, was born.[2] These babies—the first infants the Chesnuts had ever had in their home so frequently—were a delight to Mary and James Chesnut, childless themselves but both genuinely fond of children.

After the deaths of Mary's sister Kate and Kate's daughter Serena in 1876, when Mary had become so ill as to alarm the entire family, her mother, Mary Boykin Miller, had finally come to live with the Chesnuts. Mrs. Miller, who had grown up in the area and whose Camden relatives were numerous, had always been unusually close to her oldest daughter. In a sense, she took the place vacated by Kate as Mary's dearest friend, and she undoubtedly served as a buffer between Mary and Camden society as well as being of real service in helping her daughter run the household. But Mrs. Miller was elderly; in 1881 she was seventy-seven and infirm, and so a great deal of Mary's time had to be spent making certain her mother was comfortable.

Early in 1882 Miller took his family to Creswell, his wife Jane's family seat in Washington County, North Carolina, and left them there while he went to Lexington, Kentucky, to take a job.[3] His departure was probably timed to coincide with the arrival of his younger brother, David, who had been working as a civil engineer after his graduation from Washington and Lee, but who would eventually choose to live in Camden the rest of his life. Miller had almost certainly been assisting his uncle only until his brother could return. With a wife and two children and little inclination to farm, Miller was no doubt anxious to strike out on his own. Now David, twenty-three, moved into Sarsfield.

Mary and James certainly missed Miller and Jane Williams, but it was the children, Serena and Charley, for whom they most longed. Shortly after they left, James Chesnut, the cool, reserved general, wrote a letter to his three-year-old niece that shows him in an entirely new light:

MY DEAR SERENA

It is now so long since I have heard from you that I am almost afraid that you have forgotten me—and yet I so love my dear little Daughter that I will not believe that I am not still remembered affectionately by her . . . . The earth is green, here now—and covered with bright flowers that you used to admire so—and all is beautiful.

Grandmother's health seems to be much better, and Aunty about as usual. She is arranging for a Dairy Farm this Spring & Summer. She is very busy with collecting eggs, raising young chickens, & attending to vegetable & flower gardens. All we want is the presence of our little Serena to make us happy.

Do you remember the little naughty yellow cat? She has enlivened the establishment by bringing into it four young kittens. I cannot say Aunty rejoices much over their advent.

We all send love to you, Mama, Grandmama, papa—and that *splendid little Brother* of yours.

Your Affectionate Uncle Jimmy[4]

James's picture of his wife "arranging for a Dairy Farm," stepping with annoyance over four kittens, and "very busy with collecting eggs, raising young chickens, & attending to vegetable & flower gardens," is obviously written to match the interests of a three-year-old child. Yet the picture admits of little time in which Mary might sit in her library and work on her journal. And indeed, much of the energy she expended day by day was directed precisely at making ends meet. Later in 1882 she herself wrote to Jane, speaking quite matter-of-factly about the lack of ready cash. Knowing that since Miller's move to Kentucky, Jane must be lonely and bored, Mary sent along a number of gifts, including what seemed to her the best possible antidote, "two very readable books."

MY DEAR JANE.

The dress is made by one of Anna Ancrums. The ribbons are for Serena too—and Uncle Jemmy sends candy and basket. The sacque is for you. It is not very fine but may be useful in the country. I am scraping and saving to have my diamond maltese cross set as a ring—I hereby give it to Serena—If I live I will keep it and give it to her myself when she is old enough—*but*. And you know how more than usually uncertain life is to me

If I drop off—the ring is Serena's—I will tell Mr C—and he wants her to have it.

I wish I could see your great boy—who does he look like—

. . . I send two very readable books.

Yours affectionately—MBC

Mother means to send a *dollar* which Hannah owes you. More to come as she collects it . . . . .[5]

This letter is interesting for several reasons. The diamond Maltese cross to which Mary refers had been, almost certainly, James's wedding present to her.[6] That she wished to pass it on as a legacy to her grand-niece bespeaks the deep love she felt for the child. That she had to "scrimp and save" to have the diamonds reset is a measure of the extent to which the Chesnuts' scale of living had changed. Before the war, they had been heirs to one of the largest fortunes in the state. Now, Mary's mother could repay a debt only a dollar at a time, and yet in the letter there is no hint of embarrassment at these reduced circumstances.

The old antagonism toward Camden ameliorated somewhat as Mary grew accustomed to the restrictions imposed by both her health and her budget. Her greatest pleasure had always been good conversation, and now she found among her neighbors several friends to whom she could recount tales of her past and, more importantly, with whom she could debate questions of politics, of the human spirit—even of personal immortality. After her death, one such friend remembered her love of good conversation during this period. "Mrs. Chesnut and I used to talk by the hour, and . . .

she often sent me a letter every day. I remember so well how we talked in the moonlight down there at Sarsfield,—General Chesnut sometimes listening, sometimes joining in—about everything in Heaven and on earth. And then the next morning, before I was out of bed, one of those faithful colored men would make his appearance with a note supplementing some of the last evening's talk, and then it would begin over again."[7]

Without the Williams children to charm and distract James and her mother, Mary found herself constantly "on call" to the demands of both of them when guests were not present. Neither considered her writing important enough to grant her uninterrupted time for it, and one day, on the verso of a miscellaneous page of a pencil draft of the journal, she expressed her annoyance: "It is as difficult to work independently in their presence—(mother & husband) as to pursue intellectual labour in the continual presence of some over whelming human potentate—such as the Czar of Russia for example—One must have solitude at will—for intellectual work."[8] Then she added, "I have been interrupted three times in trying to *accomplish* this sentence." In earlier years, a similar moment of frustration might well have elicited a sharp remark. Now, older and more patient, she could assuage her anger by recording it on a scrap of paper to be destroyed.

Certainly one reason James interrupted his wife so often was because he was himself frustrated and bored. Although Mary in her biographical sketch of her husband had characterized him as content to retire from political life, there is evidence that James's "contented" retirement was from necessity rather than choice. During the years of Radical Reconstruction in South Carolina, he had remained active—a member of the old guard and a spokesman for the old virtues of pride, honor, and aristocratic government. As Reconstruction ended, he may well have expected that all of his behind-the-scenes correspondence and support would net him some position in which he could put his experience to good use. In the fall of 1878 he seems to have had reason to believe that public office would be forthcoming, for he petitioned the House of Representatives to remove his political disabilities. The petition was passed unanimously on December 13, but whatever office James expected (if indeed, as seems likely, he did expect one) failed to materialize. In 1882 Congress established a Tariff Commission, and James Chesnut's friends placed his name on the president's desk as a possible member. James encouraged his own nomination, and the matter was regarded as certain; Camden's youngest Civil War general John D. Kennedy (who had sold the Chesnuts the land for Sarsfield) even wrote a letter of congratulations to him, and added perceptively that he expected the move to Washington which the appointment would require might improve Mrs. Chesnut's health.[9] In any case, President Arthur did not act as anticipated, and the appointment was not made.

We do not know whether Mary was disappointed or not, for she never mentioned the Tariff Commission in writing. But certainly by 1882 her old craving for excitement away from home was mitigated by her desire to finish the journal revision—a task that, as she patiently carved an hour or two out of each day, must have sometimes seemed endless. Occasionally in the revision, she inserted a phrase far more indicative of her mood of the 1880s than of twenty years earlier. In the entry for May 6, 1862, for example, she wrote, "Oh! Peace—and a lit[er]ary leisure for my old age— unbroken by care and anxiety!!"[10]

Mary proceeded with her revision of the Civil War journals systematically, apparently working through them chronologically. For most of the journal, she would first draft an entry or series of entries on scratch pads, in purple pencil. These interim pencil drafts are very rough, often nearly illegible and unpunctuated except by dashes, with a generous amount of interlinear and marginal revision and notes to herself about additional items or passages to be included in the next draft. The evidence suggests that, having completed a segment of pencil draft, she then reworked the same segment and copied it into a bound copybook, often rearranging material so that an incident appearing on one day might well be included in the entry for the preceding or succeeding day in the copybook draft. During the three-year period from late 1881 to late 1884, she wrote well over five thousand manuscript pages, and filled nearly fifty copybooks.[11] Judging from her practice in previous literary projects, there were, for many passages, almost certainly additional interim drafts that have not survived.

Mary Boykin Chesnut's reasons for revising the journals so extensively were varied. Foremost among them was her conviction that her book should not be a record of daily domestic trifles, but rather a picture of an entire society. On June 18, 1883, she wrote in a letter to Varina Davis, "How I wish you could read over—my Journal—I have been two years over looking it—copying—leaving my self out. You must see it—before it goes to print—but that may not be just now. I mean the printing—for I must over haul it again—and again."[12] Mrs. Chesnut was well aware that the original journals were full of passages detailing her own fluctuations of mood, recording compliments or slights to herself, or simply letting off the steam of her anger at what she regarded as the stupidity of others. And she felt that these passages would diminish the importance and quality of the journals by shifting focus from the tumultuous scene around her to the ephemeral concerns of her own day-to-day life. Later in the letter to Varina Davis, she commented upon a book she had recently read, the letters of Jane Welsh Carlyle, wife of Thomas Carlyle, an author Mary Chesnut admired greatly:

> One word for the feu Carlyle—He is a better fellow than his wife. Wailing and howling—to ones family and friends—easier than writing the "French Revolution"—difference between a man's sense—and a clever woman's hysterics—when she cut old Carlyle as with a two edged sword—*I was there*—but when it is all—head aches—stomach aches—*maids* (whom *she* kisses!!)—*bugs*—housecleaning which she piles on ad nauseam. I feel—"people read all of this—because she is old Carlyle's wife" . . . . She had two motions—the one around her Sun—or brilliant husband—is delight ful—the harder she hits him—the better fun—but when she turns on her own axis—and thrusts her homely details under our noses by the guise—she is a bore.[13]

To Mary Chesnut, the horror of being a bore subsumed all other literary horrors, and she was therefore willing and anxious to "overhaul" her journal "again—and again"—as many times as necessary to breathe permanent life into it. To this end, she transformed what had originally been third-person narrative statements into dialogue, often turning her own thoughts into the words of others. To this end also, she freely rearranged incidents and thoughts within a given entry or contiguous entries to heighten their dramatic import, carefully constructing a montage of scenes in which incidents of serious importance are punctuated by anecdotes in an entirely different vein, often humorous or ironic. One feels when reading the revised journal that its author has recorded *everything*, and that the reader is to be congratulated for bringing some kind of order out of the chaos she offers. In fact, Mrs. Chesnut's major point, her central theme in the journal, might be said to be the chaos itself, the riot of emotions and events and people that *are* a disrupted society. The montage technique clearly functions as a device to produce in the reader a sense of the hectic, the confused, the fluctuating world of which Mary Boykin Chesnut in the 1860s was only a part.[14]

To achieve this chaos, though, Mrs. Chesnut exercised a rigorous selectivity on her material. For example, in one section of the journal for which we have the original and the revision, nearly half of the material in the original version is *not* used. At the same time that she cut out a great deal, she expanded what was retained so that, in spite of the considerable amount of material excised, this segment of the revised journal is more than twice as long as its counterpart in the original.[15]

A brief look at this section of the diary can illustrate well the variety of literary techniques Mrs. Chesnut applied to her original material throughout the revision process. The time is February, 1865; Mary and many of her friends have fled to North Carolina knowing that behind them, Sherman is moving inexorably to destroy their homes and, in a real sense, their lives. In the original, no sooner does she get settled in "Johnstones Hotel Lincolnton" than her maid interrupts what Mary Chesnut describes as her own constant state of weeping with a complaint: "Old Miss Jonson— 'Say in the kitchen—go away gal—dont stand there—My niggers wont work for looking at you—Now Misses—aint I a *show*."[16] In the revised journal, the scene is very different, very much longer, very much written with an eye to its humorous potential. Furthermore, it provides insight not only into the maid herself of whom we now get a vivid picture, but also into the character of the hotel proprietor:

After dinner Ellen presented herself—blue black with rage—She has lost the sight of one eye—so that is permanently *blueish*— opaque—The other flamed—fire and fury.—Heres my dinner. A piece of meat—And a whole plate ful of raw ingans. I never did eat raw ingins and I won't begin now—dese here niggers say dis ole lady gives em to em breakfast and dinner—Its a sin and a shame to do us so. She says I must come outen her kitchen—de niggers won't work for looking at me—

I'se something to look at surely—She [threw] down her odorous plate—held her fork and made a courtesy

——"Ellen—for pity sake?"—

Lord ha' mercy. She say you bring me and Laurence here to keep us from running away to de Yankees—and I say—Name o'God Ole Missis—If dats it—what she bring Laurence and me for—She's got plenty more—Laurence and Me's nothing—to our white people— De ole soul fair play insulted me" [17]

The author has turned a remark of no interest into a scene that lives in and for itself, and that also functions significantly in the whole Lincolnton section of the journal. In the original, Ellen is simply there—an adjunct to Mrs. Chesnut's other possessions. In the revised journal, however, Ellen provides comic relief and a very human tone. In the midst of the grief that the upper class Carolinians feel for the destruction Sherman is wreaking on their homes and property, Ellen is having the time of her life. This is her first trip as lady's maid, her introduction to the wide world, and she is delighted to find that the prominence of her mistress gives Ellen herself a superiority over the other servants in town.

Mary Boykin Chesnut's characterization of Ellen, like many similar characterizations in the revised journal, is also a means of "leaving herself out" of the work—shifting focus from herself to the world around her. In a passage describing the household's escape from the horrible Johnston Hotel, the original reads: "I moved here yesterday—friday morning—I swallowed my super-stitions—so anxious was I to leave the Hotel." The revised jour-nal, on the other hand, transfers the superstitions to the comic Ellen: "'Lord, Missis we can't move to day—it is friday—bad luck—all round'—but Ellen succumbed—swallowed her super-stitions—she was too keen to get away from 'dirt and raw ingans'—and the raking fire of the Landlady's sharp tongue." Ellen, in this segment, is given to singing "Massa's in the Cold, Cold Ground," the very song which had been sung as the Confederate flag was raised in Montgomery in 1861. Mrs. Chesnut uses this invented touch symbolically and to eerie effect by punctuating a "conversation" with Isabella Martin (a conversation that, incidentally, is the product of the 1880s, not an actual talk of 1865) thus:

> ——Stop Ellen—"No more Massa in the cold—cold ground"—
> Sing something else—
> ——"Well so they are most of them" says Isabella.[18]

Much of the strength of the revised journal stems directly from Mary Boykin Chesnut's development of a sustained and objective narrative voice, which had first been developed in "The Captain and the Colonel," but not fully realized until the boarding school sections of "Two Years—or The Way We Lived Then." The wit and compression with which, in "The Captain and the Colonel," the narrator described Joanna's departure to put a stop to the duel ("Mrs. Effingham was at home again in a surprisingly short time . . . . She captured the whole party") appears constantly throughout the revised journal. For example, the entry in the original journal immediately following the firing on Fort Sumter had begun, "during this time—the excitement &c was so great I had never a moment to write," never mentioning Sumter at all.[19] Its counterpart in the revision, on the other hand, is a brilliant example of Mrs. Chesnut's compression at its best:

> Home again. In those last days of my stay in Charleston I did not find time to write a word.
> And so we took Fort Sumter. —Nous autres.
> We—Mrs Frank Hampton &c in the passage way of the Mills House between the reception room and the drawing room—There we held a sofa against all comers—And indeed all the agreeable people South seemed to have flocked to Charleston at the first gun. That was after we found out that bombarding did not kill any body. Before that we wept and prayed—and took our tea in groups, in our rooms—away from the haunts of men—Captain Ingraham and his kind took it (Fort Sumter) from the Battery with field glasses—

and figures made with three sticks in the sand to show what ought to be done.

Wigfall, Chesnut, Miles, Manning &c took it rowing about in the Harbour in small boats—from Fort to Fort—under the Enemies Guns—Bombs bursting in air—&c &c—

And then the boys—and men, who worked those guns so faithfully at the Forts—they took it too—their way.[20]

As she worked toward imparting an objective narrative tone to the journal, the most serious difficulty Mrs. Chesnut faced concerned the portions of the original journal that had been written at Mulberry and Sandy Hill. There, the war had rarely intruded, and the original diary was replete with trivial and often vindictive gossip, interspersed with Mary's constant complaints at being shut off and unappreciated. As she revised the journal, she adopted the technique she had used in describing Madame Talvande's school in "Two Years," and in the Camden segments of the journal, paused to reflect on the antebellum South. The old colonel and his wife, Mary Cox Chesnut, became archetypal figures in a world that Mary Boykin Chesnut realized was irrevocably lost. Again and again throughout the revision, she unobtrusively inserted portraits of the inhabitants of that world, so that by the end of the journal, the reader has been given a thoroughly rounded picture of a large southern plantation before the war and after. And yet old Colonel and Mrs. Chesnut are, in the revised journal, not only symbols of an older, simpler society, but also three-dimensional people, with their follies, their strengths, their love for one another and, above all, their immense dignity.

Although there is a considerable amount of this essaylike material in the revised journal (almost none of which is present in the original), the author manages to insert it into her text so smoothly that the reader rarely notices the diary format has been expanded. Mrs. Chesnut took care, in the revision, to preserve a sense of spontaneity by emphasizing her role as diarist. She began her entry for March 10, 1862, for example, ingenuously: "I write daily for my own distractions. These memoirs pour servir—may some future day afford dates—facts—and prove useful to more important people than I am. I do not wish to do any harm, or to hurt any one—If any scandalous stories creep in—they are easily burned. It is hard, in such a hurry as things are in—to separate wheat from chaff. Now I have made my protest—and written down my wishes—I can scribble on with a free will—and free conscience."[21]

In light of what we know of the extremely private nature of the original journal, with its candid record of scandal and its untempered judgments of people, Mrs. Chesnut's statement here must be read as the carefully phrased remark of a narrative persona. A striking example of the extent to which she enhanced this underlying framework of the journal as a spontaneous diary occurs in the entry for February 22, 1865, which has its source in the original journal, in an entry dated February 23. In the original passage, Mrs. Chesnut testifies to the worth of her own work and to her fear that it might have to be destroyed: "For four days . . . I have been busily engaged—reading the *10* volumes of *memoirs* of the times I have written—nearly all my sage prophecies have been verified the wrong way—& every insight into character or opinions I have given as to men turned out utter folly—still I write on—for if I have to burn—& here lie my treasures ready for the blazing hearth—still they have served already to while away fo[u]r days of agony." The final revision of this passage is designed to intensify the scene and to present a thoroughly convincing narrator, Mary Chesnut, writing for her own amusement but unaware, finally, of the value of her effort: "Isabella has been reading my diaries. How we laugh [at] my sage ratiocinations—all come to naught. My famous insight into character—utter folly. They were lying on the hearth ready to be burned—but she told me to hold on—think of it awhile." Then she quotes Isabella directly: "'*Don't be rash.*'"[22]

Indeed, throughout the latter portion of the revised journal, Mary Boykin Chesnut uses Isabella Martin as a device to enable her to cast many of her own thoughts into dialogue. During the war years, Isabella had been merely one of a group of girls who flocked around Mrs. Chesnut when she was in Columbia. In the original journal, Isabella is seldom mentioned and rarely quoted. Between 1865 and the 1880s, however, Isabella had continued to

correspond with Mary, whom she admired greatly, and the friendship had grown; the older woman welcomed the compliments and
attentions of the younger, and valued Isabella at least in part because she represented a link between the glamor and excitement of
the early 1860s and the struggle with hopelessness and poverty
that the succeeding years had brought. Thus, in the revised journal, Isabella emerged as an important figure in Mrs. Chesnut's circle. Two other characters—her maids Molly and Ellen—also
played greatly expanded roles in the revised journal. Both women
had remained with Mary after the war, often working for little or
no pay and had, by their loyalty to and love for their mistress,
earned the right to fully realized portraits in her writing.[23]

When Mary Chesnut wrote to Varina Davis in mid-1883 that
her journal was not yet ready for the printer because it needed to
be overhauled again and again, she clearly envisioned spending
considerable time—perhaps years—on the task. For the time
being, her health had improved. She felt relatively well, and was
enjoying her life. On the day she wrote to Varina, she was busy
doing the kinds of things she most liked to do:

> An avalanche of company is about to over whelm us—Wade
> Hampton—Bonham—Mary Darby—Isabella—We are to unveil
> our Monument to Confed dead day after tomorrow—And to keep
> open house for a week. So my hands are full— . . . Dearest—
> would you not like to drop in on Mary Darby  Isabella and me—
> about twelve or one at night—when we are in full blast? We are to
> sleep in the same room—my house is so crowded I take them in my
> room on the first floor—away from the "Madding crowd."
>
> You do not know how glad I am to hear from you—and how I
> will parade it at the head of my table—with the *So Ca FF's* to the
> fore—"*My* friend—Mrs Davis—who is by far the cleverest wom-
> an I know—says—of Stephens &c &c &c—"[24]

In a postscript, she referred to Varina's children—and her own
childlessness once again: "You should thank God for your young
immortals—I have nothing but Polish chickens—and Jersey
calves!" Then she promised to send her friend a sample of the wine
she had been making, "as good as Rhine wine—and it is *too*
strong."

With company coming, and good wine and good conversation to look forward to, Mary Boykin Chesnut was happy in June, 1883. Work on the journal was going well. And perhaps because she was happy, she felt better than she had for years. She could not have known that she had less than a year and a half left in which to write. Furthermore, in that year and a half, her life was destined to become more complicated, and the financial stress on the family would increase. From 1881 to 1885, there were four successive years of crop failure in South Carolina,[25] and though we do not know how severely the Chesnut planting interests were damaged, certainly these were years in which the family's resources were strained.

In the fall of 1883, Mary took time to scribble a letter to her nephew Miller in the purple pencil she was using to draft the journal. The letter asks Miller to repay his brother David $83 for back taxes, and goes on to comment on a family scandal. Her aunt Charlotte Boykin Taylor's son Tom (who had had difficulty finding a job in 1876) had apparently embezzled some money, and James and Mary Chesnut considered it their duty to extricate their cousin. Accordingly, they arranged for the Boykin relatives in Camden to help them repay the money, and Mary appealed to two old friends of her Richmond days, John C. West and General Thomas N. Waul, for help. To Miller she wrote,

> I had letters from the west—John C West and General Waul—who is the first lawyer in Galveston—and an old Spotswood—Richmond crony of mine—he wrote six sheets—and for our sake will take Tom Taylor to his bosom even *now*—if he will go there—I would send the letter to Aunt C—but the ugly word *embezzlement* occurs too often—I felt hot all over as I read it—my cousin— shame and remorse are my ideas of punishment here or hereafter Aunt C is a forlorn old woman actually—I have sent her my bottom dollar to come here—where else is she to go?

The rest of Mary's letter to Miller was affectionate.

> Now dear boy, when you come—and do come—before Christmas bring Serena—The General is clean daft to see her. He had never in his life been so in love with any thing—human or *otherwise*— . . . And I have not told you of *Aunt Sally* My little sister—

The poor grey haired old woman—sad eyed—wrinkled—sallow—has bloomed out—She shows now she is a fair woman—or was her skin is pure *blonde* white again—and her eyes blue and laughing  It does me good—and to see Mr Chesnut doing the tender to this sister in law—she is inexhaustibly funny—the keenest sense of humour—I enjoy her intensely.[26]

So Aunt Charlotte, now sixty-six, came to Sarsfield, to join a growing circle of aging relatives: Mary (sixty) and James Chesnut (sixty-eight), Mary's mother (seventy-nine), and, though probably only on an extended visit, Mary's sister Sally, now in her early fifties.[27] Since Miller Williams and his family had left in 1881, the only young person in the house was Miller's brother David, twenty-five, who more and more assumed a role as the mainstay of the family. Almost totally deaf, David had always been perhaps Mary's favorite nephew. Since childhood, he had been kind and obedient, and had grown to be the sort of thoroughly natural gentleman Mary Boykin Chesnut liked and respected. In her *Index Rerum* daybook, she recorded an anecdote about him that embodied his gentlemanly qualities:

> Yesterday David looking spick & span from his bath—with white linen cuffs &c &c—resplendent—met an old negro woman who had grappled a dead limb of a tree—It was too much for her to lift—and it broke her heart to leave it. She was a horrible old crone of ninety. So he shouldered the huge piece of wood—and toted it home for her—*on Littleton St.* People stared at him—as the old Negro could not keep up with him—there was no apparent reason for his staggering under a huge log—and the thermometer in the nineties. but he was deaf as a post—and answered no questions— Though he was immensely amused at the amazement his human freak awakened.[28]

With so many people dependent on the income that the Chesnut farming and planting enterprises could bring in, Mary Boykin Chesnut felt the lack of ready cash for herself as keenly as ever. Accordingly, when she learned—probably in December, 1883— that the Charleston *Weekly News and Courier* was soliciting wartime sketches and anecdotes for a series entitled "Our Women in the War," she quickly chose an incident from the revised Civil War journal, expanded it, and submitted it to the paper's editor, Francis Warrington Dawson. Dawson acknowledged receipt of the article on January 21, 1884, and in April accepted it for publication and paid Mary $10. In 1885, after its appearance in the paper, the sketch entitled "The Arrest of a Spy" was collected along with the other sketches in the series (including one by Isabella Martin) in book form.[29]

"The Arrest of a Spy" is, in essence, the description of an incident recorded in the revised Civil War journal, excerpted from narrative segment of 1862–63, corresponding to pages 287–89 of the Williams edition of *A Diary From Dixie*, which occurred while Mary was en route to Alabama to visit her mother in June, 1863. In the revised journal, Mary had described the incident in about fifteen hundred words. For the newspaper sketch, she expanded it to nearly three thousand words, adding dialogue, description, and minor digressions. An interesting feature of the sketch is that Mary chose to begin it with an account of her refusal to defer to her husband's better judgment:

> During the summer of 1863 there came to me a telegram from my mother, saying she was ill.
>
> Fortunately for me Col. Jefferson Goodwyn, the mayor of Columbia, his wife and his two daughters were on the eve of a journey westward, and he kindly offered to take care of me as far as Montgomery, Alabama.
>
> I telegraphed at once to my husband, who was then in Richmond, for permission to go, and he as promptly refused to give it:
>
> "No. You must not go. Railroads too dangerous. Cars too crowded. Too hot. Too great risk of fever."
>
> In utter confusion of mind I read this aloud. The silence which followed was broken by Miss Kate H——'s soft voice.
>
> "What a comfort it is to know what one's duty is. To be uncertain about that is the only trouble."
>
> Did she think my duty was to obey my husband? I did not so decide. I obeyed the natural impulse, which bore me away to my mother, who was ill and bade me come to her.
>
> After all I ventured to assume all risks, as there was nobody to be hurt but myself.[30]

In the revised journal the same point is made but with greater compression and subtlety.[31]

As nearly as we can tell, "The Arrest of a Spy" represents the only piece of writing Mary Boykin Chesnut published during her lifetime. Surely she did not consider it a milestone in her life. She didn't preserve a manuscript of the sketch, or even a clipping of its newspaper appearance. She did, however, keep Dawson's letter accepting it and enclosing the $10 payment. The money was important; it meant, in a small but concrete way, that her writing was a potential source of funds, apart from its historical value. It was the first and only money she would ever receive from the years of writing: $10 for a slight and hastily written newspaper sketch.

Late in November of 1884, James Chesnut became seriously ill. Mary was shaken. The realization of her own precarious mortality and that of her husband had been often present in her mind since the Civil War years, and now she feared deep within herself that James could not live much longer. In her own mind, her writing—the journal—paled in importance beside the mass of historical material in James Chesnut's possession which, for years, he had contemplated organizing and turning into a book. When she had written to Varina Davis in 1883, she had told her friend that James was on the verge of beginning his "*memoir pour servir*," which many people had long urged him to write. Now, with James so ill that his death seemed near, Mary wrote to an old friend for help: William Henry Trescot—the same man to whom she had refused to write in 1861 because he had told her "Frenchy" anecdotes. She asked Trescot if he could possibly help with the task of arranging James's papers and writing the memoir. Trescot's reply suggests that Mary's appeal had been muted, that she had not revealed how serious James's condition was. It also suggests that his interest in the Chesnuts was still, as it had been in 1861, primarily in Mary:

> I am very sorry of course to hear the Chesnut is sick but my concern has I am afraid been much reduced by the fact that I owe to his sickness a letter from yourself. Indeed I do not see why you should not take advantage of the same opportunity to read the mass of

lumber to which you refer and your own estimate of which corresponds with the criticism of the world.

And if you would add your own recollections of the inside history at Richmond, I think you would throw as much light upon our troubles as the history of the battles—private or public—of a dozen generals.[32]

Trescot did not know, of course, that Mary Boykin Chesnut had been working on her own insider's view of the Confederacy for the last three years. But now, she had no time to write. In mid-January, James had a paralytic stroke.[33] Mary was forced to take stock of the financial situation. Her father-in-law's will had bequeathed Mulberry to James Chesnut, Jr., only for the duration of his life. At his death, the Chesnut homes and plantations must, under the old colonel's will, be left to a male Chesnut descendant. Thus, Mary would be left without the income of Mulberry. In late January she wrote to Miller's wife Jane, reminding her of debts Miller had incurred in Camden. Miller's attempt to establish himself in the business world had not gone well, and the formality of Mary's letter suggests how loath she was to mention the matter at all. Nevertheless, she felt her own situation was growing desperate, and she wrote to "My dear Jane":

I send Miller the Bonds—Mr. Chesnut is still so ill—that I get him to make David his attorney (that is gave him power of attorney) to effect this . . . Miller must send me his note for $330 . . . I am not a hard creditor—but I am old and infirm now—and except this house—and a lot which rents for forty dollars—& three houses which altogether rent for ninety dollars—I will not have a cent in the world if I am left alive—the last of the two—of us—just now—it seems hard to tell who will go first. I hope it will be me—I will leave the note to Serena—in case of my death—but if I live it must be paid. This is all strictly business.[34]

In a postscript, she added, "God grant Miller success—for his own sake—and for his family."

The same day this letter was written, matters at Sarsfield grew worse. Mary's mother began to hemorrhage and was confined to bed. With the two people most dear to her fatally ill in the same house, Mary Chesnut's physical and mental resources were strained to the utmost. A friend of thirty years, Caroline Perkins, came every day and, on the night of January 30, decided the General was so ill she had best remain. That evening she wrote to Mary's niece in Baltimore, Mary Williams Harrison, describing the situation:

> You cannot imagine how very, very sad it is here, dear Mary . . . . The Drs. say there is great pressure on the brain—he has been very incoherent, but conscious most of the time until within the last day or two. It was so pathetic, his semi-consciousness of his condition. Mrs. C. is utterly broken down with anxiety, & watching night & day . . . .
>
>    David is very kind, but owing to his deafness cannot help much in the sick room. The Gen. lies in a sort of stupor, from which he rouses once in awhile—we cannot understand what he says when he tries to speak. I thought this afternoon he cd not live an hour—but he now, at 8 P.M., lies very quietly. Mrs. C., David & I are here in the dining room—Mrs. C. so white & worn it wd make yr heart ache to see her. Her patience, tenderness, strength are wonderful—[35]

Caroline Perkins had assessed the situation well. James Chesnut died on February 1, and was buried in the family cemetery at Knight's Hill, near Camden. But there was little time for Mary to grieve now for her husband of forty-five years, because her mother grew worse. Caroline Perkins and other friends continued to come daily. Mary's niece Kate Williams Kirkpatrick, now living in Charleston, came and brought a servant to help. And Mary's aunt, Charlotte Boykin Taylor, who had left Sarsfield after Christmas to act as tutor to a local family, returned to stay as long as she might be useful. On February 6, five days after James's death, Charlotte wrote to Miller about his grandmother:

> To be plain with you, I consider her very ill . . . . From the time it was known that Mr. Chesnut could not live—the dear old lady just gave up. She has such vitality however that I can't help hoping she may yet rally. Your Auntie has been suffering very much from difficulty of breathing—and that horrid cough of hers—which will not let her lie down—is very nervous as you may know—but I hope will be better in a few days . . . . I fear your Auntie will be left very

badly off—but if she can keep this house—and recover a little she has energy enough to make a living for herself & give a home to her Mother.[36]

Three days after this letter was written, Mary Boykin Miller died. Not many days later, her daughter opened her daybook and carefully wrote one phrase: "February 1885—the black year of my life."[37]

The ordeal of the previous two months had taken its toll on Mary. The day before her mother's death, David Williams had written to his brother Miller that "Auntie is in a very nervous condition & I fear this last trouble so close on the other will have most injurious effects upon her." But now, grief notwithstanding, General Chesnut's affairs must be put in order. The will in force at the time of his death had been written fifteen years before, in 1870.[38] An unusual feature of the will (unusual, at least, in nineteenth-century South Carolina), and one which bore witness to the confidence he had in her business acumen, was that James appointed Mary sole executrix, naming one of her cousins to assist her. Copied in his own hand, the will was simple and eloquent. It began thus:

> In consideration of the love and devotion which my wife, Mary B. Chesnut and myself have mutually borne to each other, during our married life, I give, devise and bequeathe to her and her heirs forever all my estate, both real and personal, wheresoever being and lying—with a request, that she will give to the male representatives of my father, James Chesnut, and to such of them as she may deem most worthy all the portraits of General Washington by Stuart, and those of my Grand-father, my father and my mother by the same artist, to them and their heirs for ever, and other heir-looms which ought to descend to my father's family.[39]

James's actual bequest to Mary was very small, since under the provisions of his father's will, the Chesnut lands were not his to give.

Thus Mary retained only Sarsfield. Furthermore, James had, in his nephew David's words, "left nothing but debts . . . between 35 & 40 thousand dollars in debt to the estate & the judgments against him will cover 4 times the property he owned."[40] Before she could possibly have recovered from the shock of the deaths of her mother and husband, Mary found herself embroiled with law-yers and financial entanglements. In March, to relieve her outrage at what seemed to her to be ghoulish proceedings, she wrote to an old friend, one to whom she could speak plainly—Varina Davis. Her letter to Varina (it has apparently not survived) must have railed against old Colonel Chesnut's will, which she could well consider the cause of all her financial woes, for Varina Davis' reply minced no words on the subject. Varina had herself been through the harrowing ordeal of breaking her brother-in-law's will, which had failed to give Jefferson Davis title to his plantation, Brierfield. The Davises had taken the case to the Supreme Court in 1878, after four years of litigation in lower courts, and had finally won title:

> It is a shame that a cranky old creature can by the law, with his will control, after he has been mouldering in dust so long, the destinies of his descendents, who have the same right that he had, to "liberty and the pursuit of happiness". The miseries that old men entail by their unbridled wills would be understood by mankind if the sex were reversed and women did it, the world would not hold the tirades that men would utter to condemn, or the books full of stat-utes which they would enact against us.[41]

By June, matters had not improved, but Mary had at least found out the full extent of her plight, and once she was able to assess her situation, she began to recover some of her old spirit. And yet, harsh blows continued to fall. Her "sweet Williams," her nieces and nephews, were now all the family left to her. All but David lived too far for her to see them. But from Baltimore, she heard that spring of the suicide of Mary Williams' husband Thomas Bullitt Harrison.[42] And from Kentucky, she also heard that Miller had severe financial problems (he had probably lost his job). On June 21, she wrote to Miller's wife Jane, trying by putting it all on paper to come to grips with what seemed to her to be the rapid disintegration of a family:

> I have just read over the 6 sheets of a long letter I got up this morning to write to you. *But* sober second thought forbids me to send it—I have just been stopped too to find *Serenola* the beautiful

little calf. Your letter was a bitter disappointment to me—I actually thought Miller that I love so well—settled—and prosperous. apparently that is not to be, for any of us. Still Miller is young and strong and catches on his feet throw him where you will—so I will hope for the best. This has been a year of bitter experiences. From December to February what a life for me—and then the dreadful end of it all—then the blow to my pride and affection—My poor husband hardly in the ground when these insolent—insulting [one illegible word] placed in stall over his fathers affairs & his— through Henry Nelson—that took away all hope from me awhile—Oh the bitter mortification of it.[43] the stinging pain! What was to become of me?—then as I grew hardened to this cruel world again. Mary's awful disaster—and then I gave it up—one by one the things my husband thought he left me have been taken away from my by these Camden lawyers—by a cruel spirit of a pen— The Insurance money then my dower lands—as soon as I showed them where they were—*legally* they seized them for a *bad* debt of Old Mr C to Dr Deas. So I am stripped naked—but the hundred a year for the negro house rents—and what I can make by the Jerseys—about twelve dollars a month—by strict attention to my dairy. You tell me of your troubles and I feel emboldened to weep and wail—still I can laugh & gird at the world as of Yore.[44]

Mary's income since James's death was a source of astonishment to her. She mentioned it in almost every letter, stating the total over and over again as if to make herself believe it. And well she might be astonished. Now, in a whole year, her income would almost precisely equal the cost of either of the capes of Alençon lace she had casually bought in 1859 when James was a senator in Washington. Thus her dairy enterprise, which had grown from the small butter-and-egg business she had run with the help of her maid Molly just after the war, and which had for twenty years provided additional money for "extras," now became crucial. The dairy business required a great deal of time. A letter to Jane (apparently Miller assisted Mary with legal aspects of the business) reveals the extent to which Mary was involved with the care and rearing of her cattle:

I am glad to hear through Miss Sally Chesnut who was here to day that you are with Miller. We are so scattered and tossed about.

My sister Sally speaks of sending her daughter Mary to stay with me awhile.

This however is a business letter—Do get Miller to send me the certificate of Serenola's register. It is a paper he has to sign—May be I have miscalled it—Also—a calf was dropped by Olly on the 14th July and I want her registered too—as it adds to to the value of this herd to be registered. Serenola is a perfect beauty.

Rex died after a few days fever—he was very fat—& had grown tremendously altogether was pronounced the handsomest animal ever seen—Peter—Moses—and myself did all we could to save him. Now Olly's calf—being the last of Rex's progeny—(may be) I want this calf—of the 14th July—named—Renée—Do I make it plain—Renée—

Virginia Dare has fever & is very ill in point of fact she is under the oak tree at my back door—I dare say she will die too.

About these animals not being insured—I blame myself hard and heavy—When I found it was not done for me as I begged so to have it—I ought to have taken matters in my own hands and written to friends in Columbia or Baltimore—& had it done—I am too poor now to stand on trifles—My income minus the cattle being one hundred and ten dollars—the loss to me has been heavy indeed—besides Rex was such a splendid creature.[45]

And to Miller the next day, she wrote: "Virginia Dare is alive yet and I hope she may not die. but she is a sick cow still. Nettles thinks the Bull Rex was poisoned because he was such a terror to the people crossing the field. I had such an intimation before—but I do not believe it." Later in the letter, she indicated her sense of helplessness in the face of legal proceedings following her husband's death: "I am awfully tempted to sell out to some rich Yankee for cash—and run away—but I am too old—and too ill . . . . I am awfully unlucky every thing I try to do—every letter I write, or note—makes things worse some times I determine to sit down & let it all go—but one acts according to one's nature and not according to one's resolutions . . . . I am extremely anxious to sell my cattle all but three or four cows. Some how I fail now to accomplish any thing—Some time I hope it will all come right. It will take very little for *me* to live on—This year we have lived as before—but that must all be over—and we must economise bitterly. I know you want to hear so I am talking of myself."[46]

Her financial straits in 1885 led Mary to think of her writing. The ten dollars she had earned the previous year for one newspaper sketch would almost equal her monthly income now. Accordingly, she tried to find time to write. But now, over and above the need for money, she felt her first duty was to organize her husband's papers with an eye toward publication. In December, 1884, just after James Chesnut became ill, she had written to William Henry Trescot asking that he help her with the project, and he had responded by suggesting that her *own* recollections of the war years would be far more interesting than those of "a dozen generals." Immediately following her husband's death, she had mentioned the project to Varina Davis, and Mrs. Davis responded in the same vein: "It has occurred to me that you might, if you get the *right* man, get your Husbands papers arranged and condensed so as to make a book which would bring you something, but I think your diaries would sell better than any Confederate history of a grave character. Between us no one is so tired of Confederate history as the Confederates—they do not want to tell the truth or to hear it."[47]

Trescot and Varina Davis were, of course, quite right. But Mary had first conceived the idea of a biography of her husband in the late 1870s, and now it seemed a fitting memorial to him. Her own Civil War journal would have to wait at least until his papers were organized. In July, 1885, she wrote to Edward McCrady, the state's most prominent historian, and asked him to help. McCrady replied that he could not spare the time and suggested Trescot. Finally, in August, Trescot agreed to arrange the general's papers, and it seems likely that he did come to assist Mary in the task. Sometime during this period, Mary went back over the biographical sketch she had written of her husband in 1877 or 1878, and revised it slightly, but though she made some hasty notes for an expanded biography, she apparently did not actually begin to write one.[48]

In the meantime, Mary was concerned about her own revised journal. In mid-July, she went to Columbia to visit Isabella Martin and Mary Preston Darby, both of whom returned with her to

Camden about the first of August for a brief visit.[49] It was very probably during this visit that Mary Boykin Chesnut asked Isabella to take the journals, in the event of her death, and see to their publication.

Because she had been able to sell one excerpt from the journal in 1884, Mary now determined to prepare another segment for separate publication. This time, instead of a single anecdote, she chose a longer and very complicated portion of the journal—the two-week period from January 1 to January 14, 1864. During this two-week period, the military climate in the Confederacy had been bleak. The losses at Gettysburg and Vicksburg the preceding summer had deeply discouraged the South. In Richmond, despair was almost palpable. To defy that despair, Richmond ladies had devised elaborate social functions designed to entertain the elite of the Confederacy, government officials as well as military officers of high rank. Two elegant charade parties were held, and Mary Boykin Chesnut had been intimately involved in the planning and preparation of them. Now she saw in this two-week segment of her revised journal an excellent picture of the chaos of the period, with its giddy entertainments juxtaposed on a society almost exhausted by the grief and destruction of a hopeless war.

Mrs. Chesnut made at least three complete drafts of this segment, entitling the last one "The Bright Side of Richmond. Winter of 1864—Scraps from a diary."[50] Though "The Bright Side of Richmond" does not include any new material and could therefore be considered merely an excerpt from the journal, it also possesses in this form a structural unity of its own. The piece uses historical events to suggest the sense in which the war at this point in time was, for the South, a sombre charade.

In some respects even the last draft of "The Bright Side of Richmond" is not a polished work; there are many places where the prose is confusing, where it is unclear who is speaking or just where a bit of dialogue begins and ends. But there is abundant evidence that Mary Boykin Chesnut revised her piece with an excellent sense of its unity and theme. This can most clearly be illustrated by the care with which she searched for an ending. In the interim pencil draft of the revised journal, she wrote a note to herself to copy out in full the rhymed program for the concluding evening of charades, and she ends the last draft of the revised journal with this rhymed program. In the three drafts of "Bright Side," however, she experimented with various alternative endings, all of which convey some sense of the incongruity of playing charades in the middle of a war. First she tried closing with a picture of General John Bell Hood blushing with embarrassment as he realized that his heroism at Chickamauga was being praised in rhyme. In the next revision, she ended the piece on a sarcastic note; a Confederate belle, Hetty Cary, was being courted by General J. E. B. Stuart, and her cousin Conny remarked, "she likes stars—and all that." Mrs. Chesnut finally decided to conclude with irony, and from the rhymed charade program she extracted these verses: "One only syllable I am. By way of Interlude—*A dram.*" By closing "The Bright Side of Richmond" with this rhyme taken from the interlude charade, she finally focuses both on the sense in which the entire two-week period is an interlude, and on the insignificance of each individual—a mere dram—in the midst of the struggle of the Confederacy for its very life.

"The Bright Side of Richmond" is probably the last piece of writing Mary Boykin Chesnut ever did, though she may have worked further on her revised journal occasionally. Perhaps her health was too uncertain for her to keep up with her household duties and the care of her cattle and still have enough energy to write. Perhaps she devoted what little writing time she could spare to going over her husband's papers. Now she no longer had James and her mother to interrupt her constantly; perhaps she simply found that she could take no pleasure in writing, since it no longer served as a very private means of removing herself from her family when she found them wearisome.

In any case, the last year of her life, though a terribly diminished one in many respects, had happy moments. Her recently widowed niece Mary came in the fall with her three children for a long visit, and at Christmas Miller wrote with muted hope for the future:

> We send you a Christmas letter to wish you all the good things that can come with the event—& wish we could send you a nice Christmas present but it is a hard thing to say that we are not able

to do so this Christmas—Maybe next time it comes around the times will have changed & we will be able not only to send you the present but to help as need so much now. It makes me feel badly dear Aunty to think how much you have done for us all & how little we are able to return it now. The prospects are brighter for the future however & let us hope the cry with all of us wont abide for-ever "hard times." [51]

With the new year came news which elated Mary. David was to be married in July to Ellen Manning, daughter of John Manning, the former governor and friend whose elaborate and persistent at-tentions to Mary had so annoyed her husband in 1861. Ellen and David had courted for almost four years, and Mary liked the bride-to-be immensely. In a letter to Jane in February, 1886, she wrote as if Ellen were already a member of the family, and spoke of the pleasure the whole family, albeit scattered, gave to her: "Ellen asked David to show her *all* the letters of this family. She wanted to see—And really it is a blessing—as one after another come from the padre [Kate William's husband, David] down—what splendid letters the family write."

But as she continued, Mary revealed how much she missed her mother and James. The letter was written the day after the anni-versary of James's death, a particularly difficult time:

> This all came well for the old Aunty—I have been so ill—and am still so feeble. And these awful anniversaries take the little life out of me that is left—Last night Mothers clock sounded every hour—and when I dozed—it was "Yes Master! I am coming Sir"—as I heard Moze tearing thru the passage—& Mr Chesnuts impatient calls. Strange to say—at first Mother was here most—now she seems to have gone to her rest in Heaven—I never see or hear her—But Mr Chesnut—I have to sit with my back to the door not to see him come in. It is all bodily weakness I know.

It was David and Ellen who cheered Mary at such times, charm-ing her with stories, and with their sheer youth and hopefulness. [52]

David and Ellen's wedding on July 14 marked an ending, of sorts, and finally a satisfactory, happy ending. David was the last of Kate's children to marry, the child Mary had spent more time with than any other, the one child who chose to live in Camden with his "dear Aunty." She expressed her pleasure in him to Virginia Clay, a friend from the Washington days now living in Alabama: "My nephew who is the son of the nephew of Mr C who inherited his land—(Sarsfield is mine) lives with me—or I live with him—for I furnish only house & gear—he has to feed us—pay insurance taxes &c &c—He is just married—David R Williams jr his name—His wife a daughter of Ex Gov John L. Manning—as splendidly handsome & clever as he is—he is nearly deaf—the only draw back." In the same letter Mary complained of her bad heart (her angina pectoris was now severe), but her mood was a happy one: "old Grey beards—young delight to talk to the old woman yet—My home—Sarsfield—such a handsome brick house—A splendid library. No end of old china glass—silver—Stuarts portraits &c &c—50 acres—4 Jersey cows—and an income of $140. for Negro house rent—dont mistake—one hundred & forty dollars! I would not have known your picture I am far more changed than that however."[53]

Two months later, on November 22, 1886, Mary Boykin Chesnut died. For twenty years she had mentioned imminent death as likely, but when it came, it surprised her. David's new wife Ellen was sick with a cold that week, and Aunt Charlotte had come for a weekend visit, taking time off from her tutoring job.[54] As Charlotte wrote several days later to Miller, she had found Mary quite as well as usual:

> We had our chat that evening—each telling all that had occurred since our last seeing each other. On Friday morning she complained a little saying she feared the swelling was coming back—wrote to Dr. Talley[55] in Columbia describing her symptoms and asking him to send by Ex. the remedy he had used last summer to reduce the swelling—but saying if she did not feel better the next week—would go over to see him again. She seemed cheerful and talking pleasantly all day Saturday until about 6 O'Clock—when she complained of being cold.

Charlotte made up the fire, but Mary's chills persisted, and she finally went to bed. Charlotte's letter continues:

> she had an uncomfortable night—next day—(Sunday) quite a fever—but told me not to be anxious it would pass off and she

would feel the next morning as well as ever—slept the whole day—only rousing to speak occassionally. About 9 O'Clock Sunday night—she sprang up in bed saying she could not breath—and from that time until about 9 O'Clock Monday morning her sufferings were intense—from heart and right lung—she thought she was going to have pneumonia. About day light—I sent for the Doctor—who came immediately—gave her a third of a grain of morphine to quiet the pain—telling me to repeat the dose in half an hour if she was not relieved. At the expiration of that time she seemed quiet and dosing so I did not disturb her. About 9 O'Clock she aroused and[56]

The rest of the letter is missing. It was obviously passed from family member to family member, for in the margin of the page which survives, someone wrote, "Please return this letter. Miller wanted you to see it—David says it was bitterly cold & raining when she was buried."

The will had been written in January. It was simple and straightforward—she had very little to leave. Mary wrote it on the same paper she had used for the drafts of her novels; having copied out so many legal documents connected with her husband's law practice over the years, she knew the correct form to use:

> I Mary B Chesnut widow of the late James Chesnut of the State and county aforesaid, do make and ordain this to be my last Will and Testament.
> 1. I devise, and bequeath my nephew David R Williams Jr son of my late sister Catherine Williams, my whole Estate, both real and personal, not hereinafter otherwise disposed of.
> 2. I give and bequeath to My niece Serena Chesnut Williams, daughter of S. Miller Williams, my diamond ring, and my two Jersey cows. Olly and Flora and what issue they may have unsold at the time of my death. Also a note that I hold of her father's. (S. Miller Williams) for the sum of three hundred and thirty dollars, interest from date & The furniture called "the Gov Miller furniture"—consisting of two round mirrors—two mohair sofas—eight mohair chairs—and a gilt marble topped centre table—belongs now to S. Miller Williams. I gave it to him—and he left it at this my house—called Sarsfield.
> I desire to be buried at Knights Hill—by my husbands side—and

I desire a marble slab placed over me similar to that over the mortal remains of my husband—the late James Chesnut.

I desire that Moses Nelson should have a house free of rent during his life time—and that he may choose among those that I now own—on Factory Lane—[57]

Three days after David and Ellen's marriage, Mary had added a codicil to her will, specifying that though Sarsfield should be David's, he was to hold it in trust "to and for the use and behoof of his wife Ellen for and during the term of her natural life" and, in the event of her death, in trust for her children.[58] Testifying to the love Mary Boykin Chesnut held for Ellen, the newest addition to her family, the codicil also indicated how shaken the older woman had been by the last two years of her life. Though he had every intention of leaving Mary comfortable, James had instead left her almost nothing. Now she, in turn, had almost nothing to leave, but she could do as much as possible to make sure the woman who followed after her in Sarsfield would be assured of at least one small measure of independence and security, two qualities that Mary had often found lacking in her own life, and which she had struggled almost daily, in the last twenty-five years, to achieve.

Mary Boykin Chesnut's life was not an unusually long one. She died at sixty-three. But by any standards, hers was a life rich with varied experiences fully savored, a life lived with vigor and determination by a woman of unusual will, intelligence, and imagination. In her later years, she had become something of a character—even an eccentric—to the townspeople who had never understood her. Stories were told and chuckled over about the old lady, always dressed in black with "gaiter shoes and a little baby lace cap." Camden residents remembered only glimpses of her, gardening in a large shade hat and a pair of her husband's pants, or sitting in her library on many occasions, talking with great animation through the open window to her friend Caroline Perkins who would drive into the yard, and converse with her, never descending from her carriage.[59]

To her "sweet Williams," scattered so widely about, Aunty remained a fond memory, and the stories told about her sharp intelligence and her independence of spirit grew over the years. Serena Williams, Miller and Jane's first child to whom Mary had left her diamond Maltese cross, had been only six when Mary died; she remembered nothing of her aunt except being thoroughly spoiled by her: "I would have to be spanked when I had been visiting her." When Serena later asked one of her Pettigrew aunts to describe Aunty Chesnut, she was rewarded with Annie Pettigrew's memories of arriving in Camden for Serena's christening in March, 1879. "Well she was a remarkable old lady," said Miss Pettigrew. "When she came to meet us when we arrived, it wasn't raining, but she had on an old western mackintosh and a funny old hat. I just thought she looked like an old market woman." Somewhat dismayed, the Pettigrew relatives accepted Mary's invitation to dine at Sarsfield that night. After all, "she was who she was," and deserving of respect, so they arrived promptly. "Your Auntie sat in the hall—she had on a velvet gown, and a fan. She looked like a grand dame, and she was one. We had the most beautiful dinner, beautifully served; everything was perfect." In utter contrast to her attire of the afternoon, Mary Boykin Chesnut sat regal in her antebellum dinner dress and presided over the conversation with the same sharp tongue and overriding charm which had entranced Richmond society nearly twenty years before. The Pettigrew ladies emerged from the experience impressed, and "terribly in awe of Mrs. Chesnut."[60] Miller's son David remembered in mid-twentieth century a story his father had told about his ride from Columbia to Flat Rock in 1865. Mary Boykin Chesnut had included the incident in her wartime journals, and in her memoir of her sister, "We called her Kitty."[61] In Mary's accounts, Miller had, at the age of eleven, determined to act as guide for an elderly party of refugees who were bewildered and frightened at Sherman's advance. By the time Miller, himself elderly, had related the tale to his children, the ride to Flat Rock had ceased to be simply an escape from Sherman, and had become instead the daring rescue of a million dollars in gold. As the generals and treasury agents were debating how the gold might be moved without capture by the northern army, or by stragglers and bushwhackers, Aunty Chesnut spoke up: "Now you are all wrong, let me tell you. You go and get a lot of young negroes, nobody wants to buy young negroes anymore, and you go and get a lot of horses and cover their backs with tar or something and put sticks and pebbles in there and then put another piece of canvas over it so it looks like it has a sore back. Nobody wants to buy those horses." And so, disguised as a poor boy trying to sell a group of sore-backed horses, Miller made the trip to Flat Rock, and the gold was saved; pure legend—probably carved from assorted conversations Miller heard as a child—but indicative of the way in which Aunty Chesnut was remembered by her family.

To the rest of the world, Mary Boykin Chesnut was all but forgotten. She had asked Isabella Martin to oversee the publication of her journal, but for almost twenty years, the journal remained unknown. Finally, in 1904 when a New York journalist and writer, Myrta Lockett Avary, stumbled quite by accident upon the existence of the journal and persuaded Miss Martin to publish it, Mary Boykin Chesnut, once again, became known and admired. For no matter how extensively its publishers, aided by Mrs. Avary and Miss Martin, cut and edited the revised journal, the author's clear insights, her close observation and understanding of human nature, and above all her wit and intelligence showed through.

The experience of reading *A Diary From Dixie* brought to a few of her friends vivid memories of the Mary Boykin Chesnut they had known. One old friend wrote to Miss Martin to say the book had "made me just desperately homesick for her." "She used to talk often and often of 'the human document,'" wrote Mrs. L. S. W. Perkins. "Now *that* is what *she* was, and I don't believe you can give us too much of her." Mrs. Perkins had been surprised by the immediacy of the journal, by the way day-to-day events often seemed in it to obscure the war as a whole. "In her later years of looking back on that time she took a larger view,—large as the view was which she always took. I think she seemed to see the whole thing [the Civil War] in a great big image, and almost as if creating itself without the volition of man." Mrs. Perkins closed her letter with an assessment of Mrs. Chesnut which testified to how well she had known her friend. "There surely was never anyone like her,—physically and intellectually so perfectly fearless,—

fearless of facts and fearless of the truth,—never afraid where it would lead her or land her. We have no proof of immortality, but . . . who can think of that clever, quick mind not going on somehow, somewhere . . . how can one think that she would not welcome us when she saw us coming?"[62]

In 1905, the same year *A Diary From Dixie* was first published, a much lesser memoir by Louisa Wigfall Wright appeared, written at almost the same time *A Diary* was being edited. As a young girl, Louisa had visited Mrs. Chesnut frequently in Richmond, and in her book, *A Southern Girl in '61*, she characterized Mary thus: "Mrs. Chesnut was one of the most brilliant women of her time and as warm-hearted as clever."[63] Mary would have been immensely pleased with the assessment; Louisa was remembering her in 1861, in her glory, when her very presence called forth the great men and women of her world, when life was utterly exciting and hope was high. But Mary Boykin Chesnut's greatest triumphs were yet to come. For it was the last twenty years of her life that required of her real endurance, consummate strength of will, absolute honesty. Through 1865 she was a restless, questing woman, gathering together the materials and tools with which to build a life, but she was a woman unable to find peace within herself. After 1865 she watched her options disappear one by one, watched with regret, but without despair. And in her last years, with her resources so greatly diminished, she put every experience and every ability she possessed to productive use, holding together a family and, through her writing, giving life to an entire era.

# Notes

QUOTATIONS FROM LETTERS, diaries and other nineteenth-century holograph manuscripts are transcribed exactly, and readers should make allowance for the vagaries that creep into any handwritten documents. A glance at the sample journal pages among the illustrations will give readers an idea of the eccentricities of Mary Boykin Chesnut's hand. To adapt the hand to the printed page, superscript letters have been lowered and underlined words have been italicized. Inadvertent repetitions (when, for example, a "the" at the end of one line is repeated at the beginning of the next) have been silently omitted. Bracketed insertions are mine.

ONE

1 Mary Boykin Chesnut's original Civil War journal, dated May 18, 1861, South Caroliniana Library, University of South Carolina, Columbia, hereinafter cited as "Journal," followed by date of entry. Mary Boykin Chesnut will hereinafter be cited as MBC. A full transcript of the surviving portions of her original Civil War journal, edited by Elisabeth Muhlenfeld and Thomas E. Dasher, is available at South Caroliniana Library, the Library of Congress, and Yale University Library.

2 *Ibid.*

3 MBC's revised Civil War journal, written between 1881 and 1884 (see Chap. Eight herein), entry dated December 12, 1864, South Caroliniana Library, University of South Carolina, Columbia, hereinafter cited as "revised journal," followed by date of entry.

4 Isabella Donaldson Martin, June 21, 1839–March 4, 1913, was the daughter of the Reverend William Martin and Margaret Maxwell. Information on Miss Martin is scant. Her obituary in the Columbia *State*, March 6, 1913, p. 16, provides the best biographical sketch about her. Archie Vernon Huff's *Tried by Fire: Washington Street United Methodist Church, Columbia, S.C.* (Columbia: R. L. Bryan, 1975) offers isolated anecdotes about her church activities as an elderly woman. The Martin Papers in the South Caroliniana Library contain little information about Isabella. See affidavit, July 14, 1940, in Myrta Lockett Avary Papers, Atlanta Historical Society. Most of the information I have provided about the first publication of MBC's revised Civil War journal has been drawn from the Avary Papers, which include various letters and copies of letters to and from Miss Martin, Mrs. Avary, and several editors at D. Appleton and Company, publishers of the first edition of *A Diary From Dixie.*

5 Isabella Martin to Mrs. Avary, October 22, 1904, in Avary Papers. The letter states that Miss Martin had had the journals for "over ten years."

6 Isabella Martin to Francis W. Dawson, July 23, 1887, in Dawson Papers, Duke University Library, Durham, N.C. The letter states, "There is so much however that is personal in the journal that I could not allow it to go into any one's hands but my own and it will be entirely re-written." Miss Martin had apparently not yet taken possession of the journals when she wrote to Dawson, the year after MBC's death, but had almost certainly read many parts of them on her visits to Camden. Miss Martin told Mrs. Avary she was "on the eve" of burning the journals, "in despair at publishers' indifference," when Mrs. Avary "found" them. Affidavit, July 14, 1940, in Avary Papers.

7 [Isabella D. Martin], "Sketch of Mrs. [Louisa S.] McCord, by Miss I. D. Martin" in [Louisa McCord Smythe (comp.)], *For Old Lang Syne: Collected for My Children* (Columbia, S.C.: [Lucas and Richardson], 1900), 13–16; Mrs. Thomas Taylor *et al.* (eds.), *South Carolina Women in the Confederacy* (Columbia: State Co., 1903); Mrs. Avary, the daughter of Howard Alexander Lockett and Augusta Harper, wrote *A Viriginia Girl in the Civil War* (New York: D. Appleton, 1903).

8 Five long excerpts from the book appeared in *Saturday Evening Post* on January 28, February 4, 11, 18, 25, 1905. *A Diary From Dixie, as Written by Mary Boykin Chesnut, wife of James Chesnut, Jr., United States Senator from South Carolina, 1859–1861, and afterward an Aide to Jefferson Davis and a Brigadier-General in the Confederate Army*, ed. Isabella D. Martin and Myrta Lockett Avary (New York: D. Appleton, 1905; London: Heinemann, 1905).

9 M. M. Kirkman to Isabella Martin, March 28, 1905, in Williams-Chesnut-Manning Collection, South Caroliniana Library, hereinafter cited as W-C-M Collection.

10 Ben Ames Williams, *House Divided* (Boston: Houghton Mifflin, 1947); *A Diary From Dixie*, Ben Ames Williams, ed. (Boston: Houghton Mifflin, 1949).

11 Alfred Hoyt Bill, "The Journal of the Confederacy," *Saturday Review*, December 31, 1949, p. 19.

12 Edmund Wilson, *Patriotic Gore: Studies in the Literature of the American Civil War* (New York: Oxford University Press, 1962), 279, 280.

13 C. Vann Woodward, ed. *Mary Chesnut's Civil War* (New Haven, Conn.: Yale University Press, 1981).

14 Quoted in Bell Irvin Wiley, *Confederate Women* (Westport, Conn.: Greenwood Press, 1975), 3.

15 MBC to Varina Davis, June 18, 1883, in Museum of the Confederacy, Richmond. This letter has been included in Allie Patricia Wall, "The Letters of Mary Boykin Chesnut" (Master's thesis, University of South Carolina, 1977), 83. Wall's thesis contains nearly two dozen MBC letters and appropriate annotations. Since Wall's work was completed, many more letters by MBC have been found in private collections. Transcripts of all letters and manuscript material quoted herein are my own.

16 Prior to the publication of a sketch by Margaretta P. Childs in Edward T. Jones *et al.* (eds.), *Notable American Women: 1607–1950* (Cambridge, Mass.: Harvard University Press, 1971), 327–30, the most extensive biographical sketch of Chesnut was in Isabella Martin's introduction to the 1905 edition. Subsequent to

Mrs. Child's pioneering article, Bell I. Wiley included a long chapter on MBC in *Confederate Women*. Both Childs and Wiley used the collection of Chesnut manuscripts at the South Caroliniana Library, but both focused on the Martin-Avary and the Williams editions of *A Diary From Dixie* and have little to say about MBC's life exclusive of 1861–1865.

TWO

1 The only source of information about Mary Boykin Miller Chesnut's birthplace is a statement in her unpublished autobiographical novel "Two Years—or The Way We Lived Then," hereinafter cited as "Two Years." Quotations from "Two Years" will be taken from the edited text of the novel which comprises Part III of Elisabeth S. Muhlenfeld, "Mary Boykin Chesnut: The Writer and Her Work" (Ph.D. dissertation, University of South Carolina, 1978); see p. 118 of edited text. Mount Pleasant is sometimes called Pleasant Hill. Statesburg (early nineteenth-century spelling) is today called Stateburg.

2 Published sources give Stephen Decatur Miller's father's name as William. However, other documents prove that his name was Charles. The error apparently arose from a missing comma in a letter from Stephen Decatur Miller to his daughter Mary, dated White Sulphur, July 23, 1835, Chesnut Family Papers, State Historical Society of Wisconsin; a MS copy of the letter in MBC's hand is in the W-C-M Collection. One brother, Charles, served as state senator from Claremont prior to Stephen Decatur Miller's election in 1822. Another, John L. Miller, was a doctor. Some sources claim that Stephen's father died when Stephen was still a boy, and that Miller sold his modest inheritance of three slaves to attend college. *A Brief Memoir of Stephen Decatur Miller, Whilom Governor of South Carolina, and United States Senator from the Same State* (no author, publisher, or date; probably published in the 1870s) describes a family scene around the dinner table in which Stephen's father said, "'wife, I can only send one of these boys to college, which shall it be?' and his mother replied 'Let it be Stephen.'"

3 Little biographical information about Stephen Decatur Miller is available. Elias Dick Miller seems to have been born in 1815 because according to John Belton O'Neall, *Biographical Sketches of the Bench and Bar of South Carolina* (Charleston: S. G. Courtenay, 1859), II, 413, he died in 1832, and in a manuscript fragment of six pages in the W-C-M Collection, MBC says he was seventeen when he died. Of the published biographical sketches of Miller, O'Neall's is probably the most accurate. O'Neall had access to Miller's letter of 1835 (see note 2 above), which MBC must have lent to him, and we may therefore assume that she was in correspondence with O'Neall about the sketch and probably gave him much data not available in other sources. A brief sketch of Miller in Thomas J. Kirkland and Robert M. Kennedy, *Historic Camden*, (Columbia, S.C.: State Co., 1926), II, 107–13, is useful because it quotes from several of Miller's most important speeches.

4 Elizabeth H. Jervey (ed.), "Marriage and Death Notices from the *City Gazette* of Charleston, S.C.," *South Carolina Historical and Genealogical Magazine*, XLVI (1945), 15.

5 Here and for many other specific dates used in this biography, I am indebted to Martha Williams Daniels, great-great-granddaughter of Stephen Decatur Miller, who graciously made available unpublished genealogical tables compiled for

the Williams family. Sources for these tables vary but include such materials as family Bibles not available to me. Burwell Boykin's service in the Revolution is mentioned in Kirkland and Kennedy, *Historic Camden* (1905), I, 348.

6 Died October 7, 1838, daughter of William Whitaker and Catherine Wiggins. Mary Whitaker was the sister of Elizabeth Whitaker, first wife of Burwell Boykin, by whom he had three children.

7 MS memoir about Catherine Miller Williams, MBC's sister, written in 1876, pp. 3–6, in W-C-M collection. The memoir will be referred to as "We called her Kitty." MBC's statement that her grandmother died when she was eight is incorrect. Mary Whitaker Boykin's tombstone records her date of death as October 7, 1838; her granddaughter would have been fifteen at the time.

8 *Ibid.*, 5; Revised journal, undated narrative covering August, 1862–mid-September, 1863.

9 MS fragment of six pages dealing with Elias Dick Miller and other members of her family, written July, 1876, now in W-C-M Collection.

10 "We called her Kitty," 1–2, 27. Governor David Rogerson Williams (1776–1830) was the grandfather of David Rogerson Williams (October 3, 1822–November 24, 1907), husband of MBC's sister Kate. See Kirkland and Kennedy, *Historic Camden*, II, 108–12. For a discussion of the nullification movement in South Carolina, see William W. Freehling, *Prelude to Civil War: The Nullification Controversy in South Carolina, 1816–1836* (New York: Harper & Row, 1966). A brief discussion of the period may be found in David Duncan Wallace, *South Carolina: A Short History, 1520–1948* (Chapel Hill: University of North Carolina Press, 1951), 383–401.

11 Deming & Bulkley to S. D. Miller Esqr., Charleston, April 26, 1829, in Chesnut Family Papers, State Historical Society of Wisconsin; Revised journal, May 8, 1864; S. C. W. Faust to Miss Mary Miller, undated letter in Chesnut Family papers.

12 Kirkland and Kennedy, *Historic Camden*, II, 110, 111. Exact dates of birth are known only for MBC and her sister Catherine (May 24, 1827). Catherine's name is spelled *Katherine* in most published sources and in many family records. However, MBC spelled the name with a *C* in "We called her Kitty" and again in her last will (see p. 219 herein).

13 Kirkland and Kennedy, *Historic Camden*, II, 272.

14 "Two Years," 78–79 of edited text.

15 *Ibid.*, 79–80.

16 W-C-M Collection, transcribed in Wall, "Letters of MBC," 1.

17 Stephen Decatur Miller to "My dear Mary," April 26, [1883], in W-C-M Collection.

18 MS fragment dealing with E. D. Miller.

19 Series of MS fragments in W-C-M Collection written by MBC in reply to a series entitled "Old Times in Camden" by William M. Shannon which appeared in the Kershaw *Gazette* from April to July, 1876. These MSS represent incomplete versions of several drafts and bear various page numbers. One of the drafts is entitled "Let *Sleeping dogs* lie." These MSS are discussed on pp. 163–66 herein, and will hereinafter be referred to as "Let sleeping dogs lie."

20 Kirkland and Kennedy, *Historic Camden*, II, 26.

21 John Potts to Stephen Decatur Miller, "Cedar Shoals, Miss," November 3, 1833, in the W-C-M collection, discusses Miller's Mississippi lands and gives a description of the plantation before he took over on-the-spot control: "I find the plantation in a very ruinous condition—the negro houses nearly all gone not more than three or four habitable—the screw cotton & the gin house not much better . . . . I think there must have been very bad management on the place either before or since you left it or perhaps both by the land being so much gullied." Between 1833 and 1835, Miller must have made improvements on the place, for in a second letter from Potts to Miller, March 27, 1835, Potts remarked "I have heard that you mad six hundred bags of cotton last year."

22 Ann Marson Talvande, born in Santo Domingo prior to 1800, died November 15, 1850. Buried in St. Patrick's churchyard, Charleston, S.C. See also Harriott Horry Rutledge Ravenel in *Charleston: The Place and the People* (New York: Macmillan, 1906), 365. Steven Decatur Miller was in Virginia in late July, 1835 (note 2 above). Mrs. Miller was in Camden at Christmas of that year, and, since a one-way trip to Mississippi with the family took four or five weeks (see "Two Years," 4), it is unlikely that the family went and returned between August and early December. All published sources, however, state that Miller took his family to Mississippi in 1835. Mary Cox Chesnut to James Chesnut, Jr., December 20, 1835, in W-C-M Collection. James Chesnut, Jr., will hereinafter be cited as JC, Jr.

## THREE

1 "Two Years," 46, 47 of edited text.

2 *Ibid.*, 47–48.

3 *Ibid.*, 49.

4 Katherine Wooten Springs, *The Squires of Springfield* (Charlotte, N.C.: William Loftin, 1965), 62. School receipts from Madame Talvande's, 1828–31, in Kincaid-Anderson Family Papers, South Caroliniana Library. John England (1786–1842), Roman Catholic Bishop of Charleston from 1820, when he arrived from Ireland, until his death. See "Two Years," 49–50, for MBC's description of Bishop England's visits.

5 Chapters 9–12 of "Two Years" provide an excellent description of Madame Talvande's school. Little recent detailed scholarship is available on female education prior to 1840; most discussions of the subject emphasize the dearth of good secondary schools and the curriculum concern for ladylike accomplishments. See "The Contradictions in Ladies' Education" and "The Domestic Ideology and Women's Education" in Sara Delamont and Lorna Duffin (eds.), *The Nineteenth-Century Woman: Her Cultural and Physical World* (New York: Barnes & Noble, 1978), 134–87; see also Nancy Green, "Female Education and School Competition: 1820–1850" in Mary Kelley (ed.), *Woman's Being, Woman's Place: Female Identity and Vocation in American History* (Boston: G. K. Hall & Co., 1979), 127–41; Carl Deglar, *At Odds: Women and the Family in America from the Revolution to the Present* (New York: Oxford University Press, 1980), 307–11. An example of MBC's script appears in a letterbook she kept in the 1870s, in possession of Katharine Herbert of Florence, S.C., photocopy in W-C-M Collection.

6 See "Two Years," 72–73, for descriptions of Maum Jute and Dédé. Some of the characters in "Two Years" are fictional, or are given fictional names, and it is possible that Maum Jute and Dédé are fictional names.

7 Sue Petigru King (1826–75) was the daughter of James Louis Petigru under whom James Chesnut, Jr., read law. Her works include *Busy Moments of an Idle Woman* (1854), *Crimes Where the Law Does not Reach* (1854), *Lily* (1855), *Sylvia's World* (1859), and *Gerald Gray's Wife* (1866). Mary Serena Chesnut Williams (November, 1821–September 13, 1887) was the daughter of JC, Jr.'s oldest sister Esther Serena Chesnut (September 29, 1796–October 29, 1822) and Colonel John Nicholas Williams (July 2, 1797–April 12, 1861), son of Governor David Rogerson Williams. In February, 1840, just two months prior to MBC's wedding, Mary Williams married John Witherspoon, a distant cousin of MBC. The two girls were almost certainly attendants at one another's weddings. Mary was the sister of David Rogerson Williams, who would marry Kate Miller in 1846.

8 Mary may have gotten to know James Chesnut, Jr., in Camden in the summer of 1836. In a letter to Edward Anderson from John McCaa of Camden dated April 13, 1836, McCaa writes, "You will confer a particular favor on me by calling at Madame Talvande's and making the necessary arrangements for Miss Mary Millers leaving town with my friend W. J. Grant Esq.—If Mr. Millers agent (Fraser) will not advance the money, you will please do so on *my acct*," in Kincaid-Anderson Family papers. Thus Mary was apparently brought back to Camden at the end of the spring term in the company of W. J. Grant, who was James's brother-in-law, the husband of his sister Harriet Serena (January 7, 1809–December 2, 1835). Mary's family returned from Mississippi for the summer months. Mary Serena Chesnut Williams to JC, Jr., Sandy Hill, July 26, 1834, in Chesnut Family Papers, Wisconsin. See Chapter I of "Two Years." The degree to which "Two Years" is autobiographical is discussed on pp. 172–78 herein. See also "We called her Kitty," 20, where MBC, speaking of her relationship with JC when she was fifteen, says her courtship had already lasted two years.

9 "We called her Kitty," 6–7.

10 "Two Years," 6 of edited text.

11 "We called her Kitty," 7–8.

12 Greenwood LeFlore (1800–1865) eventually amassed over 15,000 acres of land and 400 slaves, and served in the Mississippi legislature. LeFlore died in 1865, having remained loyal to the Union throughout the Civil War. Mrs. N. D. Deupree, "Greenwood LeFlore," *Publications of the Mississippi Historical Society*, VII (1903), 141–52.

13 "We called her Kitty," 9–10. MBC gives a description of the "double log house" in "Two Years," 29, 30, 32, edited text; also "Two Years," 130, in MS not included in edited text. Mary Williams Harrison Ames Papers, privately owned. For a corroborative account of life on a Mississippi plantation in the 1830s, see Mary J. Welsh, "Recollections of Pioneer Life in Mississippi," *Publications of the Mississippi Historical Society*, IV (1900), 343–56. Miss Welsh, like MBC, was born in 1823 and was brought to what is now Kemper County, Mississippi, in 1834. Her account includes a detailed description of the log homes first built by planters in the Choctaw Nation which accords with MBC's description.

14 "We called her Kitty," 10.

15 In "Two Years" the narrator says she had been absent from Madame Talvande's for six months, but the date of Mary's return to Charleston cannot be
fixed precisely. The trip is described in unedited portion of "Two Years," 29, 30,
32 (see note 13 above).

16 "We called her Kitty," 10.

17 "Two Years," 93–94 of edited text.

18 *Ibid.*, 71.

19 "We called her Kitty," 11; "Two Years," 71–72 of edited text.

20 "We called her Kitty," 11.

21 Mary Cox Chesnut's sisters had married Horace Binney (1780–1875), a renowned Philadelphia lawyer; John Stevens (1749–1838), an engineer, inventor,
and pioneer in transportation, who had been instrumental in the setting up of the
patent laws and procuring the first American railroad act, and was the founder of
the Pennsylvania railroad system; and John Redman Coxe (1773–1864), a Philadelphia physician of national reputation who had studied with Dr. Benjamin
Rush (*DAB*). Letters in the W-C-M Collection dating from the period James was
at Princeton indicate that he frequently visited these relatives.

22 "We called her Kitty," 11, 14.

23 *Ibid.*, 13.

24 The daybook is now in the possession of Katharine Herbert of Florence,
S.C.; a photocopy is in the W-C-M Collection.

25 "We called her Kitty," 20.

26 *Ibid.*, 20–21.

27 Francis Boykin (1785–1839), son of Burwell Boykin's first wife, Elizabeth
Whitaker. Francis (usually called Frank) may have moved to Alabama as early as
1810. (Richard Manning Boykin, *Captain Alexander Hamilton Boykin* [New York:
privately printed, 1942], 7). Kirkland and Kennedy, *Historic Camden*, I, 348,
states he moved to Conecuh County, Alabama, in 1818.

28 Boykin, *Captain A. H. Boykin*, 43.

29 "We called her Kitty," 18, 19. See also "Two Years," 100–101, for a slightly
different account.

30 Boykin, *Captain A. H. Boykin*, 44–45. T. J. Withers to JC, Jr., January 7,
1859, indicates that certain aspects of the Miller estate were still under litigation
in 1859. See W-C-M Collection.

31 Kirkland and Kennedy, *Historic Camden*, II, 121.

32 JC, Jr., to Mary Miller, May 9, 1839, in W-C-M Collection.

33 *Ibid.*, June 28, 1839.

34 Mary Serena Chesnut Williams to JC, Jr., July 1, 1839, Chesnut Family
Papers.

35 Mary Serena Chesnut Williams to Mary Miller [fall, 1839], Mary Serena
Chesnut Williams to JC, Jr., November 19, 1839, in Chesnut Family Papers.

36 John Chesnut, Sr., to Colonel James Chesnut, Philadelphia, October 24,
1839, in W-C-M Collection; Kirkland and Kennedy, *Historic Camden*, II, 121.

37 Will of Ellen Whitaker Chesnut, John's wife, lists six children living in
1850, eleven years after John's death: Serena Haile (wife of Thomas E. Haile),
Mary Whitaker Chesnut, Ellen Chesnut, Thomas Whitaker Chesnut, James

Chesnut, and John Chesnut ("Johnny" of the Civil War journal).

38 John Cox (1732–93), a Philadelphia merchant who owned iron works in New Jersey, served as assistant quartermaster general under General Nathanael Greene. Chapter 1, Colonial Dames of America, *Ancestral Records and Portraits* (New York: Grafton Press, 1910), 31–35; Kirkland and Kennedy, *Historic Camden*, I, 336.

39 Kirkland and Kennedy, *Historic Camden*, II, 70, states that James Chesnut was the only boy to participate in a ceremony honoring General Lafayette when he visited Camden in 1825, "he alone having the white trousers and black coat required by Reverend Jonathan Whitaker, the principal of the town schools." A twenty-two-page MS sketch of JC, Jr., by MBC in W-C-M Collection states, "Capt Partridge had established early in this century a military school at Rice Creek Springs midway between Camden and Columbia. Capt Lattimandi then taught French and Fencing. And a light hearted, stout limbed, boyish battalion, the elite of southern youth, they camped, drilled, stood sentinel, and played at soldiering." The sketch is included as an appendix in Muhlenfeld, "MBC: The Writer and Her Work." James Chesnut, Sr., to JC, Jr., April 11, 1832, in Chesnut Family Papers; James Chesnut, Sr., to JC, Jr., February 12, 1832, in W-C-M Collection.

40 Bailey Dana & Blodgett Superintendents to Rev. Dr. Carnahan, May 12, 1832, in Chesnut Family Papers.

41 Mary Cox Chesnut to JC, Jr., August 5, 1833, James Chesnut, Sr., to JC, Jr., June 17, 1834, John Chesnut to JC, Jr., June 30, 1835, all in W-C-M Collection; "Chesnut, James" in *DAB*, II, 57. MBC says in MS sketch of JC, Jr., that he gave the valedictory address.

42 Family letters in the Chesnut Family Papers, mention the trip. Samuel D. McGill, in *Narrative of Reminiscences in Williamsburg County* (Columbia, S.C.: Bryan, 1897), 114–18, describes being shown great hospitality by James Chesnut, Jr., and his father in the fall of 1836 when he, as a boy, found himself stranded near Camden.

James Louis Petigru (1789–1863) was a lawyer of national reputation and "undisputed head of the state bar for nearly forty years" (*DAB*). He had been graduated from the South Carolina College in 1809 (one class behind Stephen Decatur Miller), had served as attorney general of South Carolina in the 1820s, and had assumed leadership of the Union party in 1832 to protest the nullification ordinance. The Chesnuts were also strong union men. *Oration by James Chesnut, Jr. delivered in the Presbyterian Church on the Fourth of July, at Camden, S.C.* (Camden, S.C.: L. M. Jones, 1837).

43 JC, Jr., to Mary Miller, April 22 [1840] in Virginia Historical Society, Richmond.

44 "Two Years," 119, of edited text.

FOUR

1 Revised journal, November 28, 1861. Other contemporary descriptions of Mulberry will be found in Esther S. Davis, *Memories of Mulberry* (privately printed, n. d.; repr. Camden Archives Commission, 1975), McGill, *Narrative of Reminiscences*, 116–18, Cato D. Glover, *The Stray and the Strange from "Mulberry"*

(Camden, S.C.: privately printed, 1972), and Margaret Maxwell Martin, "Rides about Camden" in Harvey S. Teal (ed.), *Rides About Camden, 1853 and 1873* (n.p., n.d.), 3–5. Cato Glover was the son-in-law of David Rogerson Williams III, a nephew of MBC who eventually inherited Mulberry. Margaret Martin was the mother of Isabella D. Martin, who used her mother's description in her introduction to the Martin-Avary 1905 edition of *A Diary From Dixie*.

2 Revised journal, November 28, 1861; Kirkland and Kennedy, *Historic Camden*, I, 11.

3 Glover, *The Stray and the Strange from "Mulberry,"* 24–25.

4 Davis, *Memories of Mulberry*, 2. Davis provides an excellent and extensive description of antebellum Mulberry, and much of the information herein is culled from here and from MBC's descriptions in the revised journal. Revised journal, November 28, 1861.

5 Revised journal, December 6, 1861, May 18, 1865.

6 *Ibid.*, November 28, 1861.

7 *Ibid.*, November 28, 1863.

8 *Ibid.*, December 8, 1861. Old Colonel Chesnut is described throughout the revised journal. For other descriptions, see Davis, *Memories of Mulberry*; Percival Reniers, *The Springs of Virginia* (Chapel Hill: University of North Carolina Press, 1941), 147–49; and *South Carolina Historical and Genealogical Magazine*, LXII (1961), 247–48. See Journal, November 7, 1861; "I read to JC's father. I should do it for no other man living."

9 Revised journal, September 24, 1861; Davis, *Memories of Mulberry*, 12.

10 Revised journal, September 24, 1861.

11 *Ibid.*, November 28, 1861.

12 *Ibid.*, September 24, 1861.

13 Kirkland and Kennedy, *Historic Camden*, II, 28–29.

14 "We called her Kitty," 26. Mary's relationship with Kate, which remained extremely close and loving until Kate's death in 1876, seems to have been a good example of what Carl Degler calls "sorority." Degler identifies sorority as an exclusively nineteenth-century phenomenon among women which seems to have developed as a result of the concept of the "woman's sphere," whereby the woman's role in life was strictly limited to home and family. Sorority as a social phenomenon seems to have passed away in the twentieth century as women's opportunities and roles expanded (*At Odds*, 144–50).

15 Revised journal, May 6, 1862. References to MBC's love of music and to playing the guitar are scattered throughout the journal and the revised journal. See, for example, revised journal, February 18, 1865. MBC mentions teaching blacks several times in the revised journal (e.g., December 13, 1861). In a MS fragment of eight pages, apparently a draft of a letter to a newspaper, she writes: "I was never in any house where any servant could not learn to read if he wished it—the children were ready to teach—more ready than they to learn. We taught negro Sunday school—I confess mine ran principally to singing hymns—they liked that and so did I—I was a poor teacher and they were not apt scholars—I have for more than forty years taught negroes to read up to a certain point they got on very well," in W-C-M Collection.

16 This summary of MBC's reading is based on the reading she referred to,

quoted, or alluded to throughout her letters, daybooks, journals, the revised journal, and her unpublished MS novels. In February 1894, MBC's nephew David Williams wished to sell the Chesnut library "of about 1500 volumes for the most part English editions handsomely bound in calf," and for the purpose he had a list made of the books in the library (in a bound book now in South Caroliniana Library). However, the list cannot be relied upon as an actual indication of the books which JC, Jr., and MBC owned before their deaths, as MBC gave many books away and traded others for new or different titles. Further, we have no way of knowing how much of the library was divided at the death of JC, Jr., or at MBC's death. Many titles which MBC mentions throughout her writings do not appear in the list (which contains only short titles and/or authors' last names). A large portion of the 1,500 volumes—perhaps all—were not sold, and are still in the possession of the family.

17 "Two Years," 75–76 of edited text. See Revised journal, April 15, 1861, in which MBC says Mary Cox Chesnut locked up Eugene Sue's novel *Le Juif Errant* (1844–45) and returned a presentation copy of Washington Allston's *Monaldi* (1841) "with thanks and a decided hint that it should be burned."

18 Revised journal, January 7, 1865; Journal, April 29, November 23, 1861.

19 Emma Chesnut, April 11, 1812–April 9, 1847. Letters in W-C-M Collection indicate she died of a lingering pulmonary disease. Emma Chesnut to James Chesnut, Sr., July 20, 1845, in W-C-M Collection.

20 James Chesnut, Sr., to JC, Jr., August 29, 1845 in W-C-M Collection. Although James had written to his father that he and Mary did indeed have sufficient funds, Mary recalled in the revised version of her Civil War journal his being stranded in Europe without letters of credit. Letters of credit and introductions were immediately dispatched; one such letter, from Secretary of State James Buchanan, who would become president in 1856, to the American minister to Great Britain, Louis McLane in London, Washington, September 3, 1845, sought to introduce "Mr James Chesnut, junr. of South Carolina, who, in pursuance of medical advice, has suddenly left our country for Europe accompanied by his lady & child." Mary Cox Chesnut to "My dear children," August 29, 1845, in W-C-M Collection.

21 Of course, this statement by Mary Cox Chesnut does not constitute real evidence for such an assertion, but, as is discussed on p. 62, herein, MBC later in speaking of her own childlessness, said "sometimes hope told a flattering tale." See also note 20 above.

22 Revised journal, March 9, December 30, 1861, "Two Years," 54 of edited text.

23 "We called her Kitty," 27.

24 T. J. Withers to James Chesnut, Sr., August 19, 1848, in W-C-M Collection. For the fact that Withers acted as guardian to MBC prior to her marriage I am indebted to Martha Williams Daniels.

25 James Chesnut, Sr., to JC, Jr., September 16, 1848. For a discussion of the prevalence of invalidism among nineteenth-century women, see Lorna Duffin, "The Conspicuous Consumptive: Woman as an Invalid," in Delamont and Duffin (eds.), *The Nineteenth-Century Woman*, 26–56. James Chesnut, Sr., to MBC, September 20, 1848, in Chesnut Family Papers.

26 Joseph Hall (1574–1656), bishop of Norwich. The daybook is in the possession of Katherine Herbert of Florence, S.C.

27 This home, a private residence, is now called Frogden. However, MBC always referred to it as Frogvale.

28 See, for example, revised journal, undated narrative covering August, 1862–mid-September, 1863, where MBC describes a trip to Charleston to see "Adrienne Lecouvreur."

29 Robert Leighton (1611–84) was archbishop of Glasgow.

30 MS sketch of JC, Jr.

31 MBC to JC, May 28, 1850, in W-C-M Collection. Quoted in full in Wall, "Letters of Mary Boykin Chesnut," 5–6. While many husbands might object to having their wives thoroughly rearrange their books and papers during their absence, James seems to have frequently turned such tasks over to Mary. Few plantation records survive that are not at least in part in Mary's hand.

32 Stephen D. Miller, Jr., to MBC, March 9, 1850, in Chesnut Family Papers.

33 Catherine Miller Williams to MBC, July 10, 1852, *ibid.*

34 Revised journal, September 9, 1861. See Sally A. Miller Boykin to Mary Miller, July 25, 1852: "Tell Mary I have met a lady here that knows her, Mrs Shackelford from Charleston says her friend Mrs Harrison has a little daughter—two years old—she was married a great many years before she had any."

35 William Joshua Grant to "My dear Children," December 4, 1852, in the possession of Mary Chesnut Philips Britton; Memoir of Mary Miller Withers Kirkland (1838–1925) in possession of Pauline Trotter Wooten, Charleston.

36 Memoir by Mary Williams Harrison Ames (Mary Williams Harrison Ames Papers, privately owned).

37 Revised journal, March 18, 1861; Journal, March 21, 1861.

38 MS sketch of JC, Jr.; Journal, June 13, 1861.

39 Kamchatka was sold in 1859 and shortly thereafter was bought by Mary Withers' husband, Thomas Kirkland, whom she married in April, 1859. The present owners, the Buckley family, bought it in 1938.

40 W-C-M Collection.

41 Journal, December 6, 1861; Mary Withers Kirkland memoir; Revised journal, March 5, 1862.

42 Journal, March 18, 1861.

43 For a good description of the congressional mess at Brown's Hotel, see Virginia Clay-Clopton, *A Belle of the Fifties* (New York: Doubleday, Page, 1904), 42, 50, and *passim*. "[Mrs. Chesnut] was the only daughter of Governor Miller, of South Carolina, and having been educated abroad, was an accomplished linguist and ranked high among the cultured women of the capital. Moreover, Mrs. Chesnut was continually the recipient of toilette elegancies, for which the bazaars of Paris were ransacked, and in this way the curiosity of the emulative stay-at-home fashionables was constantly piqued. Her part in that brilliant world was not a small one, for, in addition to her superior personal charms, Mrs. Chesnut chaperoned the lovely Preston girls of South Carolina, belles, all, and the fashionable Miss Stevens, of Stevens Castle, who married Muscoe Garnett of Virginia."

44 Journal, February 20, 1861; Revised journal, November 28, 1863.

45 Revised journal, July 13, 1862; Journal, February 20, 1861.

46 JC, Jr., to James Chesnut, Sr., January 19, 1860, John L. Manning to his wife, May 14, 1860, in W-C-M Collection; Journal, October 12, 1861; John Laurence Manning (1816–89), son of Richard I. Manning and Elizabeth Richardson Manning, was governor from 1852–54. He had attended Princeton with JC, Jr.

47 A letter from John L. Manning to JC, Jr., written in 1858 shortly after Chesnut's election as senator indicates that Manning had entertained hopes of being elected himself. John L. Manning to his wife, May 18, 1860, in W-C-M Collection.

48 "We called her Kitty," 31.

49 Sally A. Miller Boykin to MBC, June 22, 1853, in Chesnut Family Papers.

50 Revised journal, November 8, 1861.

51 William Randolph Withers (1846–77), then fourteen.

52 "We called her Kitty," 33–34.

53 Journal, February 18, 1861. Both internal evidence and external evidence such as the type of paper it is written on suggest that this entry was not written on February 18, 1861, but rather was composed later, probably during the war, to serve as an introduction to the journal.

FIVE

1 Journal, February 18, 1861. JC, Jr.'s return to South Carolina was immediate. On November 12, 1860, he delivered a speech in Columbia. Camden *Weekly Journal*, November 13, 1860, p. 2. See page 10 of a volume which MBC had been keeping as a daybook in 1860. Sometime thereafter, she wrote on the flyleaf of the red volume, "November 10th 1860 James Chesnut Jr resigned his seat in the U.S.A. Senate—'burnt the ships behind him' The first resignation—& I am not at all resigned," in W-C-M Collection.

2 Journal, February 18, 1861.

3 MBC referred to the upcoming conflict as "civil war" as early as February 25, 1861. *Ibid.*, March 12, 1861.

4 Entry for February 25, 1861, begins, "Since I last wrote in my journal." Two earlier entries survive, dated [February] 19 and 20. See note 53, Chapter Four, herein. Journal, February 25, 1861.

5 *Ibid.*, March 11, 1861; cf. Dryden, *Marriage a la Mode* [1673], Act II, sc. 1: "Our souls sit close and silently within,/ And their own webs from their own entrails spin."

6 Ishbel Ross, *First Lady of the South* (New York: Harper & Brothers, 1958), 14; Journal, March 5, 1861.

7 Journal, March 28, February 28, March 12, 1861.

8 *Ibid.*, March 18, 1861.

9 *Ibid.*, March 19, 20, 1861.

10 *Ibid.*, June, 14, 15, 1861. A letter from Serena Williams to MBC dated Flat Rock, October 1863, in W-C-M collection says, "Is it not funny my writing in bed like you Aunty." In journal, July 3, 1861, MBC complains that JC has gone and has accidentally taken her keys so that she cannot get to her journal. Journal, April 4, March 12, February 26, 27, 1861.

11 *Ibid.*, March 6, 1861.

12 *Ibid.*, February 28, March 7, 8, 1861.

13 *Ibid.*, February 25, March 5, 1861. MBC probably refers to Robert Josselyn (1810–84), author of several books of poetry, among them *The Faded Flower, and other Songs and Little Poems* (Boston, 1849). Josselyn, born in Massachusetts, was a member of the bar in Virginia and had served with Jefferson Davis during the Mexican War. *Library of Southern Literature, Volume XV, Biographical Dictionary of Authors*, 232. However, she may possibly be referring to Jep Josselyn, author of *Tar-Heel Rhymes in Vernacular Verse* (1866). William Henry Trescot (1822–98), a South Carolina historian and diplomat, was appointed assistant secretary of state in June, 1860. When South Carolina seceded in December, he resigned his post, but remained in Washington until February, 1861 (*DAB*).

14 Journal, March 26–April 2, August 7, 1861. Apparently Manning's attentions to MBC caused his uncle to speak with him, for Manning wrote a letter to his wife on April 3, 1861, in which he made light of the flirtation: "I have seen but little of Uncle John . . . . Uncle John says that I have spent most of my time attending upon Mrs. Chesnut, because she gave me a good seat coming down on the cars. She is staying at this house [Mills House] and is very busy electioneering and frankly confesses that she wants to go back to Montgomery" (W-C-M Collection).

Several passages dealing with Manning were written in pencil and later erased by MBC. Most of these have been recovered by careful study under infrared light: for example, "Mr C came home so enraged with my staying at home he [said] to flirt with John Manning that I went to bed in disgust" and "JM would whisper to me to the disgust of Mr C" (April 1, 1861).

15 Revised journal, October 1, 1861. December 21, 1863, December 25, 1861, January 24, 1862.

16 *Ibid.*, January 1, December 12, 1864.

17 *Ibid.*, August 1, March 12, 1864; although we have no real evidence, there are hints in the revised journal that JC, Jr., may have indulged in his own flirtations from time to time. Furthermore, in a daybook kept in a volume entitled *Index Rerun* from 1878 until her death, MBC wrote: "Forgiveness, is indifference—in love matters—Forgiveness is impossible—while *memory* lasts—Forgiveness is *almost impossible* while love lasts—Eh?" in W-C-M Collection.

18 Journal, March 26, 1861.

19 *Ibid.*, April 9, 1861.

20 *Ibid.*, April 13, 15, 10, 27, 1861.

21 In an entry in Civil War journal dated December 2, 1861, MBC wrote that she was destroying old letters, including some from Mary Witherspoon, "cold & formal & fantastic—frantic with an attempt at fine writing even in her religious ravings."

22 The Chesnut plantation was regarded as one of a number of model plantations, examples that proved slaves and their masters both benefited from the institution of slavery. See, for example, John Belton O'Neall's statement in 1853 to that effect quoted in Thomas H. Pope, *The History of Newberry County, South Carolina* (Columbia: University of South Carolina Press, 1973), I, 326, and Boykin, *Captain A. H. Boykin*, 38. Two doctor's daybooks from the 1840s in W-C-M Collection also indicate that slaveowners were charged the same fees for medical

services to family members as to slaves. JC to MBC, June 12, 1861, quoted in revised journal, June 27, 1861; revised journal, November 28, 1863, November 27, 1861.

23 Daybook entitled *Index Rerum.*

24 Described in "Two Years," 66–68 of edited text. No other evidence of this having happened exists, and the incident may possibly be fictional, but in every verifiable particular, MBC's description of Madame Talvande is accurate. See Explanatory Notes for "Two Years," entry for 67.8, in Muhlenfeld, "MBC: The Writer and Her Work."

25 Journal, March 4, 1861. Mary Chesnut's linking of slavery and women's rights was unusual among southern ladies, but by no means unique. Recent scholars have begun to study the relationship between abolitionism and feminism in the nineteenth century. See, for example, Blanche Glassman Hersh, *The Slavery of Sex: Feminist-Abolitionists in America* (Urbana: University of Illinois Press, 1978); Degler, *At Odds*, 303–307 and notes; Ann Firor Scott, *The Southern Lady: From Pedestal to Politics, 1830–1930* (Chicago: University of Chicago Press, 1970), 46–63; and Mary Elizabeth Massey, *Bonnet Brigades* (New York: Alfred A. Knopf, 1966), 15–24 and Chapter 13.

26 *Journal*, March 21, 18, June 15, 1861.

27 *Ibid.*, June 27, 1861.

28 *Ibid.*, July 22, 1861.

29 *Ibid.*, August 15, 1861.

30 *Ibid.*, July 26, August 31, September 1, 1861.

31 *Ibid.*, April 7, 1861.

32 *Ibid.*, August 12, 1861.

33 *Ibid.*, August 13, 19, 29, 1861.

34 *Ibid.*, September 19, 28, 1861.

35 *Ibid.*, October 17, 1861.

36 See Revised journal, December 6, 16, 1861, May 12, 1862; Journal, December 6, 7, 8, 1861.

37 Published in truncated form as "Memories," Chap. 16 of Ben Ames Williams' edition of *A Diary From Dixie*, the revised journal entry covering this period reads like an essay composed with great care. It contains perhaps the finest sustained writing of the entire revised journal. Much of the specific information contained in this section was obtained from letters, notes, and newspaper clippings which MBC kept and which are now in the W-C-M Collection. Had she written a draft of the section in October, 1863, as she says she did, she would have been unlikely to keep so many of these letters and clippings (similar materials have not survived in such numbers from other periods during the war—when, presumably, she *had* kept a journal). Furthermore, and perhaps more important, her statement that "Fredericksburg was over—And the Wilderness not dreamed of" proves the section could not have been written until after the Battle of The Wilderness, in May of 1864.

38 Undated letter, MBC to JC, later identified in MBC's hand as "Flat Rock 1862," included in Wall (ed.), "Letters of MBC," 29–30. MBC to JC September 18, 1863 [actually 1862], quoted by MBC in revised journal, undated narrative covering August 1862–mid September, 1863; original letter no longer exists.

39 Journal, August 27, July 29, 1861.

40 Revised journal, undated narrative covering August 1862 to mid-September, 1863.

41 *Ibid.*, January 5, 1864.

42 *Ibid.*, July 26, 1864.

43 *Ibid.*, October 7, 1864.

44 Varina Davis to MBC, October 8, 1864, quoted in revised journal, November 6, 1864. Original letter no longer exists.

45 Mary Williams Harrison Ames memoir.

46 *Ibid.*

47 Many letters to and from MBC are concerned in part with the lending and procuring of books. In 1862, for example, she wrote to C. S. Venable, professor of mathematics, asking him to get her some novels from the South Carolina College library. He replied, "The South Carolina authorities acknowledge but two authorities in the art of fiction—Walter Scott and Gilmore Simms. Other novels the library does not contain. After much labour I have persuaded my colleagues of the Library committee that Bulwer had a reputation scarcely inferior to Simms . . . . I tried my neighbour who is a great novel reader but failed" (letter copied in MBC's hand in a letterbook in possession of Mrs. Herbert). Revised journal, March 12, 1864.

48 See Revised journal, September 18, 1861. When MBC refers to "Lord Rawdons letters," she may be referring to his 1813 letter to Henry Lee defending his (Rawdon's) role in the British occupation of South Carolina during the Revolution. Rawdon's letter was printed in the revised edition of Lee's memoirs, entitled *The Campaign of 1781 in the Carolinas* (Philadelphia, 1824).

49 Revised journal, May 6, 1862.

50 *Ibid.*, November 25, 1864.

51 Journal, February 25, November 7, 1861.

52 Revised journal, January 21, 1864.

53 MBC read many American authors, but rarely praised them. *Ibid.*, May 12, 1862, January 18, 1864, November 6, 1861, March 11, 1864.

54 *Ibid.*, March 12, February 26, March 6, 1865.

55 *Ibid.*, April 19, 1865.

56 Civil War journal, undated entry on flyleaf of last surviving journal volume, entitled Book of Recipes, containing entries dated May 7, 1865 through June 26, 1865.

57 Union General Edward Elmer Potter, commanding Negro troops, plundered Camden on April 18, 1865. Kirkland and Kennedy, *Historic Camden*, I, 25; Revised journal, May 9, 1865. See also original journal of the same date; "JC was so bitter last night—said if he had come home a year ago & saved his property as *some* did—I said he did right to lose it—he replied—'I wont go & dine with the ones who did it'—'Yes, because Uncle H [A. H. Boykin] is the only one I know who did so'—but I think still as you aided in bringing on this war—you were bound to sacrifice all & stick to it no matter where you were placed no matter how unpleasant your position . . . he then said—'he had staid—& from his own conviction of duty—& not from my persuasion'—which is the honest truth— but he cannot forbear the gratification of taunting me with his *ruin*—for which I

am no more responsible than the man in the moon—but it is a habit of all men to fancy that in some inscrutable way their wives are the cause of all the evil in their lives." Journal, May 7, June 1, 1865.

58 See MBC's letters from Flat Rock to JC quoted in Wall (ed.), "Letters of MBC," 17, 29. Journal, May 15, 1865.

59 Journal, May 21, 1865. Harriet must indeed have been difficult to live with. On June 26, 1865, Mary wrote, "Hecate told John [JC's nephew John Chesnut] when he first came—that she had made sure that detestable person her uncle [JC]—would be killed—now to think he was to come back—and walk over them as if every thing belonged to him—(as it does) They had managed that poor old blind man [Chesnut, Sr.] so long they could not bear the return alive of the men of the family." Harriet Grant married Richard Stockton on July 10, 1865.

60 Journal, June 10, May 18, 1865.

61 MBC heard on June 10, 1865, that General Howell Cobb had been arrested; thereafter, she feared JC would suffer the same fate.

62 Revised journal, April 23, 1865; Journal, May 16, June 12, 1865.


SIX

1 In an entry dated June 26, 1865 (the last entry in the Civil War journal, which has survived from 1865), MBC writes, "We have so much more than this establishment consumes—I am enabled to carry baskets of vegetables to my destitute friends—That is the one pleasure left me."

2 Revised journal, February 25, 1865. One of the few contemporary mentions of MBC is in a sketch entitled "The Last Bazaar" by Grace Elmore in Mrs. Thomas Taylor et al. (eds.), *South Carolina Women in the Confederacy* (Columbia, S.C.: State Co., 1903), 244. Mrs. Chesnut is recalled as a "starry-eyed matron," characteristically laughing at the bazaar held in Columbia in January, 1865.

3 Journal, March 18, 1861.

4 Will of James Chesnut of Mulberry and Petitions to Probate Court by JC, Jr., March 5, October 22, 1866, Probate Records, Kershaw County Court House.

5 MBC to Virginia Caroline Tunstall Clay, *ca.* April, 1866, in Wall (ed.), "Letters of MBC," 73; undated letter to "my dear boy," first page of which is in JC's hand, second page (recto and verso) in MBC's hand, in Stephen Miller Williams Papers, estate of David R. Williams (1885–1969), privately owned. The letter, presumably to JC's nephew John Chesnut in Charleston some time in 1866, seems to have been written while JC and MBC were visiting in Columbia.

> [JC's hand]
> My dear boy—Your letter was fwrd here so I forward it to you, as you say you are to return to Camden before coming here—I am sorry not to see you as soon as I expected. I hope your stay with your beauty—this long, means a life long copartnership—Do please write at once & say—& tell every thing you can—& how Mary [Williams] is—Give her this letter from Mary [MBC]—We are still at Jarvis & go to Louisa's [probably Louisa McCord] Saturday till after 1st—Still utterly at sea as to future— see no haven where we would be—at rest—[marginal note of two words:] For [one illegible word] Yours

[MBC's hand]

I am sorry you did not come in last night I was sitting up looking for you—tho the lamp was out—Miss Susan had told me of the "reading" *dansante.*

besides you had better stay here when you come up—I had something to say *bacon* wise—may be Aunt Sally C [JC's older sister, Sarah Chesnut] might wish to make the percentage between the price now & next fall & lend you bacon money—that was & is my idea—Also I can find just these two envelopes. So I send some postals—also—wherewith to buy more I have but ten cents current greenbacks of this model republic. *Also.* Mose has to stay tomorrow to dig asparagus roots so come up to the meeting Mr. C *also* wants you to sign some of his liens as witness—he wished so heartily this morning that you were here—Your's MBC.

You need never mind disturbing us at night— We like our young man so well he never comes amiss—too often too soon—or too late—

6 MBC to Virginia Clay, *ca.* April, 1866, in Wall (ed.), Letters of MBC," 73.

7 Among the Chesnut papers in the W-C-M Collection is an advertisement for settlement in British Honduras, "as many people have despaired of repairing their broken fortunes in the Southern States . . . ." New Orleans, November 20, 1867. Undated letter from JC and MBC, presumably to John Chesnut (see note 5, above).

8 JC to MBC, July 13, 1867, in Chesnut Family Papers.

9 Mary Williams Harrison Ames memoir, in Mary Williams Harrison Ames Papers; "History of the Chesnut Family of South Carolina" in Joseph Sweetman Ames Genealogical Collection, Maryland Historical Society.

10 David R. Williams to "Dear Auntie," April 13, 1881, in W-C-M Collection.

11 Journal, May 18, 1865. John Chesnut died June 22, 1868.

12 See letters from Margaret Howell in MBC's letterbook, XLIX, in W-C-M Collection, February 25, March 23, 1867, and J. S. Preston to JC from Paris, July, 1867, both in W-C-M Collection. Isabella Martin's Columbia High School for Young Ladies and Little Girls was in operation from 1866 to 1890 in the Martin residence at the corner of Blanding and Henderson streets. (Isabella Martin's mother, Margaret, had conducted a school there from time to time during the late 1850s). Though it remained small, Miss Martin's school came to be highly regarded, attracting pupils from as far away as Florida, Pennsylvania, and Rhode Island. Most were day students, though a few boarding students lived with the Martins in a family setting. Genevieve A. McCaw, "Miss Isabella Martin's School," *State Magazine*, February 20, 1955, pp. 6–7; Martin Family Papers.

13 See Revised journal, November 28, 1861. In an entry dated February 23, 1865, in Civil War journal MBC wrote "To day is thursday & for four days I have not written—I have been busily engaged—reading the *10* volumes of *memoirs* of the times I have written." The volume in which this entry occurs contains entries from January 17–February 23, 1865. At least two other volumes followed this one. One later volume containing entries from May 7, 1865, to June 26, 1865, also survives, and there must have been at least one intervening volume between these two. There may have been entries in another volume covering the period after June 25th. Only six volumes survive, in W-C-M Collection.

14 Journal, entries dated October 12, November 26, and December 2, 1861, all record that MBC was sorting letters and papers. The November 26, 1861, entry reads: "*ill*—stayed at home—arranged boxes of old letters & destroyed quantities—what a stirring up of ghosts those old letters are— I read letters from people who called themselves my dearest friends whose existence I had forgotten—I read my old letters—twenty & fifteen years old—& find I must have been quite an interesting creature." Among the Chesnut papers in the W-C-M Collection there is evidence that MBC went through them systematically to find material of use in the journal revision. For example, on the back of a letter dated November 19, [1866], from S. M. Capers to MBC is a note in MBC's hand which reads, "Private Letters *No use*."

15 Journal, October 22, 23, 1861. "Brady" was undoubtedly James Topham Brady (1815–1869), a New York lawyer and advocate of states' rights who, like many southerners, had supported John C. Breckinridge for president in the election of 1860, and who made many war speeches. Edwards Clarke, "A Great Advocate: James T. Brady," in *Galaxy*, May, 1869, in a collection of miscellaneous pamphlets made by LeRoy Youmans, South Caroliniana Library. "Wilson" probably refers to Joseph Ruggles Wilson (1822–1903), a South Carolina minister who delivered a speech on January 6, 1861, entitled *Mutual relations of masters and slaves as taught in the Bible. A discourse preached in the First Presbyterian church, Augusta, Georgia* (Np., n.d. [presumably Augusta, Ga., 1861]). No evidence exists that MBC's critique was published. She was at Sandy Hill when her journal entry was recorded, but neither the Camden *Weekly Journal* nor the Camden *Confederate* for 1861 contain any such critique; nor has it been found in Columbia, Charleston, or Richmond papers during this period.

A two-page fragment, pp. 10 and 11, in W-C-M Collection, seems to be a book review. A three-page fragment (one page bears the number "3"), appears to be part of what is at least a second draft of an essaylike journal entry of late 1865 or early 1866; it relates family anecdotes about slavery and the first aftermath of the war.

16 Émile Souvestre (1806–1854). MBC read *Au bord du lac* (Paris: Giraud et Dagneau, 1852) in December, 1861 (Civil War journal, December 7, 1861). This is a collection of tales which MBC felt was designed to show human progress. One of the tales, "Le Chevrier de Lorraine," she translated and sent to Isabella Martin for comment (see p. 141). In the W-C-M Collection is an eight page fragment of another translation headed "From Emile Colombey's 'Histoire Anecdotique du duel.'" This fragment contains part of a corrected draft of a translation of Émile Laurent's (1819–1897) *Histoire anecdotique du duel, dans tous les temps et dans tous les pays* [par] *Émile Colombey* [pseud.] (Paris: Hetzel, 1861). It seems likely that this translation dates from late 1870s or early 1880s; the subject may have been suggested to her by the fact that her nephew was involved in a duel in 1878 (see p. 184), or by the famous Cash-Shannon duel of 1880.

17 Easterby, "JC," *DAB*. One interesting letter from C. C. Church to JC, July 18, 1869, says that he has enclosed a copy of a draft of a preamble for a proposed revised United States Constitution. Church states that the revision of the Constitution is a nationwide project, and elicits JC's comments and support.

18 November 16, 1869. A letter from J. R. Trimble to MBC, Baltimore, November 11, 1869, pays his compliments to MBC whom he has just met in

Staunton and mentions the forthcoming ceremony. JC's account book (W-C-M Collection) contains entries from December 4, 1866 through December 22, 1885, many of which are in MBC's hand.

19 [MBC] to [Mary Withers Kirkland], undated, *ca.* 1873 (Kirkland Family Papers, South Caroliniana Library). Two volumes, one entitled *Account Expense Book* (W-C-M Collection), contain MBC's personal and household accounts from January, 1870, through 1872, including accounts for the book club and lists of books and periodicals purchased. The *Saturday Review* was a London journal; *Blackwood*'s was published in Edinburgh; *L'Express des Modes* was a Paris woman's magazine. The other journals mentioned were published in New York. Undated letter [March, 1873], in Wall (ed.), "Letters of MBC," 77. The books to which MBC refers are John Hall Gladstone's *Michael Faraday* (London, 1872) and Thomas Henry Huxley's *Evidence as to Man's Place in Nature* (London, 1863).

20 MBC to Mary Withers Kirkland, March 31 [1873], in Kirkland Family Papers. Ann Firor Scott in *The Southern Lady*, 150–58, links the evolution of women's clubs—most of the earliest of which were literary—to women's growing need for self-development, for expanded educational opportunities. Scott dates the growth of such clubs in the South from about the mid-1880s. Mrs. Chesnut, by founding her book club, was thus in the vanguard of what was rapidly to become a national institution for social change.

21 MBC's *Annual Expense Book*. MBC's Account book.

22 Easterby, "JC," DAB. In W-C-M Collection is a ticket for the South Carolina Rail Road issued September 21, 1871, entitling JC to ride 1,000 miles. About 800 miles were used up on the ticket. Deed in W-C-M Collection.

23 Invoice of March 11, 1873, from John H. Devereux, a Charleston architect, "for plans, specifications & Estimate on Norman villa located near Camden SC/ Est Cost $6614" (Chesnut-Miller-Manning Papers, South Carolina Historical Society). See Wall (ed.), "Letters of MBC," 84, 91.

24 [MBC] to [Mary Withers Kirkland], undated, *ca.* 1873, in Kirkland Family Papers.

25 Single page (W-C-M Collection) numbered '5,' which appears to be a transcription in MBC's hand of a letter from her mother, contains such anecdotes, and reads in part, "When I see you I will tell you many things. Young as I was he talked freely & openly to me on all subjects. He always begged me to keep his letters some days they would be useful. I gave them to you as the oldest & feeling Mr C would act with you." Isabella Martin to MBC, "Wednesday" [1874]. See note 16 above. "The Goatherd" is undoubtedly MBC's translation of "Le Chevrier de Lorraine." Isabella Martin's letter reflects the opinion of many Southern women that writing was an acceptable and relatively easy way of earning a living. See Ann Firor Scott, *The Southern Lady*, 118.

26 Journal, October 3, 1861. MBC refers here to the Columbia *Banner* (the weekly edition of *South Carolinian*). Dr. Robert Wilson Gibbes (1809–66) was, in 1861, publisher of the paper, but had given up editorship in April, 1858.

27 Revised journal, January 1, 1864.

28 "The Captain and the Colonel," 13–14, edited text in Muhlenfeld, "MBC: The Writer and Her Work." The MS of "The Captain and the Colonel" is in the W-C-M Collection.

29 Mary Williams Harrison Ames memoir. A letter from Mary Preston to

MBC, copied in MBC's hand (letterbook in possession of Katharine Herbert) dated September 18, 1863, announces her engagement and describes her seal ring.

Revised journal, February 12, 1864, December 6, 1861, March 5, 1862. See explanatory notes to "The Captain and the Colonel" in Muhlenfeld, "MBC: The Writer and Her Work," 438–80, for identification of specific events, characters, quotations, etc., in the novel.

30 John Chesnut's date of birth is approximate; his tombstone in Chesnut Cemetery, Knight's Hill, near Camden, says he died on June 15, 1868, "Aged 31 years." Charlotte Ellen Whitaker Chesnut (February 10, 1807–April 6, 1851). John Chesnut (Johnny's father) to JC, June 30, 1835 (W-C-M Collection), indicates the house at Cool Spring was built in 1834 and that the family was living there in 1835.

31 James Chesnut [JC's nephew] to "my dear sister," August 13, 1849 (Chesnut-Miller-Manning Collection), indicates that James, the eldest son of John and Ellen Chesnut, attended West Point and that Thomas, the second son, was presently attending. John Chesnut to his grandfather, JC, Sr., September 24, 1853, states that he is departing for Princeton the following week. A. Bohmar to JC, Sr., August 18, 1854, states: "It gives me pleasure, after a few months trial & observation, to be able to state to you that, since his return, your grandson John Chesnut has behaved towards all as becomes a young gentleman . . . . Having found out that he lacked the knowledge of many things necessary to the foundation of a good & solid education he is now determined to make up for time lost." Revised journal, November 5, 1863. John's service is mentioned through the revised journal. Mary Williams Harrison Ames memoir, in Mary Williams Harrison Papers; Probate Records, Kershaw County Court House.

32 Revised journal, November 5, 1863.

33 *Ibid.*, December 8, 1861; December 21, 1863; Journal, March 20, 1861.

34 "The Captain and the Colonel," 49–50 of edited text.

35 *Ibid.*, 69.

36 *Ibid.*, 115.

37 *Ibid.*, 23 (emphasis added).

38 *Ibid.*, 3–4.

39 *Ibid.*, 13, 15.

40 *Ibid.*, 25–26.

41 *Ibid.*, 81–82.

42 *Ibid.*, 57.

43 *Ibid.*, MS, 39.

44 "The Captain and the Colonel," 19, edited text.

45 Page tipped into *Index Rerum* (MBC's daybook of the late 1870s and 1880s). Bracketed words are MBC's interlinear changes.

46 "The Captain and the Colonel," 90, edited text. Revised journal, February 24, 1864.

47 "The Captain and the Colonel," 90–91, edited text.

48 *Ibid.*, 141–42.

49 These revised entries are neatly written on legal-sized sheets; MBC grouped them together into segments of approximately 50 pages each, and provided each

segment with a cover sheet. Segments 10, 11, 21, and 22 survive. In the upper lefthand corner of several cover sheets are the symbols "X75," perhaps a notation MBC made in later years to indicate that these were drafts completed in 1875.

50 R. M. T. Hunter to JC, July 12, 1876, in W-C-M Collection.

51 Lady Mary Wortley Montagu (1689–1762), English poet and letter writer. Her complete works, including her correspondence, poems, and essays, were published in 1803 and were popular throughout the nineteenth century. R. M. T. Hunter to JC, August 14, 1876, in W-C-M Collection.

52 See, for example, an early draft of a disquisition on slavery written on three tissue paper sheets, and an eight-page draft fragment (two folded leaves, numbered 3–8, 11–12) which appears to be a review of some work on slavery or reconstruction, in W-C-M Collection.

53 A number of letters in the W-C-M Collection pertain to this transaction. Eventually, the Washington portrait was sold, probably after MBC's death. Letter copied in MBC's hand (with signature in JC's hand) to J. M. Caldwell and Sons from JC, March 14, 1875 (Chesnut-Manning-Miller Collection, South Carolina Historical Society).

54 Will dated December 4, 1875, in Chesnut Family Papers.

55 Isabella Martin to MBC, July 3 [1875] in W-C-M Collection. Miller Williams, who was graduated from Virginia Military Institute in 1873, had worked as a Civil Engineer for the Shenandoah Valley Railroad until the company failed, had then completed a two-year law course at Washington and Lee in less than a year, and had been licensed to practice law in Virginia in September, 1875. He arrived in South Carolina about mid-November of that year. I am indebted to Martha Daniels for this information.

56 Charlotte Boykin Taylor (MBC's aunt) to Mary Boykin Miller (MBC's mother and Charlotte's sister), January 23, 1876, Thomas Taylor to MBC, February 11, 1876, MBC to Kate Williams, September 26, 1875, all in S. Miller Williams Papers.

57 A copy of the oration, *An Address Delivered Before the Literary Societies of the College of New Jersey by the Hon. James Chesnut, of South Carolina on Tuesday, June 27 [28], 1876* (Princeton, N.J.: The "Press," 1876), in the South Caroliniana Library, is inscribed in MBC's hand to "His Honor Judge Bryan with respects of The Authors." Though it cannot, of course, be proved that the setting copy was in MBC's hand, such a supposition seems likely. Many characteristics of MBC's hand (but not of JC's) are preserved in the printed document: punctuation resembles that in MBC's carefully copied MSS; there are numerous sentence fragments—which JC usually avoided; capitalized words tend to be those beginning with letters for which (in MBC's hand) capitals cannot be distinguished from lower case letters; one typographical error, *yon* for *you*, is suggestive—the two words are indistinguishable in MBC's hand. James McCosh to JC, May 26, 1876, in W-C-M Collection.

58 *An Address . . . Before the Literary Societies*, 25–27.

59 Harvey S. Teal (ed.), *Old Times in Camden, Pen Pictures of the Past* (N.p., 1961), 5–6.

60 W-C-M Collection. It is unclear exactly why MBC so despised William Shannon's role in writing these memoirs. Shannon (1822–1880, killed in a duel

by Colonel E. B. Cash) had been a friend of the Chesnuts for many years. A letter from Shannon to JC, January 13, 1858 [1859], states, "Present my kindest regards to Mrs Chesnut and allow me to say to her that as Mr Clay stood sponsor for you in the Senate I hope she and Mrs Clay will be great friends. I have often heard that Mrs Clay *was* the first woman in Washington." In an entry dated March 20, 1861 in the original Civil War journal, MBC called Shannon "one of the best & purest men that ever lived." However, during the war Shannon served as president of the Bank of Camden rather than in the army. After the war, JC had loans outstanding for which Shannon held security. MBC may have resented this. (See statement of JC to Bank of Camden, May 5, 1868, in W-C-M Collection.)

61 JC's grandfather had, as a boy, been a clerk in Joseph Kershaw's store. MBC refers to this fact several times in these Shannon rebuttals. For example, she writes: "John became a clerk of the oft mentioned Joseph Kershaw. he was a lad then of 12 years old—he became a partner in the *store* & then bought out his former employer—one of the chief feathers in the Kershaw glory cap of Mr Shannon's weaving—is that this magnificent old Carolinian was once a clerk of the Kershaws. Does any body remember the name of the printer who first employed Franklin or the baker whose rolls he carried."

62 "The Captain and the Colonel," 6, edited text. In a revision of part of Chapter I, made several years after the novel was written, the pun is more obvious. Joanna says, "Pappa says if we tell any story concerning them we must invent it." And Frank replies, "Let sleeping dogs lie. I beg your pardon—that was malapropos."

63 Interestingly, this format (beginning with a similar "Advertisement") is one followed in an anonymous translation of a work by Émile Souvestre entitled *An Attic Philosopher in Paris, or A Peep at the World from a Garret, Being the Journal of a Happy Man* (New York: D. Appleton, 1856).

64 Revised journal, April 1, 1865.

65 Written in 1876. The MS was written after Kate's death in April and before Serena's death in September of that year. Muhlenfeld, "MBC: The Writer and Her Work," 802-47, and, herein, note 9, Chap. II.

66 Index Rerum (MBC's daybook of the late 1870s and 1880s). See pp. 185-86, herein. That MBC was also conscious of her role as historian is evidenced by the fact that she sought books and materials concerned with South Carolina history. For example, in the W-C-M Collection there is a five-page MS, neatly copied in MBC's hand, of "The high minded Young Carolinian. From Judge [William Dobein] James' interesting unpublished manuscripts," dealing with General Zackariah Cantey of the Revolution—an extract from the *Southern Chronicle and Camden Aegis*, July 28, 1824. In March 1876, MBC and JC joined the Southern Historical Society (invoice in W-C-M Collection).

67 See Easterby, "JC," *DAB*, and MBC's MS sketch of JC. JC served as Hampton's campaign manager for Kershaw County.

68 Mary William Harrison to MBC, October 17, 1876, in S. Miller Williams Papers.

69 MBC to S. Miller Williams, December 7 [1876], *ibid*. The letter is very faint and, in large part, illegible.

SEVEN

1 Letters to James Chesnut during this period often express regret over Mrs. Chesnut's health. See pp. 218–19 for a description of her death, in which she is said to be suffering from recurring illness in her heart and lungs.

2 Undated form letter and MS in W-C-M Collection.

3 Two onionskin pages of notes, written in purple pencil, with the heading "anecdotes for the life of *James Chesnut*" are preserved in the W-C-M Collection. The notes on these pages are sketchy and, in many cases, illegible, and make little sense to the modern reader. In MBC's daybook kept during the late 1870's and 1880's, several notes pertain to JC, including one page entitled "Scrap for the life of James Chesnut."

4 Anthony Trollope, *The Way We Live Now* (London: Chapman and Hall, 1875). Apart from the title, the book seems to have no connection with "Two Years." Mrs. Chesnut mentioned Trollope's book in her letter to Kate of September 25, 1875, "When the girls finish—the 'Way we live now' make them send it to you—I found it vastly amusing—bitter bad as it is—it is not *worse*—or nasty. Trollope never is."

5 "Two Years," 2, of edited text in Muhlenfeld, "MBC: The Writer and Her Work."

6 *Ibid.*, 16–17, of edited text.

7 *Ibid.*, 19.

8 *Ibid.*, 20, 25.

9 See "We called her Kitty," MS 15–16 for a description of a frightened man who joined Mrs. Miller and Mary en route to Mississippi in 1838, who was given to lifting up his hands and saying, "Thou God seest me." "Two Years," 26, 33–34, edited text.

10 Thomas Campbell, "Song of the Greeks" (1822).

11 Campbell, "Speech of the Chorus in the Same Tragedy [Medea]" (1830).

12 Thomas Moore, "A Canadian Boat-Song," stanza I (1805).

13 "Two Years," 60–61, edited text.

14 *Ibid.*, 56–57.

15 *Ibid.*, 66.

16 George Gordon, Lord Byron, "The Waltz" (1813).

17 "Two Years," 70, edited text.

18 *Ibid.*, 73–74.

19 *Ibid.*, 81–82.

20 *Ibid.*, 84.

21 *Ibid.*, 122.

22 Jane North Pettigrew (November 5, 1855–May 5, 1890), daughter of Jane Caroline North and Charles Lockhart Pettigrew.

23 Kirkland and Kennedy, *Historic Camden*, II, 234. All information on Miller's duel is taken from this source, pp. 234–36.

24 W-C-M Collection. The volume, with an introduction by John Todd, D.D., is entitled *Index Rerum: or Index of Subjects; Intended as a Manual, to aid the Student and the Professional Man, in preparing himself for usefulness* (Northampton, Mass.: Hopkins, Bridgman, 1850).

25 *Index Rerum*, pp. Aa, Eo, Ae.

26 Thomas Drayton to JC, November 10, 1879, in W-C-M Collection; Letter from David R. Williams to S. Miller Williams, December 19, 1879, in S. Miller Williams Papers.

27 F. W. Dawson to "Madam" dated July 2, 1880, in W-C-M Collection.

28 W-C-M Collection.

EIGHT

1 All journal manuscripts are on deposit in the South Caroliniana Library, and are available on microfilm through interlibrary loan. Complete transcriptions of these manuscripts have been made by students in the Southern Studies Program of the University of South Carolina under the direction of James B. Meriwether. The entire revised Civil War journal has been edited by C. Vann Woodward and published as *Mary Chesnut's Civil War* (Yale University Press, 1981). There are four extant drafts or portions of drafts of the first entry in the journal. The earliest is a rather formal essay, probably written about 1864, which contains most of the materials of pp. 1–4 of Ben Ames Williams' edition, but which conveys little sense of "diary." The second, third, and fourth appear to have been written in the 1880s; they are all very different from each other and from the first draft. Only two of them contain what is, in the Williams edition, the opening paragraph of the journal, a vignette (which may be fictional) used by Mrs. Chesnut to establish the tone of an eyewitness account: "on the train just before we reached Fernandina a woman cried out—'That settles the hash.' Tanny touched me on the shoulder.—'Look out!' 'Lincoln's elected.' 'How do you know?'—'The man over there has a telegram.'" The earliest draft is carefully copied in a group of pages stapled together; the second is a series of loose pages in pencil; what is apparently part of another draft written about the same time as the interim pencil draft is a single page containing the "That settles the hash" passage; the last, page one of the last revised journal draft, has been lost, but was reproduced in facsimile in the first edition of the journal, edited by Isabella Martin and Myrta Lockett Avary in 1905.

2 *Index Rerum*, p. Ci. Caroline Pettigrew Williams was born on June 2, 1880, and died the following day. Charles Pettigrew Williams, November 1, 1881–June 17, 1927.

3 Miller and his family were in Camden at the time of Charles' birth in November, 1881, but departed before Christmas.

4 JC to Miss Serena Chesnut Williams, dated Camden, April 18, 1882, in S. Miller Williams papers.

5 MBC to Jane Williams, undated, in S. Miller Williams papers. The letter is dated tentatively by MBC's statement "I wish I could see your great boy—who does he look like." Assuming Charles was taken from Camden as an infant of two months, the statement seems a likely one for MBC to have made within the next several months.

6 Only evidence for this assumption is MBC's statement in the final chapter of "Two Years" that "The bridegroom's present was a diamond cross."

7 L. W. S. Perkins to Isabella Martin, April 4, 1905, in Mary Williams Harrison Ames Papers, privately owned.

8 W-C-M Collection.

9 *House Resolution* 5503, "An act to remove the political disabilities of James Chesnut of South Carolina." Letter from General M. C. Butler to JC, May 10, 1882, informs him that JC's name has been placed under consideration. J. D. Kennedy to JC, May 29, 1882, all in W-C-M Collection.

10 Revised journal, May 6, 1862.

11 The scratch pads bear the copyright date 1881, the only piece of evidence that definitely dates the work on the journal. Of the revised Civil War journal, notebooks numbered 2–9 and 13–47 (with two notebooks numbered 46) survive. Sections of the revised journal corresponding to notebooks 10, 11, and 12 have been prepared in fair copy form, on loose sheets bound together (and numbered 10, 11, and 12) by brads. The section corresponding to notebook 1 exists on loose sheets, in rough draft only.

12 MBC to Varina Davis, June 18, 1883, in Museum of the Confederacy.

13 *Ibid.*

14 Some of the material in this discussion of the revisions of the journal was first developed for a paper presented at a conference, "South Carolina Women Writers," in October, 1975, at the University of South Carolina. The paper, entitled "Literary Elements in Mary Chesnut's Journal," has been published in the proceedings of that conference, James B. Meriwether, ed. (Spartanburg, S.C.: Reprint Co., 1979).

15 Journal, January 17–February 23, 1865, and its counterpart in the revised journal. A typed transcription of the original version is nineteen pages long, and a typed transcription of the revision is forty pages.

16 Journal, February 16, 1865.

17 Revised journal, February 16, 1865.

18 Journal, February 18, 1865; Revised journal, February 18, 19, 1865. In the original journal, MBC simply remarks to herself, "'Massa in the cold– cold ground'—The time they sung when they elevated our flag at Montgomery—They are *most* of them there—young & old."

19 This passage in the original journal appears under the date "Monday 15th–16th–17th–18th–& 19th–20th 21st–22nd–23rd."

20 Revised journal, April 15, 1861.

21 *Ibid.*, March 10, 1862.

22 *Ibid.*, February 23, 1865.

23 The only evidence we have that Molly and Ellen remained with MBC until her death is Isabella Martin's statement to that effect in her Introduction to the 1905 edition of *A Diary From Dixie*, p. xix.

24 MBC to Varina Davis, June 18, 1883.

25 A letter in the W-C-M Collection from Richardson Miles (probably to JC) dated June 23, 1883 states, "It has been very long since I have enjoyed such pleasure as I did in your Muse and Company in the time I was in Camden. I have been very glad to report to Mrs Chesnut's friends in Charleston how much better she is, and how charming she was in her entertainment." Miles had undoubtedly been one of the Chesnuts' guests at the unveiling of the Confederate Monument the preceding week. Wallace, *S.C.: A Short History*, 615.

26 Undated letter, MBC to Miller Williams, in S. Miller Williams papers. Dated by MBC's opening remarks, "David gave me a bunch of Tax receipts to keep for you. He paid Ned Cantey—from '78 for you—Ned Cantey having paid

it himself before to save you annoyance—the whole amount is $83—so you are clear for the fiscal year of '82."

27 The house servants were also elderly. In letters written in 1885, MBC refers to "Peter," whom she has been trying to get rid of for some time; however, Peter was probably not a house servant. Moses Nelson, "Mose," served as James Chesnut's personal servant and as butler. MBC was to mention him in her will. As has already been noted, according to Isabella Martin, Ellen and Molly also remained with MBC until her death. The Civil War journals suggest that Molly was about MBC's age, and Ellen perhaps 10 or 15 years younger.

28 *Index Rerum,* pp. Oo and Ou.

29 F. W. Dawson to MBC, January 21, April 8, 1884, in W-C-M Collection; F. W. Dawson (ed.), *Our Women in the War* (Charleston: *Weekly News and Courier,* 1885). MBC's sketch appears on pp. 344–47; Isabella Martin's on pp. 3–10 is entitled "The First Wayside Hospital."

30 MBC, "The Arrest of a Spy," Dawson (ed.), *Our Women in the War,* 344.

31 Revised journal, undated narrative covering August, 1862 to mid-September, 1863.

32 William Henry Trescot to MBC, December 6, 1884, in W-C-M Collection. Trescot (see note 13, Chap. V), the nephew of the state's most prominent historian, Edward McCrady, served on several diplomatic missions throughout the 1880s, to China, Panama, Chile, and Mexico (DAB).

33 A letter from Caroline Perkins to Mary Williams Harrison dated January 30, 1885 in S. Miller Williams Papers states, "As you know, Gen. C. had a stroke of paralysis about two weeks ago."

34 MBC to Jane Williams, January 20, 1885, in S. Miller Williams Papers.

35 Caroline Perkins to Mary Williams Harrison, January 30, 1885. Caroline Perkins had been one of the young girls whom Mary had enjoyed chaperoning and entertaining in the 1850s. A friend of Mary Withers Kirkland, Miss Perkins had also been a regular member of Mary's book club/lending library in the late 1860s and early 1870s.

36 Charlotte Boykin Taylor to S. Miller Williams, in S. Miller Williams Papers.

37 *Index Rerum,* p. Mo.

38 David R. Williams to his brother Miller, February 8, 1885, in S. Miller Williams Papers. In the letter, David writes, "His last will left the Mulberry & Sandy Hill plantations to you & I but as that will cannot be found the next of date leaves them to Papa" (Kate's husband and JC's nephew, David R. Williams).

39 Probate Records, Kershaw County Court House.

40 David R. Williams to S. Miller Williams, February 8, 1885.

41 Varina Davis to MBC, March 25, 1885, in W-C-M Collection.

42 Harrison died on February 25, 1885. He had been ill for several years (information provided by Martha Williams Daniels from family letters).

43 Probably P. H. Nelson, II, who served as one of Kershaw County's representatives to the state legislature, 1886–88. However, the reference to Nelson here is unclear.

44 MBC to Jane Williams, June 21, 1885, in S. Miller Williams Papers.

45 MBC to Jane Williams, August 16, 1885, in S. Miller Williams Papers.

46 MBC to Miller Williams, dated Sarsfield, August 17, 1885, in S. Miller Williams Papers.

47 Varina Davis to MBC, March 25, 1885.

48 Edward McCrady to MBC, July 21, 1885, William Henry Trescot to MBC, August 3, 1885, in W-C-M Collection. An undated two page typescript in the W-C-M Collection written after JC's death is based on MBC's biographical sketch of her husband, sometimes borrowing wording from it, and may have been written by MBC.

49 David R. Williams, Jr. to Jane Williams, July 16, 1885, in S. Miller Williams Papers.

50 MSS in journal materials, South Caroliniana Library.

51 S. Miller Williams to MBC, December 22, 1885, in W-C-M Collection.

52 MBC to Jane Williams, February 2, 1886, in S. Miller Williams Papers. At the end of the letter, MBC writes, "When David comes & finds me fretting—he begins at once with his funny Clarendon tales." Ellen's father, John L. Manning, lived at Milford, in the High Hills of the Santee, in Clarendon County.

53 MBC to Virginia Clay, September 1886, Perkins Library, Duke University. In Wall (ed.), 90–91.

54 Charlotte Boykin Taylor to Miller Williams, November 26, 1886, in S. Miller Williams Papers.

55 Dr. Alexander Nicholas Talley (1827–97), a Columbia physician, served as medical director of South Carolina during the Confederacy, and as president of the army board of medical examiners. From 1869–73, he was professor of medicine at the University of South Carolina. Isabel C. Patterson, "Dr. A. N. Talley: Physician, Soldier, Benefactor" in *State Magazine* (December 11, 1949), 9.

56 Charlotte Boykin Taylor to Miller Williams, November 26, 1886, in S. Miller Williams Papers.

57 Will in Probate Records, Kershaw County Court House.

58 *Ibid.*

59 Description attributed to Creola Bracey by Jane B. Trantham in a talk given to the Kershaw County Historical Society on January 17, 1974. According to Mrs. Trantham, "'Cre' looked across the neglected fields to the empty house one day and remarked [to her] 'Ain't nobody live there now. When I was a girl, Miss Mary Chesnut lived there. I took her some eggs and she asked me what they was worth. I told her fifteen cents a dozen and she say that ain't enough and she gimme a quarter.'"

60 Transcription of a taped discussion with Serena Chesnut Williams Miles (1879–1957) made in 1956, loaned by the estate of David Rogerson Williams IV.

61 Transcription of a taped discussion with Miller's son, David Rogerson Williams IV (October 29, 1885–August 21, 1969), loaned by the estate of David Rogerson Williams IV. See revised journal, January 17, 1865, and "We called her Kitty," 28.

62 L. S. W. Perkins to Isabella Martin, April 4, 1905, in Mary Williams Harrison Ames Papers.

63 Louisa Wigfall Wright (Mrs. D. Giraud Wright), *A Southern Girl in '61* (New York: Doubleday, Page & Co., 1905), 83. Mrs. Wright also includes one letter from MBC and pictures of MBC and JC taken in Charleston in 1861.

# List of Sources

ARCHIVES, REPOSITORIES, AND MANUSCRIPT COLLECTIONS

Joseph Sweetman Ames Genealogical Collection, Maryland Historical Society, Baltimore.

Mary Williams Harrison Ames Papers, privately owned.

Myrta Lockett Avary Papers, Atlanta Historical Society.

Catalogue of American Portraits, National Portrait Gallery, Smithsonian Institution, Washington, D.C.

Chesnut Family Papers, State Historical Society of Wisconsin, Madison.

Chesnut-Miller-Manning Papers, South Carolina Historical Society, Charleston.

James Chesnut, Jr., letter, Virginia Historical Society, Richmond.

James Chesnut, Jr., Papers, Robert Woodruff Library, Emory University, Atlanta, Ga.

Mary Boykin Chesnut Journals, South Caroliniana Library, Columbia.

Mary Boykin Chesnut, letter, Museum of the Confederacy, Richmond, Va.

Clement C. Clay Papers, William R. Perkins Library, Duke University, Durham, N.C.

Francis Warrington Dawson Papers, William R. Perkins Library, Duke University, Durham, N.C.

Kershaw County Probate Records, Kershaw County Court House, Camden, S.C.

Kincaid-Anderson Family Papers, South Caroliniana Library, Columbia.

Mary Withers Kirkland Papers, South Caroliniana Library, Columbia.

Martin Family Papers, South Caroliniana Library, Columbia.

*News and Courier* Charleston: Ledger; *News and Courier* Receipt and Invoice Book, South Caroliniana Library, Columbia.

Preston Family Papers, Virginia Historical Society, Richmond.

South Carolina State Department of Archives and History, Columbia.

Webber Family Papers, South Carolina Historical Society, Charleston.

Wigfall Family Papers, Library of Congress, Washington, D.C.

Bell I. Wiley Papers, Robert Woodruff Library, Emory University, Atlanta, Ga.

Williams-Chesnut-Manning Collection, South Caroliniana Library, Columbia.

Stephen Miller Williams Papers, privately owned.

SOUTH CAROLINA NEWSPAPERS

Camden *Confederate*
Camden *Weekly Journal*
Charleston *Daily Courier*
Charleston *Mercury*
Charleston *Weekly News and Courier*
Columbia *Banner*
Columbia *State*
Camden *Kershaw Gazette*

UNPUBLISHED PAPERS AND MONOGRAPHS

Johnson, William H., Jr. "Dr. Robert Wilson Gibbes: Southern Editor and Publisher, 1852–1864." M.A. thesis, University of South Carolina, 1969.
Meriwether, James B. "The First Edition of Mary Boykin Chesnut's *A Diary From Dixie*."
Muhlenfeld, Elisabeth S. "Mary Boykin Chesnut: The Writer and Her Work." Ph.D. dissertation, University of South Carolina, 1978.
Trantham, Jane B. "Mary Boykin Chesnut." Kershaw County Historical Society. January 17, 1974.
Wall, Allie Patricia, ed. "The Letters of Mary Boykin Chesnut." M.A. thesis, University of South Carolina, 1977.

PUBLISHED MATERIAL

*American Literary Manuscripts; a Checklist of Holdings in Academic, Historical, and Public Libraries in the United States.* Austin: University of Texas Press, 1961.
Andrews, Matthew Page, comp. *The Women of the South in War Times.* Baltimore: Norman, Remington, 1920.
*Appletons' Cyclopeadia of American Biography.* Ed. James Grant Wilson and John Fiske. 6 vols. Revised ed. New York: D. Appleton, 1900.
Avary, Myrta Lockett. *Dixie After the War.* New York: Doubleday, Page, 1906.
———. *A Virginia Girl in the Civil War.* New York: D. Appleton, 1903.
Barnwell, Stephen B. *The Story of an American Family.* Marquette: n.p., 1960.
Bearss, Edwin C. *Osceola at Fort Moultrie.* Washington, D.C.: Office of Archeology and Historic Preservation, 1968.
Bill, Alfred Hoyt. "The Journal of the Confederacy." *Saturday Review*, December 31, 1949, p. 19.
*Biographical Directory of the American Congress: 1774–1949.* Washington, D.C.: U.S. Government Printing Office, 1950.
Blosser, Susan S. and Clyde H. Wilson, Jr. *The Southern Historical Collection: A Guide to Manuscripts.* Chapel Hill: University of North Carolina Library, 1970.
Boatner, Mark Mayo. *The Civil War Dictionary.* New York: David McKay Co., Inc. 1959.

Boyd, Mark F. "Asi-Yaholo or Osceola." *Florida Historical Quarterly*, XXXIII (1955), 249–305.

Boykin, Richard Manning. *Captain Alexander Hamilton Boykin: One of South Carolina's Distinguished Citizens.* New York: privately printed, 1942.

*A Brief Memoir of Stephen Decatur Miller, Whilom Governor of South Carolina, and United States Senator from the Same State.* [United States]: n.p., n.d.

Brooks, U. R. *South Carolina Bench and Bar.* Vol. I. Columbia, S.C.: State Co., 1908.

Campbell, Thomas. *Descendents of Capt. Angus Campbell of Laurens, South Carolina.* Charlottesville, Va.: Thomas Campbell, privately printed, 1955.

Carson, James Petigru. *Life, Letters and Speeches of James Louis Petigru, the Union Man of South Carolina.* Washington, D.C.: W. D. Lowdermilk, 1920.

Cauthen, Charles Edward. *Family Letters of the Three Wade Hamptons.* Columbia: University of South Carolina Press, 1953.

———. *South Carolina Goes to War: 1860–1865.* Chapel Hill: University of North Carolina Press, 1950.

Channing, Steven A. *Crisis of Fear: Secession in South Carolina.* New York: Simon and Schuster, 1970.

*Charleston Directory; and Register, for 1835–6.* Ed. James Smith. Charleston: David J. Dowling, 1835.

*Charleston Directory, and Stranger's Guide for 1840 & 1841.* Charleston: T. C. Fay, 1840.

Chesnut, James. *An Address Delivered Before The Literary Societies of the College of New Jersey by the Hon. James Chesnut, of South Carolina on Tuesday, June 27 [28], 1876.* Princeton: The "Press," 1876.

———. *Oration by James Chesnut, Jr. delivered in the Presbyterian Church on the Fourth of July, at Camden, S.C.* Camden, S.C.: L. M. Jones, 1837.

Chesnut, Mary Boykin. "A Diary from Dixie." *Saturday Evening Post*, January 28, 1905, pp. 1, 2, 3, 22, 23; February 4, 1905, pp. 6, 7, 24; February 11, 1905, pp. 6, 7, 27, 28; February 18, 1905, pp. 8, 9, 22; Feb. 25, 1905, pp. 12, 13, 38.

———. *A Diary from Dixie, as written by Mary Boykin Chesnut, wife of James Chesnut, Jr., United States Senator from South Carolina, 1859–1861, and afterward an Aide to Jefferson Davis and a Brigadier-General in the Confederate Army.* Ed. Isabella D. Martin and Myrta Lockett Avary. New York: D. Appleton, 1905.

———. *A Diary From Dixie.* Ed. Ben Ames Williams. Boston: Houghton, Mifflin, 1949.

Childs, Margaretta P. "Chesnut, Mary Boykin Miller." *Notable American Women: 1607–1950.* Ed. Edward T. Jones *et al.* Cambridge, Mass.: Belknap Press of Harvard University Press, 1971, pp. 327–30.

Childs, St. Julien. Rev. of *A Diary From Dixie*, by Mary Boykin Chesnut. *South Carolina Historical and Genealogical Magazine*, LII (1951), 183–84.

Clarke, Edwards. "A Great Advocate: James T. Brady." *Galaxy*, May, 1869. In collection of miscellaneous pamphlets bound by LeRoy Youmans, South Caroliniana Library, Columbia.

Clay-Clopton, Virginia. *A Belle of the Fifties: Memoirs of Mrs. Clay, of Alabama, Covering Social and Political Life in Washington and the South, 1853–66*. Ed. Ada Sterling. New York: Doubleday, Page, 1904.

Colonial Dames of America, Chapter I. *Ancestral Records and Portraits*. Vol. I. New York: Grafton, 1910.

Cook, Harvey Toliver. *The Life and Legacy of David Rogerson Williams*. New York: Country Life, 1916.

Coulter, E. Merton. *The South During Reconstruction: 1865–1877*. Vol. VIII, Louisiana State University Series: A History of the South. Gen. eds. Wendell Holmes Stevenson and E. Merton Coulter. Baton Rouge: Louisiana State University Press, 1947.

Davidson, Chalmers Gaston. *The Last Foray: The South Carolina Planters of 1860, A Sociological Study*. Tricentennial Studies No. 4. Columbia: University of South Carolina Press, 1971.

Davis, Esther S. [Reynolds]. *Memories of Mulberry*. N.d.; rpt. Camden, S.C.: Camden Archives Commission, 1975.

Dawson, Francis Warrington, ed. *Our Women in the War*. Charleston: Weekly News and Courier, 1885.

Degler, Carl N. *At Odds: Women and the Family in America from the Revolution to the Present*. New York: Oxford University Press, 1980.

Delamont, Sara and Lorna Duffin, eds. *The Nineteenth-Century Woman: Her Cultural and Physical World*. New York: Barnes & Noble Books, 1978.

De Leon, Thomas Cooper. *Belles, Beaux and Brains of the 60's*. New York: G. W. Dillingham, 1909.

De Rosier, Arthur H., Jr. *The Removal of the Choctaw Indians*. Knoxville: University of Tennessee Press, 1970.

Derrick, Samuel Melanchthon. *Centennial History of the South Carolina Railroad*. Columbia, S.C.: State Co., 1930.

DeSaussure, Nancy Bostick. *Old Plantation Days: Being Recollections of Southern Life before the Civil War*. New York: Duffield & Company, 1909.

Deupree, Mrs. N. D. "Greenwood LeFlore." *Publications of the Mississippi Historical Society*, VII (1903), 141–52.

Duyckinck, Evert A. and George L. Duyckinck. *Cyclopaedia of American Literature*. 2 vols. New York: Charles Scribner, 1856.

Easterby, J. H. "Chesnut, James." *Dictionary of American Biography*, II, 57–58.

———. *Guide to the Study and Reading of South Carolina History*. 1950; rpt with supplement by Noel Polk, Spartanburg, S.C.: Reprint Co., 1975.

Edgar, Walter B., ed. *Biographical Directory of the South Carolina House of Representatives*. Joan Schreiner Reynolds *et al.*, comps. Vol. I. Columbia: University of South Carolina Press, 1974.

Fairbanks, Mrs. A. W., ed. *Emma Willard and Her Pupils or Fifty Years of Troy Female Seminary: 1822–1872*. New York: Mrs. Russell Sage, 1898.

Foote, Shelby. *The Civil War: A Narrative*. 3 vols. New York: Random House, 1958, 1963, 1974.

Fraser, Charles. *Reminiscences of Charleston*. Charleston: John Russell, 1854.

Freehling, William W. *Prelude to Civil War: The Nullification Controversy in South Carolina, 1816–1836*. New York: Harper & Row, 1966.

Freeman, Douglas Southall. *The South to Posterity*. New York: Charles Scribner's Sons, 1939.

Gay, Mary A. H. *Life in Dixie During the War*. Third ed. (enlarged). Atlanta, Ga.: Charles P. Byrd, 1897.

Glover, Cato D. *The Stray and the Strange from "Mulberry"—Camden, S.C.* N. p.: n. p., 1972.

Green, Nancy. "Female Education and School Competition: 1820–1850." *Woman's Being, Woman's Place: Female Identity and Vocation in American History*. Ed. Mary Kelley. Boston: G. K. Hall & Co., 1979, pp. 127–41.

Greenberg, Kenneth S. "Revolutionary Ideology and the Proslavery Argument: The Abolition of Slavery in Antebellum South Carolina." *Journal of Southern History*, XLII (August, 1976), 365–84.

Greenberg, Ronald M., ed. *National Register of Historic Places*. Washington, D.C.: U.S. Department of the Interior, 1976.

Gregory, Eileen. "The Formality of Memory: A Study of Literary Manuscripts of Mary Boykin Chesnut." *South Carolina Women Writers*. Ed. James B. Meriwether. Columbia: Southern Studies Program, University of South Carolina, 1979, pp. 229–43.

Guilday, Peter. *The Life and Times of John England*. 2 vols. 1927; rpt. New York: Arno Press and the New York Times, 1969.

Hamer, Philip M., ed. *A Guide to Archives and Manuscripts in the United States*. New Haven: Yale University Press, 1961.

Hayhoe, George F. "Mary Boykin Chesnut's Journal: Visions and Revisions." *South Carolina Women Writers*. Ed. James B. Meriwether. Columbia: Southern Studies Program, University of South Carolina, 1979, pp. 211–21.

Hemphill, James Calvin. *Men of Mark in South Carolina*. 4 vols. Washington, D.C.: Men of Mark Publishing Co., 1907–1909.

Hendrick, Burton J. *Statesmen of the Lost Cause: Jefferson Davis and His Cabinet*. Boston: Little Brown, 1939.

Hennig, Helen K. *Great South Carolinians from Colonial Days to the Confederate War*. Chapel Hill: University of North Carolina Press, 1940.

Hersh, Blanche Glassman. *The Slavery of Sex: Feminist-Abolitionists in America*. Urbana: University of Illinois Press, 1978.

Hubbell, Jay B. *The South in American Literature: 1607–1900*. Durham, N.C.: Duke University Press, 1954.

Huff, Archie Vernon, Jr. *Tried by Fire: Washington Street United Methodist Church, Columbia, S.C.* Columbia, S.C.: R. L. Bryan, 1975.

Inabinet, L. Glen. "'The July Fourth Incident' of 1816: An Insurrection Plotted by Slaves in Camden, South Carolina." *South Carolina Legal History*. Ed. Herbert Johnson. Columbia: Southern Studies Program, University of South Carolina, 1980, pp. 209–21.

Jervey, Elizabeth H. "Marriage and Death Notices from the *City Gazette* of Charleston, S.C." *South Carolina Historical and Genealogical Magazine*, XLVI (1945). 15.

Jones, Hazel Parker. *Descendants of James Boyd Magill*. Clinton, S.C.: Jacobs Brothers, 1963.

Junior League of Charleston. *Historic Charleston Guidebook*. [Charleston]: Junior League of Charleston, 1965.

Kershaw County Historical Association. *Kirkwood: The Story of a Neighborhood*. N.p.: n.p., 1970.

Kimball, William J. "The End of 'Old-Time Grace and Hospitality': Richmond, 1864." *South Carolina Review*, III (June, 1971), 37–48.

Kirkland, Thomas J. and Robert M. Kennedy. *Historic Camden*. 2 vols. Columbia, S.C.: State Co., 1905, 1926.

Knight, Lucian Lamar, ed. *Biographical Dictionary of Authors*. Vol. XV of *Library of Southern Literature*. Atlanta: Martin and Hoyt, 1907.

Lefvendahl, Georgie Inabinet Adams. *The Inabinet Family of South Carolina*. Vol. III. N.p.: n.p., 1970.

Leiding, Harriette Kershaw. *Historic Houses of South Carolina*. Philadelphia: J. B. Lippincott, 1921.

Long, E. B. *The Civil War Day by Day: An Almanac, 1861–1865*. Garden City, N.Y.: Doubleday, 1971.

Martin, Isabella D. "Sketch of Mrs. [Louisa S.] McCord." In *For Old Lang Syne: Collected for My Children*. Comp. [Louisa McCord Smythe]. Columbia, S.C.: [Lucas and Richardson], 1900.

Massey, Mary Elizabeth. *Bonnet Brigades*. New York: Alfred A. Knopf, 1966.

McCaw, Genevieve A. "Miss Isabella Martin's School." *The State Magazine*, February 20, 1955, pp. 6–7.

McCrady, Edward and Samuel A. Ashe. *Cyclopedia of Eminent and Representative Men of the Carolinas of the Nineteenth Century*. 2 vols. Madison, Wisc.: Brant and Fuller, 1892.

McCrady, Edward. *The History of South Carolina in the Revolution: 1775–1780*. 2 vols. New York: Russell & Russell, 1901, 1902.

McGill, Samuel D. *Narrative of Reminiscences in Williamsburg County*. Columbia, S.C.: Bryan Printing Co., 1897.

Meminger, Edward Reed. *An Historical Sketch of Flat Rock*. N.p.: n.p., 1954.

Meriwether, James B. *South Carolina Women Writers*. Proceedings of the Reynolds Conference, University of South Carolina, October 24–25, 1975. Columbia: Southern Studies Program, University of South Carolina, 1979.

Mills, Robert. *Statistics of South Carolina*. 1826; rpt. Spartanburg, S.C.: Reprint Co., 1972.

"Miss I. D. Martin." Obituary. *The State*, Columbia, S.C., March 6, 1913, p. 16.

Molloy, Robert. *Charleston: A Gracious Heritage*. New York: D. Appleton-Century, 1947.

Moore, John Hammond. *Research Materials in South Carolina: A Guide.* Columbia: University of South Carolina Press, 1967.

Muhlenfeld, Elisabeth. "Literary Elements in Mary Chesnut's Journal." *South Carolina Women Writers.* Ed. James B. Meriwether. Columbia, S.C.: Southern Studies Program, University of South Carolina, 1979.

Myers, Robert Manson. *The Children of Pride.* New Haven, Mass.: Yale University Press, 1972.

*The National Union Catalogue of Manuscript Collections.*

Neuffer, Claude. *Names in South Carolina: Volumes I–XII, 1954–1965.* Spartanburg, S.C.: Reprint Co., 1976.

O'Neall, John Belton. *Annals of Newberry.* Charleston: S. G. Courtenay, 1859.

————. *Biographical Sketch of the Bench and Bar of South Carolina.* 2 vols. Charleston: S. G. Courtenay, 1859.

————. *The Negro Law of South Carolina.* Columbia, S.C.: J. G. Bowman, 1848.

Patterson, Isabel C. "Dr. A. N. Talley: Physician, Soldier, Benefactor." *The State Magazine,* December 11, 1949, p. 9.

Patton, Sadie Smathers. *A Condensed History of Flat Rock.* Asheville, N.C.: Church Printing Co., n.d.

Pember, Phoebe Yates. *A Southern Woman's Story.* Ed. and with intro. by Bell Irvin Wiley. Jackson, Tenn.: McCowat-Mercer, 1959.

Pope, Thomas H. *The History of Newberry County, South Carolina.* Vol. I. Columbia: University of South Carolina Press, 1973.

Pryor, Mrs. Roger A. [Sara Agnes (Rice)]. *Reminiscences of Peace and War.* Revised ed. New York: Macmillan, 1905.

Ravenel, Harriott Horry Rutledge. *Charleston: The Place and the People.* New York: Macmillan, 1906.

Reniers, Percival. *The Springs of Virginia.* Chapel Hill: University of North Carolina Press, 1941.

Reynolds, Emily Bellinger, and Joan Reynolds Faunt. *Biographical Directory of the Senate of the State of South Carolina: 1776–1964.* Columbia: South Carolina Department of Archives and History, 1964.

Reynolds, John S. *Reconstruction in South Carolina: 1865–1877.* Columbia, S.C.: State Co., 1905.

Richardson, Emma B. *Charleston Garden Plats.* Charleston Museum Leaflet No. 19. Charleston: Charleston Museum, 1943.

Ross, Ishbel. *First Lady of the South.* New York: Harper & Brothers, 1958.

Rowland, Dunbar. *History of Mississippi.* 2 vols. Chicago: S. J. Clarke, 1925.

————. *Jefferson Davis, Constitutionalist, His Letters, Papers and Speeches.* Jackson: Mississippi Department of Archives and History, 1923.

Scott, Anne Firor. *The Southern Lady: From Pedestal to Politics, 1830–1930.* Chicago: University of Chicago Press, 1970.

————. "Women in a Plantation Culture: Or What I Wish I Knew about Southern Women." *South Atlantic Urban Studies,* II (1978), 24–33.

Scott, Edwin J. *Random Recollections of a Long Life: 1806 to 1876*. Columbia, S.C.: Charles A. Calvo, Jr., 1884.

Selby, Julian A. *Memorabilia: And Anecdotal Reminiscences of Columbia, S.C., and Incidents Connected Therewith*. Columbia, S.C.: R. L. Bryan, 1905.

Shaffer, E. T. H. *Carolina Gardens*. Chapel Hill: University of North Carolina Press, 1939.

Shannon, William M. *Old Times in Camden: Pen Pictures of the Past*. Ed. Harvey S. Teal. N.p.: n.p., 1961.

Simms, William Gilmore. *The Letters of William Gilmore Simms*. Ed. Mary C. Simms Oliphant, Alfred Taylor Odell, T. C. Duncan Eaves. 5 vols. Columbia: University of South Carolina Press, 1952–1956.

––––––. *Sack and Destruction of the City of Columbia, S.C.* Ed. with notes by A. S. Salley. 2nd ed. Oglethorpe, Ga.: Oglethorpe University Press, 1937.

Skeat, T. C. *The Catalogues of the Manuscript Collections in the British Museum*. Revised ed. London: The Trustees of the British Museum, 1962.

*South Carolina Historical and Genealogical Magazine*. 1900–1967.

Springs, Katherine Wooten. *The Squires of Springfield*. Charlotte, N.C.: William Loftin, 1965.

Strode, Hudson. *Jefferson Davis*. 3 vols. New York: Harcourt, Brace, 1955, 1959, 1964.

Sweet, Ethel Wylly, *et al. Camden: Homes & Heritage*. Camden, S.C.: Kershaw County Historical Society, 1978.

Taylor, Mrs. Thomas *et al. South Carolina Women in the Confederacy*. 2 vols. Columbia, S.C.: State Co., 1903, 1907.

Teal, Harvey S., ed. *Rides About Camden, 1853 and 1873*. [United States]: n. p., n. d.

Trollope, Anthony. *The Way We Live Now*. London: Chapman and Hall, 1875.

Wakelyn, Jon L. *Biographical Dictionary of the Confederacy*. Westport, Conn.: Greenwood, 1977.

Wallace, David Duncan. *The History of South Carolina*. 4 vols. New York: American Historical Society, 1934.

––––––. *South Carolina: A Short History: 1520–1948*. Chapel Hill: University of North Carolina Press, 151.

Warner, Ezra J. and W. Buck Yearns. *Biographical Register of the Confederate Congress*. Baton Rouge: Louisiana State University Press, 1975.

Watson, Charles S. *Antebellum Charleston Dramatists*. Tuscaloosa: University of Alabama Press, 1976.

Wauchope, George Armstrong. *Literary South Carolina*. Bulletin of the University of South Carolina No. 133. Columbia: University of South Carolina, December 1, 1923.

Welsh, Mary J. "Recollections of Pioneer Life in Mississippi." *Publications of the Mississippi Historical Society*, IV (1900), 343–356.

Wiley, Bell Irvin. *Confederate Women*. Contributions in American History No. 38. Westport, Conn.: Greenwood, 1975.

———. "Diarist From Dixie." *Civil War Times Illustrated*, XVI, No. 1 (1977), 22–32.

Williams, Ben Ames. *House Divided*. Boston: Houghton, Mifflin, 1947.

Wilson, Edmund. *Patriotic Gore: Studies in the Literature of the American Civil War*. New York: Oxford University Press, 1962.

Wilson, John Lyde. *The Code of Honor; or, Rules for the Government of Principals and Seconds in Duelling*. Charleston, S.C.: James Phynney, 1838.

Woodward, C. Vann, ed. *Mary Chesnut's Civil War*. New Haven, Conn.: Yale University Press, 1981.

Wright, Mrs. D. Giraud. *A Southern Girl in '61*. New York: Doubleday, Page, 1905.

# Index